Running My Way Across the USA

*One woman's account of running a
long distance event in all 50 states
and the District of Columbia*

Bridget Simpson

Running My Way Across the USA
by Bridget Simpson

ISBN 13: 978-1517756826

Cover photo: Robert Badalucco

This book is dedicated to my beautiful mother, Delores Simpson, whose unconditional love and support blesses me beyond measure.

About the Author

Bridget Simpson has run a long distance event in all 50 states and the District of Columbia. In all, she has competed in over 75 races and placed several times in her age group, including the 10k Women's Masters Championship in 2009 in Pocatello, Idaho.

In addition to running, she's an avid hiker and tennis fan, and she rarely missess the annual U.S. Open in New York.

She holds a Bachelor of Science degree in Electrical Engineering from North Carolina State University and a Master of Business Administration (MBA) from Emory University. She has lived in Atlanta, Los Angeles, and Baltimore, and presently resides in Nashville, Tennessee.

Bridget has been an active member of the Screen Actors Guild (SAG-AFTRA) since 1999.

Table of Contents

(Races by State in Chronological Order)

Key to symbols

Special comments about the venue. Regular comments are included in my introduction to a particular race.

The details about the course and my experience as I ran it.

Things to do and see in the race city.

My personal overall assessment of the running event.

Not all topics are addressed for each race.

How My Running Adventure Began

I moved to Nashville from Los Angeles in October 2004. The move itself was simple since the company I worked for at the time picked up the entire tab, but starting a new life in a new city is always a daunting task.

Having moved nearly a dozen times upon completing graduate school, I was used to making transitions in life; however, what awaited me in Nashville was unlike anything else I had experienced up to that point. Nashville marked many "firsts" in my life; it was where I bought my first house, where I got in the best shape of my life and where a dream was born in my heart—to run a long distance event in all 50 United States. And to think it all began on my 40th birthday.

As far back as I can remember I have always loved sports, both as a spectator and as a participant. Growing up in the central part of North Carolina, just minutes from both Durham and Chapel Hill, I was influenced by the strong representation of college sports in that region. In fact, most of my early sports training took place on the campuses of UNC-CH and Duke University. My mother served on the faculty of UNC-CH as a coordinator of the summer program Upward Bound, and family members of the faculty had access to all the campus facilities. Thus, I learned how to swim and dive at the campus indoor and outdoor pools when I was around 8 or 9 years old. Shortly thereafter, the mother of a friend of mine got the two of us in a lifeguard program at Duke University where I became a certified junior lifeguard. I still adore the water and try to swim as much as possible.

My other true sports passion was and remains tennis. I adore everything about that sport and began taking tennis lessons from a local pro (a dubious title for him) in Chapel Hill when I was about 11 or 12 years old. I showed a lot of promise but never pursued it beyond recreational fun.

Other loves have included basketball, football (as a spectator), cycling, and later in life, running of course, but between the ages of about 15 to 37, however, I was watching everything from the sidelines. Sadly, that span of nearly 15 years represented the most inactive and physically unfit time of my life, and I'm not exactly sure why. I never lost the joy of watching sports, but my enthusiasm for participating in them took a nosedive, which was puzzling considering the big role they played in my life early on. Thus, slowly as the years progressed, I became more and more of a couch potato, gaining weight and losing myself in the process.

Depending on where I was living at that time, there were moments of physicality that mirrored the days of my youth. For example, when I lived in Roanoke, Virginia (the first place I lived after finishing graduate school), a friend and I would frequent the local YMCA and participate in pick-up basketball games. I still had a great set shot and could play defense well enough that one of the coordinators asked me to participate in a local women's basketball league.

A few years later when I moved to Baltimore, I got into racquetball and developed a reputation for being a decent player, but none of it was consistent. I would have a week or two where I worked out nearly every day, and then go nearly a month without doing so much as a jumping jack. Even more atrocious were my eating habits. I ate out all the time and kept my refrigerator stocked with nothing but processed foods. Thus, I continued to get larger, lazier and more lethargic as each year passed. That is until that defining moment in early 2005; the day I signed up for my first half marathon.

Since getting a graduate degree in Atlanta in 1991, my life has been comprised of a series of jobs in corporate America that facilitated a move to a new city and state every 2-3 years. That has a lot to do with why I love to travel so much. After graduation, I accepted a job in Roanoke, Virginia and remained there for nearly two years. I then accepted a job in Freeport, Illinois and was there for 18 months, before transferring to Baltimore, Maryland where I lived the next 4 years. After transferring to North Carolina for additional two years, I finally realized a lifelong desire to live in Los Angeles, where I resided for the next 6 years. From L.A., I accepted another job transfer, this time to Nashville, Tennessee. It was in Nashville that my 50 state running quest was born and nurtured.

Actually, the seed to become a runner was planted the first week after I moved to the music capital. I purchased my first home in the beautiful city of Franklin, just south of Nashville, and had handymen doing work on my house the day before my furniture arrived. One of these men was there to install my security system. As he worked to set up the various sensors and keypad, he asked me rather matter-of-factly, if I was a runner. I have to admit that I found that rather flattering, considering I had never run more than a mile without stopping.

I told him "No, I'm definitely not a runner." He replied that I looked like one, which seemed dubious to me considering I was carrying an extra 30 lbs. on my frame at the time. He suggested I enter the annual marathon in the city, to which I gave him a smug "sure" response and thought nothing else of it.

Then, about a week later, I was at my bank filling out a deposit slip, when I noticed a flyer for the race. The branch V.P. saw me reviewing the brochure and asked if I was going to run in the marathon.

"What is this, I thought? "Why is everybody asking me about this stupid marathon? As it turned out, that bank was one of the corporate sponsors of the event. I looked around and saw posters and pictures related to the event hanging from every door and wall of the building. One piece of information stood out from the rest: the date. This race was to take place on April 30, 2005 – my 40th birthday! If all the other signs – the security installer, the bank sponsorship, the branch V.P. highlighting the advantages of participation – weren't enough to grab my attention, the fact that this race would fall on my birthday certainly did. Moreover, we're not just talking any birthday; we're talking about the big 4-0, one that I was already dreading just a bit in the first place.

As I drove home with all the literature and registration information, I began to think about the irony of this situation. Generally, as a society, we consider age 40 as the start of middle age – the time when life starts to slow down, and when many goals and dreams are better left forgotten. Since I never subscribed to that way of thinking, I figured that running this race would be the perfect way to declare that 40 is not the age for slowing down. It is the

My fastest half marathon: The Baton Rouge Beach Half Marathon, December 2008 - photographer Karen Thibodeaux.

age for realizing old dreams and developing new ones.

This is a good time to mention that I knew nothing about running when all this began, a truth that would become crystal clear in the following weeks and months. In fact, I was so uneducated that I had no idea of the actual distance of a marathon. When I saw in the literature that it was 26.2 miles, I nearly dropped the piece of paper. I thought there is no way I can run that far. Thankfully, this event also included a half marathon which was 13.1 miles, and while that didn't seem realistic to me either, at least it was better than 26.2 miles. So, admitting my ignorance of the whole thing, I filled out the form, wrote my check for the registration fee and put it in the mailbox that very afternoon.

Later that evening, I had what you might call a form of buyer's remorse. I thought, "This is just too crazy, birthday or no birthday. I'm pulling out of this and getting my money back." However, the application form was clear; "There will be no refunds under any circumstances."

Oh well, I thought. Never one to waste money, I knew that I had no choice. I was going to run a half marathon on my 40th birthday. I had no idea what that would encompass, but I knew that I had about 5 months to figure it out so it would be okay.

As I look back on it now, I marvel at how naïve and just plain ignorant I was in the beginning. I knew nothing about the world of running, and I do mean nothing. It never occurred to me that there were literally hundreds of races conducted every single weekend across the country and internationally. I did not know there was an entire culture within the running community that focused on things like running shoes to match one's running style and foot strike, specific cross-training principles, heart rate monitors, and things of that nature. Nor did I realize the large number of websites dedicated solely to the sport of running.

At this point, my knowledge was limited to owning a pair of running shoes from Payless and wearing a headband, which I thought was more than acceptable since my goal was to do this just one time. It was never in my sights to run another event of any kind after this first one. My goal was to be "one and done."

I became so excited about the race that I told almost everyone I knew about the race. One of my colleagues from work had a client that was planning to run the same half marathon and was training through a running club. What a surprise to discover such clubs existed! The club provided a running schedule for members to follow over the next several months. She was good enough to share a copy of the schedule with me, giving me a metric for how many miles I should be running daily in preparation for race day. Although I would adjust as needed, I used this running guide for each race I entered during my 50 state journey.

As you read my story, note the following: My criteria for the race distance was nothing longer than a marathon and nothing shorter than a 10k. So the races include:

- Marathon - 26.2 miles
- Half Marathon - 13.1 miles
- Quarter Marathon - 6.55 miles
- 10k - 6.21 miles

Each state is represented by one key race, although I mention additional races in the states where I ran more than one event.

I pray that as you read about my cross-country adventure, it will bring as much blessing to you as it did to me; the kind of blessing that keeps on giving. Happy Reading!

Race 1

Music City Half Marathon
Nashville, Tennessee - April 30, 2005

Happy Birthday to Me!

As I started "training" for my first race, I discovered a few people I knew who were planning to participate, including a couple of my neighbors. It was good to have someone to compare stories with, although I was still looking at this as a one-time event and not taking it too seriously. Nonetheless, I stuck to the schedule as best I could and felt good about the progress I was making, considering that my primary goal for this race was simply to finish in the time allotted. I knew nothing about pace so my intention was just to complete it in one piece. The only reward I wanted was the bragging right of having run a half marathon on my 40th birthday. That was it—period.

Since it was my birthday and my mother had not seen my new house yet, she flew to Nashville to spend the weekend with me. She arrived the Thursday before the race and that entire day it rained cats and dogs. In fact, it rained so much I didn't even want to participate in the race even though it was two days later. Nevertheless, once I picked Mom up at the airport, we drove straight to the Nashville Convention Center downtown to attend the event's expo and suddenly, my enthusiasm was back in a big way.

The Music City Marathon and Half Marathon is one of the largest running events in the nation. Later becoming part of the "Rock-n-Roll" race series, these races are noted for the fact that at every mile, a live band or artist performs a musical selection, keeping the race course lively and interesting. Later, I would participate in many of these well-attended music-oriented races, as well as quite a few smaller events. While there are advantages and disadvantages to different sized races, I will always be grateful that my first exposure to the world of running was at one of the largest races in the country.

Generally, large race events are accompanied by a large expo, as I would discover the moment I walked into the convention center. After picking up my goody bag, which contained my runner's bib, timing chip, and several samples and freebies from various sponsors, Mom and I toured the rest of the expo. It consisted of rows of exhibitors displaying everything from running apparel to new energy drinks and nutrition bars. In addition, there were representatives from the fields of healthcare, communications and other races hoping to sign up new participants for their individual events. It was quite a lot to take in and I enjoyed every aspect of it;

so much so that we were there for well over an hour. All the excitement of the other runners and vendors recharged my battery and made me anxious for Saturday to arrive.

In 2005, the number of runners for both the Music City Marathon and Half Marathon reached just over 15,000. By 2014, the number of participants had grown to over 23,000. Large numbers require a wave start or corral process. A corral is a sectioned area at the race's starting line. Race participants are grouped according to their expected finishing time as indicated on their registration form. Typically, the faster runners are placed in the first few corrals and slower runners are placed in corrals toward the back.

By starting the race this way, it helps to reduce the propensity for "bottlenecking" and overcrowding on the course, especially in the first couple of miles. If people are honest in reporting their true expected finish time and get in the corral assigned to them, it is a system that works well.

Over the years I've seen people abuse this rule and line up wherever they want. However, for the most part, runners are decent folks who understand the purpose behind the wave start and begin the race when they are supposed to. Elapsed time is based on when you cross the sensor mats at the start and finish lines (there is an electronic timing chip you attach to your shoe or runner's bib), so it really doesn't matter when you start.

I was assigned to corral 18 out of 24 for this race, so I was toward the back. Although the race officially started at 7:00 a.m. with corral 1, my corral didn't reach the start line until about 7:25.

I was cold before I started to run but once I started moving my muscles, I began warming up quickly. I ran non-stop for 6 miles when I stopped for the first time and drank some water. From there, I ran when I could but I walked more than I ran. This race is known for being rather hilly, but being so new to the running game it made no difference to me. Whether the course was flat or hilly, my conditioning would only allow me to run for so long.

One humorous side effect associated with my need to walk were the numerous conversations I had while on the race course. There are people who enter races to do nothing more than meet people; running is last on their list. So when you're toward the back where the vast majority of participants are walking, you tend to meet great conversationalists who treat the race course like a singles bar. There was one guy in particular who exercised this fact exceptionally well. I think it was somewhere near the 9 or 10 mile mark, when the two of us started walking side-by-side. He asked me a ton of questions like, "Is this your first race?" and "Where are you from?" He, of course, told me his entire life story and before I knew it, we had talked for nearly 15 minutes walking at a snail's pace. While I was far from serious about my finish time, I knew that I didn't want to come in dead last, so I told him I was going to speed up a little and that it was nice talking to him. He said "likewise" and before I got out of earshot, I heard him starting a new conversation with another young lady.

I had to chuckle and will never forget that unique experience. Once I became a proficient runner and serious about my races, I seldom engaged in conversations beyond a simple reply to someone's comment. However, in this first race, I was just happy to be out there with no expectations of repeating such an experience.

Soon, I was on the homestretch and at the 12.5 mile mark, the number of spectators increased. The loud cheers made me feel like I was coming in alongside one of the great runners from Kenya. In fact, someone held up a sign that said, "Today you are all Kenyans!" I loved reading that and had to smile as I imagined it was true.

As I closed in on the finish line, I heard the announcer call out my name and time and I felt like a million dollars. Wow, I thought. I just completed 13.1 miles! I was overjoyed and I promise you that no Olympic Champion has ever felt happier, stronger or more thankful. It was a moment I'll never forget.

The following weekend, several of my neighbors had a barbeque to celebrate our participation in either the marathon or half marathon. While none of us shattered any records, most of the guys who ran had a much better finish time than me. Many of them asked if I was going to run again next year. I was starting to realize that a theme was developing here; the theme of doing this race again. I didn't entertain this theme, not even remotely, for the next several months. However, as the year rolled along, the thought of possibly trying this again kept ringing in my ears.

That evening after I had time to rest and regroup, Mom and I had a great dinner and enjoyed a wonderful performance by the Nashville Symphony Orchestra at the Tennessee Performing Arts Center (TPAC). I studied classical piano for over ten years as a youth and participated in piano competitions as a teenager, including several at Duke University.

Classical (or concert) music remains my favorite genre of music. As I traveled the country, I made it a point to attend as many symphony performances as possible. As a resident of Nashville, I'm a season ticket holder of the Nashville Symphony, not just to support the arts, but because listening to such amazing arrangements brings me joy. It was a wonderful way to end what I can only deem as a "life-changing" day.

This was my first race and it shaped my future in a positive way. I began to think that if I finished my first half marathon in 2:50:47 with only a moderate amount of training, imagine what I can do if I got serious about it. If I worked harder and became more focused, I thought that I might be able to shave 20-25 minutes off my finish time, which would be huge for me. So, somewhere between 4 to 6 months after completing my first half marathon, I decided to try it again.

On April 29, 2006, exactly 364 days after my first attempt at this race, I ran it once more. The final result: a finish time of 2:20:21, over 30 minutes faster than my first race. If you thought I was ecstatic the first time around, you had no idea how thrilled I was after the second attempt.

I would go on to take part in this event two more times, improving upon my finish time with each effort. I would participate in two additional races in the state of Tennessee (St. Jude Half Marathon in Memphis in 2007 and Covenant Health Knoxville Half Marathon in 2008) before committing to running a long distance event in all 50 states.

As I look back over the entire experience, I see how instrumental these early events were in my preparation for what would turn out to be one of the most remarkable experiences of my life. When I think how far I've come since that first race, I'm not only astounded by the progress I've made as a runner, but as a human being in general.

Race 2

Little Rock Half Marathon
Little Rock, Arkansas - March 4, 2007

The Perfect Place to Start
This Running Thing

As I look back to my half marathon race in Little Rock, I have to marvel at how green and naïve I was about road racing. This was even though, by this time, I had completed two half marathons, both at the same event in Nashville, almost a year apart (4/30/2005 and 4/29/2006). While I was proud of what I accomplished up to that point, I was still far from thinking that I could run long distances in all 50 states.

I'm thankful that my first race outside Nashville was in Little Rock, Arkansas. From the influential runners to the historical exploration of this noted city, this event showed me that running can open doors to not only meeting great people, but to discovering the diversity of various cities and towns that make our nation so unique and special.

I found out about this event in a rather odd way. I friend of mine from L.A. called to tell me he was planning to participate in a marathon in Little Rock while in town for a wedding. Since Arkansas and Tennessee are neighbors, he suggested I join him. Until our conversation, it never occurred to me to consider another race, and certainly not one outside Nashville.

After doing some research, I discovered that the Little Rock marathon and half marathon drew thousands of runners from all over the country. Moreover, several years earlier on a cross-country trip, I stopped briefly in Little Rock and really enjoyed my time there. The idea of visiting the city again, coupled with getting to spend some time with my dear friend Kris, made it a no-brainer. I registered for the race promptly.

I arranged to have some business meetings in Memphis that concluded on Friday afternoon. From there, I made the easy, 2-hour drive to Little Rock and began an interesting and educational experience in this very early stage of my 50-state journey.

Several weeks prior to the race, my friend Kris found out that he had a scheduling conflict and could not attend the race. However, by that time, I was fully invested in participating and was actually looking forward to it so I proceeded with my plans and boy am I glad I did.

The night before the race there was a pasta dinner for all participants that began at 5:00. All I was expecting was some good pasta, and while I got that in abundance, I also received the gift of meeting some wonderful folks, one of which would be instrumental in helping me develop a new appreciation for road racing that would eventually take me all over the country.

I helped myself to the buffet-style meal and found a seat at one of the empty tables. Shortly thereafter I was joined by a man I called "Dr. Rick" before the end of the evening. Dr. Rick is a dentist in Toronto who has run over 178 marathons (full, not half marathons) since 1978. His fastest time was 2:42 and it was obvious by his long, lean body that he was a serious runner. I loved listening to his stories of various races throughout the world (he had run in several countries) and soon, we were joined by his wife. She was not a runner but often traveled with her husband to keep him company. They had two grown children who had run with their father in the past but never shared the passion for it that he does. I found it amazing how this man has maintained a successful dental practice all these years while spending nearly every weekend in a different city, state and possibly country participating in full marathons.

A little later we were joined by a runner from Atlanta who was very humorous and the total opposite of Dr. Rick in that he didn't take his running very seriously; he was just out there to have a good time. He was not fast and was starting the marathon at 6:00 a.m., the start time for those runners needing more than 6 hours to complete the course. It was great listening to these two very different runners sharing their take on this avocation that brought us all to the same table. I enjoyed it very much.

As we talked, someone mentioned the weather to which I replied that I forgot to check the weather forecast before departing Nashville. Dr. Rick gently chided me about that and sternly advised me to start reviewing the weather forecasts several days in advance of the race and I took his advice to heart. He also advised that I cover my ears since the wind was supposed to be excessive on race day.

When I told him that I didn't have anything (not even a toboggan), he said that he made some additional headbands out of a sweatshirt and that I was welcome to have one of his. I gratefully accepted his gesture and followed him and his wife to their room to pick it up. To my surprise, it fit perfectly and I couldn't thank him enough; not just for the headband, but for being so open and sharing so much of his running experience with me. Although I didn't know it at the time, many of Dr. Rick's words would serve as a blueprint for me as I progressed as a runner and began my pursuit of the 50-state journey.

I was up at 5:30 on race morning and raring to go. Showing my inexperience and ignorance of road racing, I chose to catch the 6:30 free shuttle bus from the hotel to the starting area. I say "ignorance" because the race did not start until 8:00. Given the fact that the temperature was in the mid-20's at the start, it was ridiculous for me to arrive early and just sit around trying to stay warm. I would learn from this experience.

Thankfully, when I registered I paid extra for "VIP" services, which essentially was the opportunity to sit in a tent where they had a small floor heater. I think they had some extra water and liquids also but since I was freezing, I hardly paid attention to anything.

I waited until the very last minute to turn my coat and sweatpants into the gear check area, not yet aware of how important it is to warm-up before a long race. I made my way to the start line feeling miserable and started running when the alarm sounded. Since I had no concept of what my pace was or should be, I paid no attention to my watch. I just ran and tried to take in the sights along the way, including Central High School, where nine black students made history in 1957 when they integrated the then all-white high school. I felt a rush as I ran past this national historic site.

Everything was going fine until about mile 11 when a terrible pain shot through the outside of my left knee. I had no idea what it was, but it was so severe that I eventually had trouble bending my knee. Instead of running, I was hobbling. Although I finished in 2:18:19, two minutes faster than my second half marathon in Nashville, I was in a lot of pain when I finished and I would later learn why. But at that moment, I was just happy to have accomplished my goal of running my third half marathon.

Again, running a long distance event in all 50 states was not even a concept to me at this point. But from my experience in Little Rock, I would become a much more prepared and efficient runner and the lessons learned there would enable me to realize something I never thought was possible.

When I made up my mind to race in Little Rock, I made sure to schedule time to tour the Clinton Presidential Center.

Less than a mile from my hotel, I enjoyed walking along the Arkansas River to arrive at the William J. Clinton Presidential Center. What a building and what an honor to tour this institution. I stayed for over 2 hours on a self-guided tour through one of the most educational establishments in our country. With a total of three levels in 20,000 square feet, this library showcases American history at the turn of the 21st century with several interactive exhibits, including a full-scale replica of the Oval Office and a White House Cabinet Room.

Another exhibit consists of a 120-ft. timeline of the Clinton Administration through both of his terms. One doesn't have to be a fan of President Clinton to admire and appreciate all this great building showcases and represents. I found it just fascinating and had it not been for the pasta dinner ticket I'd pre-purchased, I definitely would have stayed longer, but before I left, I bought some nice souvenirs for my parents and myself to help commemorate this experience. It was a great way to spend my afternoon.

After my experience in Little Rock, I knew that I wanted to have this adventure in other great cities. I wanted to meet more "Dr. Rick's" and tour other establishments that made towns and cities so unique like the Clinton Presidential Library. Although it would take roughly another year to officially commit to running a distance event in all 50 states, Little Rock, Arkansas will always hold that special place in my journey as, "the one that triggered this whole running thing."

Race 3

Rock-n-Roll Marathon San Diego
San Diego, California - June 3, 2007

Still So Much to Learn
But Glad to Be Back In Cali

After the race in Little Rock, I ran in my 3rd consecutive Music City half marathon in Nashville, making it my 4th half marathon. Although I was still a far cry from taking running seriously or using it as a vehicle to see the country, I was pleased that with each race, my time was improving. So when a friend of mine from college called to tell me that she was planning to participate in a marathon in San Diego, I was intrigued. Although I had never run or trained beyond 13 miles, I was curious to see if I could achieve it.

The fact that this event took place in California made it even more enticing because I had not been back on the west coast since I moved to Nashville in 2004. It was an opportunity to run in my first full marathon, see an old college chum, and visit my friends in Los

Angeles all in one trip. There were too many compelling reasons to say yes to this race, so I did.

I decided to turn this trip into a mini-vacation so I flew to San Diego on Friday, ran on Sunday, drove to Los Angeles on Monday to visit with friends, and departed from L.A. on Wednesday to return to Nashville. Since I wasn't a very good runner at this point, and since the 50-state quest was far from being a reality, I was more excited about being on the west coast again than about running my first full marathon.

I elected to stay at the Embassy Suites Downtown because I had enough points through the Hilton Honors Program to stay all three nights for free. Also, the hotel provided shuttle service to the airport and I was within walking distance to the convention center (where the expo was being held) and the trolley station, preventing the need for a rental car while in town.

Upon arrival, I rode the hotel shuttle to the hotel, checked in, and walked the two blocks to the expo. Since the San Diego Marathon and Music City events in Nashville were operated by the same organization, I knew that the expo would be filled with many vendors and exhibitors. They were all eager to talk about their services and distribute samples of their products and I was eager to accept all the freebies they had to offer.

After nearly 1-1/2 hours of visiting most of the booths and loading up on sample bars and drinks, I met up with my old pal from college. She was there to walk the marathon as part of a group that raised money for the Leukemia Foundation. It was good to see her again. When we spoke before arriving in San Diego, she told me about a luncheon the organization was having for all the fund raisers and their friends and family. I was happy to purchase a ticket for such a worthy cause and looked forward to attending the next day.

I was up at 4:00 race morning hoping to catch the 5:00 a.m. shuttle to the race from the Hyatt, which was one block from my hotel. On my way out the door, I overheard the concierge arranging to have a van take runners to the race for $5.00. Yeah. About 10 of us rode in the van and got the start line about 5:30. So far, everything was working out just fine.

With nearly 16,000 runners, the starting area was huge. I had an hour to spare before the 6:30 start so I took a bite of a meal bar and turned in my gear bag with my jacket and sweatpants. I then found my corral, ready to take on the task of running 26.2 miles, or so I thought. Little did I know how instrumental this race was going to be in my overall development as a runner.

I started running about 8 minutes after the race began and found myself needing to use the restroom just 5 miles after starting. I had to stop and stand in line for about 5 minutes before rejoining the race. After running another ½ mile or so, I felt a pop in my left knee. This was the same knee that gave me trouble in Little Rock, but this time it was much worse. The pain was excruciating and I could barely bend my knee. Oh boy, was I in bad shape! Even though I could barely hobble, I was determined to not give up. I had not traveled over 3,000 miles to quit with over 20 miles left in the race. I was just going to have to dig deep and find a way to get through it.

After stopping on the side for several minutes, I finally made it to the medical aid station at mile 6.9 where I was given two Tylenol. They put a red mark on my bib to indicate to medical stations further along the course that I had been given my quota of medicine for the race. Yes, just two Tylenol! I thanked them for the help and continued hobbling along, almost dragging my left leg across the ground because of my inability to bend my knee. It was just horrible watching legions of runners pass by me, many of whom were not even running very fast. On top of the physical pain, I was mentally anguished also. I was nowhere near being the runner I would become, but I knew in my heart that I could have performed much better that day had it not been for my injury. That truth was heartbreaking to me.

The Rock-n-Roll events do a great job of placing timers throughout the course so runners can track their pace. When we reached the halfway mark, I was pleasantly surprised to see my time was 2:30 hours, which I thought was good considering that I had been reduced to a "hop" since the mile 6 area.

I kept going as best I could until mile 16 when I just couldn't take another step. I stopped on the side yet again, and this time, my face must have displayed total disgust because a very kind and caring runner stopped to ask me if I was okay. That was a generous gesture given the fact he was adding to his own time by stopping to help me.

I told him that even though I had taken two Tylenol at the medical station, the pain was still excruciating. He reached into his pocket and pulled out about ten Tylenol. He said that he could afford to give me two of his and handed them to me.

I was floored for two reasons: First, because I couldn't believe this guy had all that medicine on him. Second, because I was overwhelmed by his generosity in sharing part of his own "supply" with me.

The pain left me no option, so I graciously accepted the two he offered me and thanked him. He told me it was no problem and urged me to never run a marathon without keeping a stash of pain medication on me. Then he wished me well and told me he'd see me at the finish line. His gesture illuminates the kindness often displayed within the running community; a gesture I would see repeatedly in the many races to follow.

The last 10 miles was more of the same; hobbling for a distance then stopping on the side to let the pain subside before hobbling a bit more. It was awful and I couldn't wait to get to the finish line so the torture could end.

I came into the final stretch and crossed the finish line in 5:48:48. I was thankful to receive my finisher's medal, retrieve my things from gear check, and return to my hotel as quickly as possible. My first full marathon was no picnic!

As I look back over this first full marathon experience, I am thankful for the lessons it taught me, especially in terms of preparedness and of course, fitness. Never again would I need to interrupt my running for a bathroom break, and upon discovering a few months later that my knee pain was actually an IT band injury due mostly to tight quads, I made sure to stretch my quadricep muscles daily, preventing that injury from rearing its ugly head again. However, even with these lessons learned, it would still be another year before I'd get into the best shape of my life and seriously begin tackling a race in each state.

I would go on to run other full marathons much faster and more efficiently, but when it comes to those first few races, none were more instrumental in turning me into the runner I would eventually become than the Rock-n-Roll San Diego Marathon.

Oh yeah, and as for my friend with the Tylenol, I will always be thankful for his help but I decided to reject his advice about carrying my own stash of medicine with me during a race. Thankfully, in the 75+ races I've run since San Diego, my body has held up just fine medicine-free!

Race 4

Marshall University
Half Marathon

Huntington, West Virginia,
November 4, 2007

Still Learning but Getting Smarter

At this point, I was enjoying running but still too much of a novice to consider it as something that could take me around the country . The experiences I had in Arkansas and California let me know that I liked running in cities other than Nashville, so when my job required me to travel near the West Virginia border, I thought it might be interesting to run in an event somewhere in that area. So I checked to see if any races were scheduled to take place and one in particular caught my eye: The Marshall University Half Marathon in Huntington, West Virginia.

Marshall University is a public research university that many may know from the movie, We Are Marshall starring Matthew Mc-

Conaughey. It was about the tragic plane crash that killed 75 people, including 37 members of the Marshall University football team. The marathon and half marathon take place every November, starting with a run through the campus and concluding on the goal-line in the Marshall Football Stadium. Although I didn't find out about the movie until the day of the race from another runner, I was intrigued with this part of the country. Also, I thought it would be nice to run another half marathon before the end of the year, so I registered just two weeks before the race.

Once in Huntington, I stopped at the expo to pick up my timing chip and pertinent information about the next day's race. I had no issue with the limited expo which was essentially just a packet pickup because I wanted to explore the city of Huntington with the 1-2 hours of daylight left in the day.

Huntington's downtown is a national historic district, which is common in many southern cities and towns. From its rich architecture to its tree-lined streets, I found Huntington to be quaint and charming, and I was disappointed that I hadn't allotted more time to really explore the city more.

Because I waited so late to register, all of the hotels in Huntington (which weren't that many to start with) were already booked, so I stayed at a Hampton Inn just across the Ohio River in Ashland, Kentucky.

Since the race started at 8:00 a.m., I made sure to leave the hotel in plenty of time to accommodate the 30-minute drive to Hun-

tington and to get a good parking space. With 366 marathon participants and another 235 in the half marathon, this was the smallest
race I'd entered so far. While I liked the larger events, this race in
Huntington taught me there is much to appreciate about smaller
races as well. I'm thankful that my 50-state journey encompasses
small, medium and large races.

While trying to stay warm before the start, I met another runner who travels to races all over the country in an RV, eliminating
the need to find a hotel room for the night. He was interesting and
reminded me how much I liked and admired the running community. Also, he was the one who told me about the movie, "We Are
Marshall."

Known for being a flat and fast course, I enjoyed the scenery of
this race once we got past the industrial areas. I especially appreciated some of the downtown sights like Ritter Park and the Ohio Riverfront. However, the most memorable aspect to this race was the
finish, running through the Marshall University campus to the football stadium, with the option to carry a football the last 100 yards. It
was a nice way to end 13.1 miles.

My finish time was 2:14:22, just a minute slower than my 3rd
Music City half marathon. While I was satisfied with my performance, the desire to become a better runner was growing stronger
with each race. I wanted to become leaner and more fit. I wanted to
be faster and more proficient on the race course. Little did I know
that the tide was about to turn in a mighty big way.

Along this 50-state journey, I would spend time in many college towns and on many college campuses (particularly in the northeast), and I'm glad Marshall was my first experience in this regard. My only disappointment was that I didn't spend more time exploring the area. Once I committed to running a long distance event in every state, I made sure to add in an extra day whenever possible to ensure I experienced each city or town to the fullest.

Overall, I found the people of Huntington and the neighboring communities to be kind, caring and easy going. While my time there was very short, I'm glad the Marshall University Half Marathon was the race I chose for the state of West Virginia.

2008: My Best Running Year

2008 stands as the best running year in my career. It wasn't the year that I ran the most races but it was the year in which I made my greatest strides and established records I've yet to break, including:

- First time to stand on the podium (an honor extended to those coming in 1st, 2nd, & 3rd overall and in their age group): Corinth Coca-Cola Classic 10K Run—Corinth, Mississippi
- First time to win prize money: Corinth Coca-Cola Classic 10K Run
- First time to run a sub-two hour half marathon—Virginia Beach Rock-n-Roll Marathon
- First time to come in 1st for an age group win: Route 66 Quarter Marathon—Tulsa
- PR for the Half Marathon: Baton Rouge Beach Half Marathon (1:50:42)

2008 represents the year I made a real turnaround, not just in my avocation of running, but in my life. I became more focused and disciplined, which are practices I continue to institute to this day. I love identifying goals and then working hard (and praying hard) to achieve them. Nothing gives me greater joy than to envision something in my head and watch it come to fruition over time.

As I reflect on the races in 2008, I get very excited because it takes me back to where this quest started taking off and when I became aware of all the benefits associated with it.

Race 5

Mercedes Half Marathon
Birmingham, Alabama - Feb. 10, 2008

Blessing of Heritage

Toward the end of 2007, I became very serious about my fitness and my diet. I started working out with much greater intensity and being more diligent about maintaining a clean diet. As a result, I improved in almost every area as a runner. Though still not committed to running an event in every state, I was looking forward to entering more races within driving distance of Nashville. I found a gem when I registered for the Mercedes Half Marathon in Birmingham, Alabama.

Since I lived in Nashville, my drive to the beautiful city of Birmingham was just slightly over 3 hours. At the time, I was driving quite a bit for my job (almost 3500 miles a month) so I tried to avoid driving more than 6 hours to reach my destination whenever possible. Since the race took place on a Sunday, I left my home that Saturday morning around 9:00 so I'd have plenty of time to enjoy myself at the expo and tour the city of Birmingham, whose history greatly interested me.

Saturday was gorgeous without a cloud in the sky. The weather reached nearly 60 degrees which was just perfect. I couldn't have picked a lovelier day for a drive and as I started south on I-65, I knew this was going to be a special couple of days and race.

Upon arrival, I immediately liked Birmingham. Southern cities are intriguing to me, mostly because of their deep historical roots and the part they played in the shaping of our country. Since I grew up in the south, I have an attraction for the architecture and style that characterize most of these cities. I couldn't wait to strap on my backpack, set out on foot, and soak up as much of the city's unique charm as I could.

I stayed at the Hampton Inn & Suites downtown, a perfect location since it was within walking distance of the expo, race start and most of the historic institutions of the city. With amazing weather expected all weekend, I couldn't wait to realize all that the next two days would yield. I just knew it was going to be grand — and I was right.

In Birmingham, I started a trend the night before the race. It is a process I call "race mode." Race mode is when I start to relax and allow my mind and my body to just "let go." This is the time when I become as unburdened as possible so that I'm prepared to perform to the best of my ability the next morning on the race course. As I've grown into a stronger runner, the process of getting into race mode has become increasingly important to my success on the race course. It is a discipline I still practice today.

My preparation time the night before a race is similar no matter where I am or what distance I'm running the next day (marathon vs. half marathon vs. quarter marathon vs. 10K). I typically start by going through the swag bag and examining all the goodies I received at the expo. Then I lay out my race clothes, attach my bib to my shirt and the timing device to my shoe. The timing device is a magnetic strip attached to the bib or a strap that goes around the ankle. I prefer the strip on the bib because it is convenient and provides less opportunity for error. Once I complete these tasks, then I simply relax. I either watch television or read the Bible, or both, but ultimately, I clear my mind of all the chatter of the day and focus on why I'm there and what I hope to accomplish. In Birmingham, I read the Bible and the day's entry from my Max Lucado daily reader before retiring to bed to watch television and drift into a restful sleep.

Upon rising at 5:00 a.m., I prayed and then slowly started getting ready. I learned from Dr. Rick in Little Rock to make sure I know what to expect weather-wise on race day. On this day in Birmingham, the forecast was calling for morning temperatures in the 30's but a rapid warm-up to the 60's later in the day. Most runners will tell you that they prefer cold or cooler weather when running; however, I prefer warmer temperatures. Not hot but warm. Since it was expected to be a cold start, I elected to wear my long spandex pants, several layers of wicker shirts, gloves, and toboggan.

Around 6:00 I consumed a container of goat's milk yogurt that I brought from home and some water before heading to the start line around 6:45 a.m. As soon as I hit the outside, I noticed how warm it seemed. Clearly it was not 30 degrees, but there was nothing I could do at that point. I was dressed for 30 degrees, so be it.

I checked my bag and coat and had just enough time to warm-up and stretch (something that I would learn to do a much better job of later on) before getting into line. The race started promptly at 7:03 a.m. and we were off. I felt good, but I recognized about mile 2 that it was going to get hot out there. I didn't want to discard anything, not even my gloves, so I kept my head down and forged along.

The Mercedes Half Marathon is a tough course. It contains some of the biggest inclines of any race I'd run previously (or subsequently) but I knew it was going to be tough from the outset. Many of the posts I'd read about the course from runners in previous years made it clear how difficult it was to maneuver the hills, but there is nothing like discovering those hills for yourself. Around mile 9 or 10, I wanted to quit and in previous races, I would have started walking by that point, but this time was different. Even though I was very fatigued, I continued to maintain a very slow jog. A few sips of Powerade at a couple of race stations helped maintain my energy level.

I was so happy to see mile 13 because mile 12 had been hard. I finished strong and sprinted the final few yards for a finish time of 2:19:51. While I had run half marathons faster than that, I was still elated with my finish time and the beautiful shiny new medal I received. It just felt good to be running injury-free and strong. I was really starting to love being out on the race course.

With backpack in tow, I walked from the expo to the Birmingham

Civil Rights Institute where I experienced an unforgettable touch with my history that I'll carry with me always. I thought my visit to Little Rock was meaningful but not to the degree that it was in Birmingham. Each exhibit, from the original bars and doors of the cell where Dr. Martin Luther King Jr. penned his noted "Letter from a Birmingham Jail," to the replica of the Greyhound bus carrying the Freedom Riders, touched me. I developed a deeper appreciation and understanding of the struggle endured by others to allow me to be where I am today. I couldn't get enough of this place and left only because they were closing for the day.

I purchased some mementos in the gift store, including the book Fifty Black Women Who Changed America before exiting the building. I walked across the street to the Sixteenth Street Baptist Church where those four precious little girls died from a hater's bomb. I stood there in silence, looking at this historical structure and thinking about the changes that have taken place in our society since those days of protest, turmoil and just plain hatred.

There is no denying we still have a ways to go as a society and nation. Likewise, there is no denying that in the city where much of the racial turmoil of the 50's and 60's took place, an African American woman can now walk the streets of Birmingham freely and participate in one of the largest half marathons in the nation. Yes, progress has been made and I'm thankful my race experiences help to illuminate that fact, while simultaneously putting a small dent in all the work that is yet to be done.

On the way back to the hotel, I walked through the famed Kelly Ingram Park where many young people of color marched for their freedom in 1963. The park was clean and lovely and the weather was outstanding, thus making the walk back to my hotel that much more enjoyable.

Regardless of your race or background, I believe it is impossible to tour these amazing institutions of our nation's history and not be deeply touched in a special way. I loved soaking up the history in such a personal way. It was moving and I look forward to visiting the Institute again someday soon.

There are too many kisses to list about this weekend. The Mercedes Half Marathon and the city of Birmingham will always be special to me. I would go on to run many half marathons at a much faster pace, but no other race gave me the opportunity to explore my history in such a profound and unexpected way. This race will always be one of my favorites for that reason.

Race 6

Coca-Cola Classic 10k
Corinth, Mississippi - May 3, 2008

The Turning Point

A lthough I can't recall exactly how I discovered the Coca-Cola Classic 10k, I'm sure it had something to do with my long time interest in the state of Mississippi. I'm a rabid lover of Southern Literature. Some of my favorite authors made their home in this state, specifically William Faulkner and Eudora Welty, whose estates I would tour within the next year (keep reading). I was always on the lookout for opportunities to explore different parts of the Magnolia State and now I had a great one in road racing. Thus, when I found out about "one of the best road races in the south," I was immediately interested.

Held in the northeast Mississippi town of Corinth, this running event has all the bells and whistles of the large Rock-n-Roll events without the massive crowds and impersonal quality. In conjunction with the race was the annual Arts & Crafts May Festival, showcasing everything from pottery, candles, baked goods, and jewelry just to name a few.

Moreover, Corinth's historical features, home to Mississippi's oldest drug store and soda fountain (Borrum's) and the Black History Museum convinced me that this was one place I didn't want to miss seeing and exploring to a greater degree. Thus, I wasted no time registering for this 10k race.

Since the race started at 8:30, I was up at 6:00 to ensure I ate properly and knew where I was going before the race started. I stayed at the Hampton Inn which was about 1.7 miles from the downtown starting line. With nearly 700 runners present, I wasn't sure how the parking downtown was going to be, so I left extra early to avoid a possible last minute debacle. I easily secured a spot just a short distance from the starting line and did a quick warm-up run and a few stretches before taking my place in line.

My energy level was great and I knew that I was ready to have a great race. Of course, having never run fast enough to place, standing on a podium was nowhere in my thoughts. I just knew that I was in the best shape of my life, tipping the scales at barely 106 pounds with well-defined upper and lower strength. Long gone were the days of IT band injuries and poor running shoes. I learned over the previous 11 races about the importance of a clean diet and the proper combination of cardio and resistance training in order to be a better and faster runner. I had no idea this was the race when all of it would come together in such a pronounced way.

From the time the horn sounded, I felt amazing and sensed

there was something different about this race. I was moving more proficiently and in some ways, it almost felt like I was coasting along without the heavy breathing and tiredness that I often experienced in past races. Much of that ease was attributable to the fact that the course was relatively flat. Also, it was clear that my augmented fitness level was a major contributing factor.

Much of the first mile takes place downtown, with most of the race winding through the charming, tree-lined residential streets of Corinth, illuminating the beauty and peacefulness of this historic city. I loved the friendliness of my fellow runners and the Corinth citizens, many of whom sat out on their lawns encouraging us with cheers and applause. One highlight for me was seeing a young girl participating in the wheelchair portion of the race with her dad running alongside her with enthusiasm and encouragement. Sights like this are one of the many blessings one reaps in a road race.

As we re-entered downtown with one mile to go, I continued to feel strong. Although I wasn't keeping track of my time, I felt certain that I was running faster than I had in any previous race or training run. As we neared the finish line and could hear the roar of the crowd, I poured it on and literally sprinted the last several yards of the race. This would become semi-standard for me in future races.

After crossing the finish line and receiving my finisher's medal, I had time to go back to the hotel, take a shower and checkout before the awards ceremony and the rest of the festival. I had no expectation of receiving an award but I still wanted to attend the ceremony, which I never had a desire to do in past races.

The awards ceremony started promptly at 10:45 and officials presented trophies in the shape of gold Coca-Cola bottles mounted on dark wooden bases. They went to everyone who placed 1st, 2nd, and 3rd in their age division, which were divided in 5-year incre-

ments. In addition, cash prizes were issued in the following increments: $50.00 for 1st place, $30.00 for 2nd place, and $20.00 for
3rd place. In the many races I've run since Corinth, I've yet to find
such a generous gesture to age group winners. Usually, a trophy is
given, and perhaps a gift certificate of some kind, but never cash to
every age group winner three deep in each division. That is unheard
of, and is one of the reasons why this race is so well-respected and
has thrived for over 30 years.

As they got to my age category, 40-45 years old, I was overjoyed
to hear my name called as the 3rd place winner in my age group!
I quickly rushed to the podium to receive my beautiful Coca-Cola bottle trophy and envelope containing $20.00. Wow—what an
unexpected surprise and blessing. Instead of spending the twenty
bucks, I have it in a frame on the wall of my trophy room.

Another great blessing occurred as I was milling around the
Court Square just before the awards ceremony. I met so many incredible people that day, but none more remarkable than Barbara
and Tall, a lovely couple whose friendship I truly cherish. So when
my new friend Barbara placed 3rd in her age group also, it was a
double blessing. In the years to follow, the three of us would share
additional running experiences in Seattle and Las Vegas, as well
as another 10k Classic in Corinth. There are many things to adore
about running, but for me, nothing surpasses the joy of friendship
I've been blessed to experience through this sport. My life is much
richer with the Talls in it, and the other friends I would come to
know in future races.

With my medal around my neck and my trophy and envelope
in hand, I spent the next couple of hours enjoying the festival. I
sampled great food, engaged in great conversations, and explored
Borrum's Drug Store, the oldest operating soda fountain and drug

store in the state of Mississippi. It was a lovely day from every perspective and one that I will never forget.

In doing my research on this historical city, I was excited to see as many of these monuments as I could. First on the list was the Black History Museum of Corinth, a former home of two of Corinth's citizens before its conversion to a museum in 2003. It wonderfully showcases the African American heritage of Corinth and its surrounding communities. I was deeply touched by what I gleaned from this historic edifice and remained in touch with its director for several years.

From there, I visited the Coca-Cola Museum, where the 100+ year relationship between Coca-Cola and the city of Corinth is illuminated. This exhibit features over 1,000 pieces of authentic memorabilia with the famous Coca-Cola trademark and because of its importance of Corinth's history, Coca-Cola Bottling Works has sponsored the 10k Classic for over 30 years.

I love to learn. If I could, I would be a perpetual college student, graduating with one degree after another; that's how much I love learning. Thus, the time I spent in Corinth was fantastic. I loved being there so much.

The Coca-Cola Classic 10k was wonderful. I returned the following year with my mother so she could experience the charm and warmth of this great city. She was as moved as I was, and if that wasn't enough, I ended up placing 1st in my age group that year. Great race, great history, great new friends - there was nothing I didn't like about this stop in my journey. After this race, I knew that I wanted to have this kind of experience all over the country and decided on my drive home that I would run a race in every state of the U.S. I had no clue how long it would take; I just knew it was something I was going to work at relentlessly to accomplish.

In early 2009, I ran a half marathon in Jackson, Mississippi where I received two unexpected blessings: a 3rd place age group win and the meeting of another wonderful friend, Paula. Our friendship has been invaluable to me and from this great lady I've learned so much about kindness, courage and faith. Again, some of the greatest blessings from this 50-state journey have been the amazing friendships with people I would have never met otherwise.

Corinth, Mississippi and the Coca-Cola Classic 10k will always hold a special place in my heart. In a way, it was here that the real journey began.

Race 7

The Kona Marathon
Keauhou-Kona, Hawaii - June 29, 2008

Full Marathon Vindication with the Granddaddy Race of Them All

By far, the Kona Marathon stands out as my favorite race to date, largely for reasons that are quite easy to understand. It takes place in Hawaii and it's many hills make it one of the most challenging marathons in the world. It takes place in Hawaii and it is the same course (with minor changes) that comprises the running portion of the Iron Man competition. It takes place in Hawaii and starts at 5:30 a.m. so you have plenty of time to finish, rest and enjoy the rest of the day. And, oh yeah—did I say that it takes place in Hawaii? One word describes this race experience for me: Beautiful.

I'd like to say that I chose this race in Hawaii over the many others this gorgeous state has to offer because I wanted to run the most challenging one I could find. Also, because I wanted the bragging rights to say I ran the marathon of the annual Ironman World Championship, which some have called the "hardest day in sports."

However, if I said these things, I would not be completely honest. The truth is, I needed to find a race in Hawaii and, having never been to the Aloha state, one race was as good as another to me. I was eager to visit Hawaii and I knew that I wanted to go sometime in the summer so that I could turn it into a vacation and stay at least a week. Since the Kona Marathon took place in June, the timing was perfect. Only later did I learn about its association with the Ironman which was simply icing on the cake.

I was yearning to try the full marathon distance again since I was in better shape and was more knowledgeable about the sport of running. I knew that I could outperform my last time by at least one hour. In retrospect, had I chosen a flatter course where the temperatures were more agreeable, I'm sure that I could have improved on my San Diego marathon time by more than 1.5 hours. However, I was not that advanced in my thinking yet. My goal at this point was to shave an hour off my "less than stellar" marathon debut, and to do so in a place many call "paradise." It never occurred to me to consider the course difficulty or the extreme heat. In this case, ignorance truly was bliss.

Since my mother had never been to Hawaii either, I thought it would be nice to surprise her with this trip. It would be something I was able to do for my Mom several times throughout my 50-state quest and I'm grateful that God blessed me with such an opportunity. Unfortunately, much of my mother's adult life had been marred by disappointment and unrealized dreams. Thus, it was a privilege to have my mother along with me on this journey as much as possible. While I've always preferred to travel alone, the joy of

Holding my Coca-Cola trophy for first place in my age group at the Coca-Cola 10k Classic in Corinth, Mississippi.

seeing her experience the gift of travel for the first time in many ways was heartwarming. I'm grateful God provided me with the means to bring her blessing in this way. In so doing, I too, have been blessed.

To make this into a complete vacation, I decided to stay a full week, with the marathon falling in the middle. The Hawaiian time zone is 4 hours behind Eastern Standard Time, so I knew that I would need at least a day for my body to adjust to the change before race day. So we departed North Carolina early Thursday morning in order to arrive in Kona early afternoon HST. Including the layover in Phoenix, we spent 11 hours traveling to Hawaii and it was worth every minute! From the moment we landed in Hawaii, I found a new place to fall in love with.

We stayed at the beautiful Outrigger Keauhou Beach Resort, which was an ideal location not only to the beach, but also to the start and finish of the race on Alii Drive. Our package included a magnificent ocean front view and free breakfast each day of our stay. We couldn't have been more pleased with these accommodations and spent most of the evening unpacking and getting situated, Then we enjoyed a nice dinner in the hotel restaurant overlooking the ocean. It was a blessed day and I couldn't wait for the rest of the week to unfold.

I was up early the next morning (Friday) and ran 6 miles along Alii Drive where I encountered several other runners in preparation of Sunday's race. We greeted one another warmly (a characteristic I've found common in most runners all over the country) and caused me to be even more enthusiastic about Sunday's marathon, as if that was possible. For the first time in my life, I felt like a runner that morning. I looked more like a runner than ever before, with the long, lean body I had always wanted. Several people in the airport approached me and asked if I was a marathoner, to which I was happy to respond affirmatively. They followed up with a comment like, "I thought so because you have the lean body of a runner." I won't lie; I like being thin and healthy and recognized for my athletic prowess. It reinforces the fact that my months of training and eating right paid off.

After my run, I sat on the beach for a little while and couldn't get over all the beauty of the state. On one hand, I would love to live in Hawaii and be privy to that amazing weather all year long, but on the other hand, I think it would be detrimental to me because all I'd want to do is sit back and enjoy the great weather.

The next day (Saturday) I attended the expo and secured all my registration materials and commemorative shirt for the race. Then we decided to venture out for lunch and took a shuttle to one of the shopping districts. We spent much of the day there before returning to the hotel where I took advantage of the free massages for the marathon participants. The rubdown was so refreshing and much needed for tomorrow's race. As I was heading toward the elevator, a tall, lean man was leaving the massage area at the same time. It was obvious that he was an experienced runner with barely 5% body fat, if that much, and we struck up a great conversation about the race. As I suspected, he runs marathons all over the globe and does so in barely 3 hours. As I was getting off the elevator on my floor, he said that he would look for me in the race. I said that was fine, thinking there was no way he'd see me out there considering that he would most likely be finished before I even reached the halfway point. I would find out that I was wrong.

It's race day and I couldn't feel more energized! I was up before my 4:00 a.m. scheduled wake-up call, preparing myself mentally for what I was about to undertake. I slowly dressed and did some quad and hamstring stretches out on the balcony as I watched the waves rolling toward the shore. It was a lovely morning and was to be a lovely day, although the temperatures were already in the high 70's, notorious for The Big Island.

In over 70 races, the Kona Marathon is the only one where my top was just a sports bra. I prefer wearing some kind of mesh running shirt but with the high temperatures and humidity expected that day, the fewer the clothes, the better. Before I left the hotel room, I prayed to the Lord for a safe and healthy race, with a finish in less than 5 hours, even if it was 4:59:59. It was important to me to have a finish time in the "4" hour range and not the "5" hour. Specifically, I wanted to shave an hour off my previous full marathon time, even though I picked a tough race to do it.

After Mom and I decided she should be near the finish line somewhere near the 4th hour, I headed to the start line at 5:15 a.m. It was on Alii Drive, just above the hotel driveway. Although there were 210 participants in the marathon, the half marathon and a 10k event were also taking place, so there were many runners milling around and staying loose until the official 5:30 a.m. start time.

The race started promptly at 5:30 and I crossed the official start line at 5:31. In later races, after I developed a better handle on my form and pace, I kept strict watch over my pace time per mile. However, at this point, I was just happy to get from one mile to the next, regardless of my pace. I started off feeling good and just kept running at whatever speed felt right without taxing me to the limit.

The Kona Marathon course (in 2008) was an out-and-back course along the coast of The Big Island; meaning we ran out to mile 13, turned around, and ran back to the place where we started. I would come to favor out-and-back courses because during the second half of the race, you know exactly what to expect, having run it already in the opposite direction. The first 6 miles were relatively flat but we would begin a long, steady climb around mile 6.5. I was still feeling pretty good making sure that I stopped for water at just about each liquid station except for a couple. The water contained ice which was so needed because the temperature kept rising. Even though I lived in the south and was used to heat and humidity, this was nothing I had experienced before. Kona is in a league all by itself.

Once we got to the turnaround point, one of my favorite moments in the race took place. In out-and-back races, you pass people who are ahead of you on one side, and people who are behind you on the other. When I was about .2 miles from the turnaround spot, the guy I met in the elevator the night before was running toward me on the other side heading in the opposite direction. I had my head down and didn't see him at first, but he yelled out to me and once I looked up, it was easy to spot him due to his height. He exclaimed, "There she is. You are doing great!" and we gave each other a high-five. I loved that race moment.

There is one way to describe the second half of this race: HARD. After the turnaround point, the climb begins again at mile 14 and more or less stays that way until about mile 20. Moreover, the fan support is practically non-existent except for a few of the runner's relatives and close friends. Other than that, it is quiet except for the sound of runners panting for air and the thud of all those tennis shoes hitting the pavement. Also by this time, I was probably 2-1/2 hours into the race and it just kept getting hotter and hotter. Needing more than water to get me through, I tried the energy drink they were distributing, which was Ultima Replinisher, but I didn't like the taste so I stuck with the water.

As I ran along this tough stretch of the race and gazed at all the lava rocks along the side, it occurred to me that I had nearly used almost everything I had physically in temperatures where vegetation doesn't even grow. It was quite a moment of realization.

By mile 19, I was getting so winded that I thought I was going to have to stop, but thankfully, I was able to forge ahead. I was grateful for the good start because once I reached mile 23, I replaced my slow jog with walking. I knew that I would have a 4+ hour finish so I didn't mind slowing down some, although I was aware that I still had 3 more miles to go.

Never in a race previously or subsequently has it taken so long to get to the finish line. It appeared the more I ran, the further the finish line seemed to be. However, the crowd support was amazing from mile 24.5 to the end and all those cheers helped because physically, I was spent. I kept thinking to myself "how much further?" and then, I finally saw the finish just above the last little hill. I was so elated to see it that I started speeding up without even realizing it. Then, I heard the announcer yell out as I crossed the finish line, "Bridget Simpson, number 204 from Franklin, Tennessee." That's me, I thought. I did it! I looked up at the clock to see my official finish time of 4:45:34. Yeah! I could hardly contain myself. I achieved my goal of finishing in the 4-hour time range and I did better than my first full marathon by 1 hour and 3 minutes!

I was over the moon about my achievement and what made it even better was seeing my mother's beautiful face as I took that final step. She was clapping and cheering with the biggest smile I've ever seen her have and that made me feel so good. In fact, I started crying which surprised even me because I so seldom cry (not because I'm not emotional but sometimes it makes my head hurt so I try to avoid doing it altogether.) We embraced one another as did so many of the runners with their loved ones. A full marathon is taxing enough, but the Kona Marathon takes it to another level. Everyone who crossed that finish line felt nothing but joy—and relief!

After getting my medal and finisher's shirt, Mom and I went to the hotel restaurant and had the world's greatest breakfast. We spent the rest of the afternoon shopping and enjoying the beauty of Kona. Words can't express how overjoyed I was to have the race behind me; it had been a long time since I felt so relaxed. And I didn't take my medal off the whole day.

Mom and I spent an extra two days on The Big Island. The time included fun events like a tour of beautiful Hawaiian homes, a tour of one of the largest macadamia and chocolate factories, a visit to Hilo on the other side of Island, and the opportunity to see some volcanoes and gorgeous waterfalls up close. We were so blessed on this vacation and couldn't have asked for a better time. I learned a great deal in Hawaii, mostly that if the rest of the country treated me as well as Hawaii, I was going to have one outstanding adventure ahead of me. Little did I know that was a huge understatement.

Hawaii is a place of superlatives. The scenery is beautiful every place you look, the food is delicious and the people are friendly. The race was outstanding too; it offered tremendous challenges, and that is what makes races exciting.

Race 8

Virginia Beach Rock-n-Roll Half Marathon

Virginia Beach, Virginia - August 31, 2008

Setting a New Half Marathon Standard

Now fully invested in running in all 50 states and still experiencing a high from my Kona marathon, I was on fire to keep the momentum going. My workouts and training was better than ever and so were my results. Coupled with my commitment to a clean diet, my 105 lb. body was performing at a higher level than I could have ever hoped or expected. I loved every minute of it and wanted to return to the race course as soon as possible.

Since it was the thick of the summer, good races were harder to find so I used July and most of August as training months. I wanted to be as competitive as possible. The reward would come on the last day of August at the Virginia Beach Rock-n-Roll Half Marathon.

Before Virginia Beach, I had completed five Rock-n-Roll events:

four in Nashville (Music City Half Marathons) and one in San Diego. By now, I had enough experience with this series to know that they are always high quality, well-organized events, despite having participants in the tens of thousands per race. Other perks include large, colorful finisher medals, individualized certificates with runner statistics, booklets containing all the information about the race, and musical guests at nearly every mile to keep the race lively. Moreover, there was great swag including tech and cotton shirts. I also enjoyed the expos at these events, which are some of the largest in existence.

This race was also attractive because I could get to it relatively easy. Taking place over the Labor Day weekend, I decided to drive a few days before the race to my parent's home in North Carolina, rest there for a day before driving 3 hours to Virginia Beach. The extra day was nice to have to slowly make my way back to my home in Tennessee.

Several years ago my job required me to travel to the Virginia Beach/Norfolk region a couple of times a month, so I knew this area quite well. I always loved being there during the off-season when the beaches were relatively empty. I can remember many times overlooking the Atlantic Ocean from my hotel balcony and feeling like I was the only person in the world. It was fabulous.

I arrived in Virginia Beach the afternoon of the 30th, the day before the race, and drove straight to my hotel, the Hilton Virginia Beach Oceanfront.

The room was lovely with an ocean view, so I was more than satisfied.

From there, I walked the 1.7 miles to the Virginia Beach Convention Center where the expo was being held. Just like those in Nashville and San Diego, it was huge with vendors and exhibitors from all over showcasing their goods and services. Also in attendance were race officials from other races around the country passing out flyers about their events. I've found out about a lot of future races through this means.

After a couple of hours of talking to vendors, sampling their products, and meeting other runners, I decided to go back to the hotel and put everything away before venturing out for some dinner. I knew many great places to eat from my past visits to the area but the weather wasn't great (cloudy all day). I was tired, so I decided to go with some light seafood at a restaurant close to the hotel. Several other runners had the same idea and it was almost like a pre-race reunion of sorts. I didn't expect all the dinner conversation but it was nice to have.

The next morning, I woke up energized and feeling great. I prepared well for this race and ready to get going with it. Even though I was close enough to walk to the start (about 1.5 miles), I decided to save my legs and catch one of the free shuttles to the start. Since the shuttles were positioned all along the boardwalk, I caught the one closest to my hotel at 28th street. I arrived at the starting area about 6:15 and had 45 minutes to stretch, take a couple of bites of an energy bar and drink some water.

I also used the time to get mentally prepared. The starters village was full of runners from every walk of life, some short, some tall, some muscular, some long and lean, some older, some younger, etc. That's one of the things I love about the running community so much; its diversity and overall kindness. Quite simply, runners are some of the nicest people you will ever encounter. I felt so blessed to be a part of that community that day.

Due to the vast number of people, a wave or tiered start was necessary (as is the case with just about any race exceeding at least 5,000 runners.) I was assigned corral #5, which was a great position because it was closer to the front than the back. All runners are equipped with timing devices that affix either to their shoe or bib, so it doesn't matter where you start. Your official time begins when you cross the timing mat at the start and when you cross the timing mat at the finish. Times are recorded electronically so your place in line has no bearing on your finish time.

The race started promptly at 7:00 which was great because of how humid it gets in Virginia that time of year. Right from the start, I felt terrific and knew that I was running well although I was not clocking my pace (this is something I would start doing fervently in subsequent races.) So even though I didn't know what my pace was, I knew that I was running well and faster than I had in previous half marathons.

The Virginia Beach Half Marathon course is flat with the final mile taking place on the Oceanfront Boardwalk. Near the middle of the race, we ran around Camp Pendleton and along the Rudee Inlet Bridge, Just when runners started to get bored and tired of running, a new band appeared to help take you up a notch. That helped me run smoother and even effortlessly at times.

As we neared the finish line running along Oceanfront Board-walk, the fan support was huge, with people lined up on the both sides of the course yelling and ringing cowbells. I was totally into it and glanced at the official time clock under the finish canopy. When I saw a "1" posted as the first digit and not a "2", I knew that I was going to post my first sub-2 hour half marathon. The momentum of that fact caused me to sprint to the finish with both hands in the air. I was so elated that you would have thought I came in first of all runners that day; I certainly felt like I did.

My official time was 1:56:49! I couldn't believe it. Again, I knew I was running better than ever but I just didn't have finishing in less than 2 hours in my sights. I guess I knew it was possible but it just wasn't something I was focused on. In retrospect, I think not focusing on it helped because I was able to really relax and just settle into my pace without placing any undue pressure on myself. It was just a fantastic race and one that forever changed my expectations of this journey from a racing perspective.

Since I knew I could run a half marathon with an average pace of 8+ minutes per mile, I began training for that type of result every time. Except for one debacle in early 2010, I always ran the half marathon in less than 2 hours.

This 50-state journey was progressing better than I could have imagined with the best yet to come.

Race 9

United States Air Force 10k
Dayton, Ohio - September 20, 2008

Getting Faster Military Style

My job required me to travel throughout the states of Tennessee and Kentucky, so when I had an opportunity to organize some meetings in the northern part of Kentucky near the Ohio border, it occurred to me it would be a good time to schedule a race in the state of Ohio.

Although Ohio may not be one of the first states that come to mind when considering road racing, it should be—the opportunities to participate in marathons, half marathons, and 10ks are numerous. In fact, some of the largest races in the country take place in Ohio, none more so than the United States Air Force series of races. Taking place on Wright-Patterson Air Force Base, this race series provides participants with the opportunity to run side-by-side with many of our men and women in uniform. Also, the finisher medals are presented to runners by a senior Air Force officer.

My first participation in the USAF events was the half marathon in 2007. While I had a decent result (finish time of 2:17:04), it was before I got serious and started performing well on the race course. However, I enjoyed the race very much and when I discovered that they were adding a 10k event in 2008, I knew that I had to participate. So I've elected to use the inaugural 10k race as my Ohio event for this book.

After wrapping up some meetings in northern Kentucky that Friday afternoon, I took the short 75 minute drive to Dayton, Ohio. I was excited to return to the Dayton/Fairborn area and thankful to have a race take place on a Saturday instead of Sunday. I was even more excited that it was a 10k, a distance fast becoming my favorite.

Since I was already familiar with the area from the year before, I drove straight to my hotel, the Hampton Inn in Fairborn. It was within walking distance to the expo and a variety of dining options. I checked in and walked to the expo which was classy and well done, though small. I liked the brochure given to all participants about this grand event (the Rock-n-Roll events distribute similar booklets as well); a nice keepsake to help commemorate the race. In addition, the long-sleeve, 100% cotton shirt we received remains one of my favorites to this day and generates the most conversation when I wear it.

Another nice touch is that the first name of each runner was printed on our runner's bib, so as we ran along, spectators were cheering us on by our name. Even though I didn't know a soul at that race, you wouldn't know it by the number of people yelling, "Come on Bridget. You can do it!" I couldn't help but smile.

Since the 10k didn't begin until 8:30 a.m., I had plenty of time in the morning to warm-up and get to the starting area without being rushed. The parking area was located at the National Museum of the United States Air Force so I knew exactly where to go and gave myself enough time to secure a good parking spot. With over 6,000 participants and quite a few spectators, I thought that parking could be an issue but thankfully, it was not. I learned from one of the volunteers at the expo to enter through the gates marked "B" in blue, and that offered plenty of parking and an easy departure after the race.

Since it was a bit chilly, I stayed in the car with the heater on for as long as possible before making my way to the gear area where I checked my jacket. I then continued to stretch as I made my way to the starting line with the other 781 participants in the 10k. A major highlight was the flybys of F22s during the National Anthem where the U.S. flag appeared via a parachute. It was a memorable beginning to the day.

My energy level was great and I knew it was going to be a good race for me, even though I still wasn't keeping track of my pace throughout the course of the race. But I was healthy and strong so regardless of the outcome, I was determined to run my best and enjoy the experience to the fullest. I was also excited to be one of the first people to take part in the 10k, which was making its debut at the USAF races.

With the course being mostly flat and well marked, I never felt tired or overwhelmed, a clear sign that my fitness level was continuing to improve. This race felt great from start to finish, so much so that I didn't stop to drink once.

Once I reached the final mile in the race, I picked up my pace as much as I could, realizing that I was running better than I had before, even though I wasn't checking my time closely. Sure enough, when I crossed the finish line, my official time registered as 51:10. Wow! I was elated. With an average of 8:14 minutes per mile, this was my fastest race yet, improving upon my Corinth 10k time by almost 25 seconds per mile. I couldn't have been happier and graciously bowed my head as a top Air Force officer placed the lovely finisher's medal around my neck.

It was such a special moment and my elation must have showed because I was approached by a reporter and camera crew and asked if I would answer a few questions about the race. I said yes in between catching my breath and gave the best interview I could about the course and race in general. The interview lasted a few minutes. I asked the reporter where and when it would air and he told me they were going to use it in a military spot to promote future races. I viewed the USAF marathon website for several months after the event and never saw it, so if anyone knows what happened to this short footage of me, please let me know. I'd love to view it.

As it turns out, I placed 5th in my age group that consisted of 57 women. I was extremely pleased with that result and felt like I had come in first overall.

Since I was in the area, I decided to participate in a half marathon walk the next day in New Albany, Ohio. I discovered it about a week before it took place, and since they still had some openings, I decided that would be a great way to wrap up the weekend. I wouldn't have to run the half marathon, but walk it. I departed shortly after the ceremony to make the 80 minute drive to New Albany.

I gained so much from my Ohio race. Not only did it confirm that my running had reached a whole new level, but it also gave me a deeper appreciation of our military and their extreme importance to our nation's freedom. Being in that environment helped to make the race so much more meaningful and thankfully, I would get a chance to repeat this type of experience at the Marine Corps 10k a year later.

I was coming into my own as a runner and although I only had nine states of the 50-state quest completed, I didn't think the joy of this adventure could become any greater. Boy was I wrong.

After attending the expo, I spent the rest of the evening exploring many of the historical places on the Wright-Patterson AFB, including the National Museum of the United States Air Force and the Air Force Institute of Technology. The year before, I attended the event-sponsored pasta dinner held at the National Museum that I was able to tour just before sitting down to eat. Although it was mostly about military aviation and space, it was still uplifting to see the exhibits and understand the important role they have in our country's history and future. I enjoyed being there very much.

Race 10

Louisville City of Parks
Half Marathon

Louisville, Kentucky - October, 19, 2008

Unwanted Change Topped with a
Blessing of Kindness

There are several running events in Kentucky that are more popular than the race I chose. However, at this point in my 50-state journey I was just trying to find races that were convenient and fit easily into my schedule. I lived in Nashville and traveled to Kentucky often for business, so it made sense to get this state completed as soon as possible. I chose a smaller half marathon event that took place in Louisville—the 2008 Louisville City of Parks Half Marathon.

The drive to Louisville from my home in Franklin, Tennessee was about 3 hours. However, I always counted it as 4 hours because Louisville is in the Eastern Time Zone and Nashville is in the Central Time Zone. Since the race was on a Sunday, I drove up Saturday morning and stayed downtown at the Hampton Inn. That would enable me to walk to the start and finish line, a biggy on my list of preferences. However, I would find out later that day at the expo that I was going to be thrown a curve ball.

Due to its relative small size (approximately 618 people in the half marathon and 258 in the full marathon) the expo was small but adequate. While picking up my shirt and timing chip, one of the volunteers handed me a map indicating that the start line had been moved and those of us staying downtown would have to be shuttled to it. "Huh" I thought. "You've got to be kidding. You wait until the day before the race to announce something this critical?" So, instead of staying warm in my hotel room until about 7:45 before heading to the start line right outside my hotel door, I would now have to catch the shuttle before 7:30 and ride for about 10-12 minutes before stretching in the cold (nearly 40 degrees) and running a route that wasn't familiar to me. Needless to say, this last minute change of venue did not make me happy.

Had I known about this beforehand, I could have arranged to stay at a hotel closer to the new start line and started the race the way I prefer, by warming up in my hotel room and walking to the start line about 15 minutes prior to the starting gun. Oh well, there was nothing to do but go with it, which I did.

I didn't journal much about this race but I do remember that it wasn't a particularly pretty route or very memorable. There were many curves and turns that made it more difficult than it needed to be, but overall it was an okay race. I was thankful to finish in less than 2 hours with an official race time of 1:58:57 which earned me an age group placement of 12 out of 38. As my 50-state journey progressed, it would become important to me to earn that 1st, 2nd or 3rd place age group win, but at this point in my quest, I was thankful to finish the race in less than 2 hours, keeping that new streak going.

While the course was no great shakes, this race was a standout for a totally different reason. Once I finished, collected my medal and grabbed some water, I went to the holding area where the shuttles were supposed to pick us up to take us back downtown.

I wrapped myself in the thermal blanket given to us at the finish line so we could stay warm, and then waited for nearly 45 minutes for the shuttle. Most people drove to the race so just a handful of us were there waiting. The longer I waited, the more irritated I became. All I wanted to do was hop in the shower and warm up my cold body.

Just as my frustration was about to reach a boiling point, a wonderful fellow-runner drove out of the parking lot and rolled down his window to ask if I needed a ride. I told him I was staying downtown. He said he was heading in that direction and I didn't hesitate to take him up on his offer. If I hadn't been so cold and frustrated, I may have taken a pass but at this point, I wasn't even sure if this race was providing shuttles back to the downtown area. So I hopped in full of thanksgiving and ended up having a wonderful conversation with my new friend about this race and running in general.

It is always refreshing to talk to someone who knows exactly what you go through as a runner. As our conversation progressed, my frustration about the shuttle all but disappeared. I became grateful that the shuttle never arrived because if it had, I would have missed the opportunity to make a new friend and end the race on a happy note.

As we turned into the driveway of the hotel, I thanked my new friend and asked him his name. He said, "Otha."

Once I returned home that evening, I looked up the results online and discovered that Otha finished 4th in his age group with a time of 1:34. Not only was he a super nice guy, but also an outstanding runner.

Running in Kentucky reiterated that racing is about more than just running; it's about making new friends and being touched with unexpected kindness that transcends a medal or a first place finish. Thankfully, I would see this type of kindness repeatedly several more times before completing my 50-state quest.

Race 11

Daytona Beach Half Marathon
Daytona Beach, Florida - October 26, 2008

Combining Business with Pleasure
is a Pleasure Indeed

B ecause I financed this 50-state journey myself, it was always a welcome blessing when I could coordinate a race around travel for my job, especially when it was a considerable distance from where I lived. Such was the case with the state of Florida when I ran the Daytona Beach Half Marathon, my first time running in an inaugural event. The USAF Marathon added the 10k race in 2008 but the Air Force series of races have been around since 1997.

The company I worked for at the time decided to hold our National Sales Meeting in Orlando the last week of October. Since Orlando is a tourist city, we were allowed to fly into Orlando for the weekend if we wanted to enjoy some of the city before the meeting started on Monday morning. This was great for me because it prevented me from having to pay for a plane ticket to Florida so I knew that I had to find a race that fit into that weekend.

The great thing about Florida is that there is never a shortage of races so once I knew the date of the meeting, I began searching all the running websites to find the perfect race within a short driving distance to Orlando, and boy am I glad I chose the one I did.

As I mentioned earlier in the book, part of what I wanted to get out of this experience was a chance to see various cities and landmarks that I had read about, seen in pictures, etc. So when I found the race in Daytona, it jumped out at me immediately. Although I had been to Orlando several times and other cities in southern Florida, I had never been to Daytona Beach and always wanted to see it. I was long past the years to enjoy it as a 20-year old on Spring Break, but I was curious to see what was so intriguing about this beach town. It was only an hour drive from Orlando and it was an inaugural event, making it a first for all of us. Deciding to participate in this half marathon was a no-brainer.

I flew into Orlando on Saturday morning (left my home at 6:30, arrived at the airport at 7:30, flight left on time at 8:50) and rented a car at the Orlando airport. The 1-hour drive to Daytona Beach was lovely and the weather couldn't have been nicer. It wasn't very warm but it was sunny and clear. I decided to stay at a Hilton Garden Inn (they upgraded me to a lovely suite) which was close to dining, shopping and the starting line, although I decided to drive there instead of walk.

The expo, which was only a packet pickup (no vendors), was held at the Daytona 500 experience which race participants could tour for free. If race-car driving was more my thing, I definitely would have gone on the tour. Honestly, there were other things I wanted to see and do.

First on my list was touring the historic campus of Bethune-Cookman University. Founded by educator and civil rights leader Mary McLeod Bethune, it was a campus I'd wanted to see for a long time and I enjoyed exploring this historical institution. Then, I drove to the hotel and checked in. I walked across the street to the Volusia Mall on West International Speedway where I ended up buying a compilation CD of dance mixes that I still listen to today.

After logging several more miles of walking along the beach and through parts of some residential neighborhoods, I decided it was time to retire to the hotel. I watched some of the college football games as I settled into race mode. It was a great day and I liked what I saw of Daytona Beach. However, I would see it from a totally different perspective during the race.

I received my wake-up call at 5:00 and had to get to the start line somewhere between 5:30-6:00 in order to get the timing chip. This is the only negative thing I can say about this event because in the vast majority of races, the timing device is included with your packet/swag bag that you pick up 1 or 2 days prior to the race. That way, you have one less thing to worry about on race morning.

However, given all the things that can go wrong during a race, something like this is only inconvenient; not catastrophic. Once I got my chip, I returned to my car to stay warm, even though it was in the mid-50's by the time the race began. I started warming up around 6:50 and by 6:58, we were off and running.

As with just about every race I've run, I started to question during mile 1 why I keep putting my body through such an arduous task. Although that questioning wanes as I settle into my rhythm, it doesn't completely go away until I cross that finish line and officials put a medal around my neck.

The course was beautiful. There were two steep hills at miles 6 and 8 that slowed me down by approximately 2-3 minutes, but I still finished with a time of 1:57:56, good enough for 9th (out of 38) place in my age group and 203 (out of 530) overall.

Actually, I believe my real time was more like 1:55 because there may not have been a sensor mat at the beginning and I started near the back. I never verified it one way or the other, so I just let it go. Either way, I was very happy with my finish time and thankful that I was still finishing the half marathon in less than 2 hours.

So the great state of Florida was now complete. I enjoyed everything about the Daytona Beach Half Marathon and I'm thankful to have been a part of the very first one. Moreover, I'm glad to see that it is still going strong nearly 7 years later.

Race 12

Route 66 Quarter Marathon
Tulsa, Oklahoma - November 16, 2008

First Place Never Felt so Good

About 10 years prior to running in this race, I drove by myself across country from North Carolina to California. It was an amazing adventure that I videotaped and turned into an amateur documentary. I guess you could say that trip whetted my appetite to see more of this great country of ours, although I had no idea at the time that running would be the vehicle that would take me on that journey.

One of the highlights from that cross-country trip was a stop I made to a small town off I-40 in Oklahoma . I knew I wanted to get to Amarillo before stopping for the day, so I decided to visit a small town to see what Oklahoma looked like up close and personal, even though I had no idea where I was in Oklahoma.

Shortly after exiting from the freeway, I spotted a Walmart and decided to stop there for some notions and a snack. I noticed that the parking lot was rather unpopulated which seemed odd for a Walmart parking lot, especially during the day. Nonetheless, I parked the car and began walking toward the entrance. I couldn't get over how sparsely populated the parking area was and I was getting a bit suspicious of this place.

Just a few feet from the door, I heard a deep voice exclaim, "Don't open that door." "Uh oh" I thought. "Is this a serial killer behind me?" Suddenly a man's hand grabbed the door handle as he said "No woman ever opens a door in my presence." I was so relieved and thankful for his kindness, which extended to every person I encountered in that store. I never forgot this experience, and because of it, I looked forward to visiting the state of Oklahoma again.

One major advantage I had while on this running pursuit was my job. As a field sales engineer, my primary responsibility was to oversee sales within a given territory. When I started on this journey, my territory consisted of the states of Tennessee and Kentucky, in addition to a few counties of Arkansas and Mississippi. I didn't realize what a blessing it was to have a job like that until I started registering for races. I was often able to use work as a way to get to a race, or closer to it without having to incur the expenses all on my own. The Route 66 Quarter Marathon in Tulsa is a good example of this advantage.

My journey to Tulsa started the Thursday before the race when I left my home in Franklin, Tennessee and drove to Memphis. Since my territory included the entire state of Tennessee, I arranged to meet with a customer in Memphis that Thursday afternoon.

The next morning I had meetings that extended well into the afternoon. By 5:00 p.m., I was on the road to Clarksville, Arkansas, which was 4 hours west of Memphis. I stayed at a nice Hampton Inn and got a good night's rest.

I woke up that Saturday feeling very relaxed because I knew that I didn't have to workout since it was the day before the race. So, I had a little breakfast and used the hotel's computer to search for the nearest Whole Foods Market. I was thrilled to discover that it was just 4 miles from my hotel in Tulsa.

The day was gorgeous for driving; lots of sunshine but very cold. After about 2.5 hours I arrived in Tulsa and headed to Whole Foods where I got a great salad. I ate there and then shopped for a few additional items to keep in the hotel refrigerator for race day.

My diet rarely changed over the course of the 2.5 years I spent pursuing a race in all 50 states, so the items I purchased that day were not unlike what you'd find in my shopping cart today: Kombucha Synergy drinks, cottage cheese, fiber bars, watermelon, cantaloupe and a broccoli/cauliflower mix.

I then drove to my lodging and was very pleased with my suite at the Doubletree Hotel, right across the street from the expo, which was excellent. It wasn't huge like those associated with the 20,000 registrant races, but it was large enough, with one vendor that would become very instrumental in my goal to complete my 50-state quest.

Life Speed Sports is a company that specializes in custom made medal display. The owners had an exhibit showcasing their various models and I found it very impressive.

By now, I had earned 18 medals and needed a way to display them in a neat and professional manner. What sold me on these displays was not just the high quality of the custom wood finish, but the fact that the owner could personalize it with whatever heading you wanted.

After reviewing their entire offering, I purchased two 3-foot displays with the heading "Bridget's Medals." About a year later I purchased an additional 30" plaque with the title "Last of the 50" to house the final 9 medals of my 50-state journey. I also had them design me a 12" display entitled "My Full Marathons." I am thankful to say that all four plaques are prominently displayed in my home and always will be. Those medals represent the fruit of my loins, so to speak.

I purchased a ticket to the pasta dinner but it was uneventful as I recall, so I ate rather quickly and retired to my room at about 6:00 p.m. I began my routine of getting into "race mode." I was tired but totally at peace. It felt good to be in Tulsa and I was thankful for God's blessings.

Race morning was typical for me—waking up early and taking my time to eat something (a few spoonfuls of goat milk yogurt and some coffee) before heading to the start line. Once there I warmed up with a very short run prior to getting in line.

There was one thing that set the race start apart from other events: the music. Most races have some kind of music playing at the start and sometimes throughout the entire course, but I don't recall any music being more appropriate than what was being played in Tulsa. It started with Rihanna's "Don't stop the music" and continued with Michael Jackson's "Don't stop 'til you get enough." Both have the perfect beat to get you ready for a run and because they were playing it very loudly, you couldn't help but get energized. Just about everybody was jumping around and moving their arms to the music and even though it was cold, I was very ready for this race, although I didn't realize just how ready until later in the day.

When the horn sounded, I started strong and was somewhat surprised by how high my energy level remained throughout the whole race. Now that I was running faster and more efficiently, I started monitoring my pace to ensure I would meet my performance goals, so I kept a good eye on my time and noticed that I was maintaining my goal of an 8:00-8:30 minute/mile pace. While I didn't think I broke any records, I knew that I was on pace to finish where I had hoped. In fact, Tulsa was the first race I can remember literally passing people frequently, especially in the last 2 miles. When I crossed the finish line, it was pure joy and because it was a quarter marathon (6.34 miles), I still had quite a bit left in the tank.

Once I got to the hotel and settled down, I checked the race website for my results. To my astonishment, I secured FIRST PLACE in my age group! While I had earned a 3rd place finish in Corinth, Mississippi about 6 months earlier, it wasn't within my realm of thinking that I could ever come in first. What a surprise and what a blessing!

A couple of days later, the race director contacted me to indicate that he had just put the 1st place trophy in the mail to me, and what a trophy it was. Shaped in a diamond, this glass structure, accentuated with the intricate design of a runner next to the race date, title, and running category, is the most beautiful of all the awards that adorn my trophy cabinet. Not only is it the most beautiful, it is also the most special because it represents my first time earning the top spot in my age group. Thankfully, it wouldn't be the last.

I wish that I had been able to spend more time in Tulsa. There was much more of this city that I wanted to see. Nonetheless, I am thankful this is the race I chose to run in Oklahoma. Along with my infamous stop at Walmart off I-40 nearly ten years prior, the Route 66 Quarter Marathon gives me another rich memory to commemorate my time in the "Sooner" state.

Race 13

Baton Rouge Beach Half Marathon
Baton Rouge, Louisiana - December 6, 2008

A Half PR with Alligator Meat To Boot

I was in overdrive after my unexpected win in Tulsa and couldn't wait to get back on the race course. However, races are hard to come by in December due to the colder temperatures and often inclement weather. Still, if you look hard enough, you can find a few out there and I was fortunate to find what I consider an absolute gem.

I checked out all the running websites in hopes of locating a race that I could get to by car since there wasn't much time to book a flight at the cheaper fares. After searching and searching, I spotted a race in Baton Rouge, Louisiana. This intrigued me because the only city I had visited in Louisiana was New Orleans. As I mentioned before, part of my objective in running the 50 was to see cities and towns that are somewhat off the radar. Not that this applies to Baton Rouge, especially, given the fact that it is the capital of

Louisiana and is the second-largest metropolitan city in the state. Still, New Orleans is the city that comes to mind most often when one thinks of places in Louisiana.

I logged onto the race's website and was unable to access some of the information I needed so I sent the race director an email to inquire how I could get the necessary information.

This is a good time to talk about the importance of a good race director. While there are many people hard at work to make a race happen, no one is more important to a race's success or failure than the race director. Ultimately, the bulk of the responsibility falls squarely on his or her shoulders and often, it is a thankless job. I think many race directors will agree that they are usually contacted or mentioned only when something goes wrong and seldom when everything moves along smoothly. This is a trend that I hope changes because the many months of hard work a race director puts in warrants far more than the obligatory pat on the back, and even those are probably few and far between.

For me, any contact I have with a race director typically occurs when I email them a question regarding the race. If it takes forever to get a response or if the response never comes, I will remove that race from contention.

When I emailed the race director a question about this event, his response was warm, prompt and detailed. So his response, coupled with the many good reviews from the marathonguide.com comments section, helped solidify my decision to register for the Baton Rouge Beach Half Marathon right away.

I soon began mapping out the details of this race, including how to get there, where to stay, etc. From my home in Franklin, Tennessee to Baton Rouge, I was looking at an 8-hour drive which exceeded my 6-hour-a-day driving rule. When I drove across country from North Carolina to Los Angeles, California, it was nothing for me to drive 12 hours in one day, but that was 10 years and about 500,000 miles ago. As a runner over the age of 40, I understood the importance of maintaining good body posture which is practically impossible when you are behind the wheel too often. I knew that in order to get to Baton Rouge by car, I would have to divide the trip into segments and I knew exactly how I wanted to accomplish that task.

The weather was perfect for running; clear skies and cool. In fact, it was cold enough to require a thick tech shirt with two additional pullovers, running toboggan, and a pair of gloves given to us in our goody bag at the packet pickup. At the start line, I took a short jog to prepare my muscles before running. This pre-race jog became a major part of my preparation in all future races.

If there is one word that encapsulates my spirit throughout this race, it would "relaxed." In fact, I can't recall being more relaxed for a race previously or subsequently. I was at my ideal weight of 105 lbs, my body was well-nourished, and I was so thankful to be in Louisiana getting ever closer to my goal. Although I had no way of predicting how the race would end, I knew that it was going to be a great one—I just knew it.

The course was lovely, and true to the description provided by the race director, flat and fun. We looped around the LSU campus and surrounding neighborhoods which provided enough scenic diversity to prevent one from getting bored out there.

I didn't follow my watch as closely as I would in later races, but

I knew that I was running well within my goal of 8 to 8:30 minutes per mile and the best part was that my energy level was through the roof.

I was breathing heavily during the second half of the race but nothing like in past races. I felt great out there and once I crossed the finish line, I went straight to the electronic posting area to see how well I did. When I got there, I asked the official in charge of the postings if it was too early to see where we finished in our age group. I told him I was wondering if I should stick around for the awards ceremony. He did a quick check with the computer and said, "Oh yeah, you'll need to stick around for sure."

Yeah! I was thrilled with that bit of news and also famished, as I usually am when I finish a race of this distance. I ventured over to the post-race food area where I was privy to the BEST food I've ever had at a racing event. I was not shy about partaking in all that was offered, with the highlight being alligator sauce piquante. It is similar to shrimp gumbo but with alligator meat instead of shrimp. You might think a dish like this wouldn't be very appetizing after a hard fought 13.1 miles, but you would be wrong. That alligator was so good I had a second helping!

After refueling my body with some good nutrition and talking to other finishers, it was time for the awards ceremony. The top 3 finishers (male and female) overall, and the top 3 finishers for each age group (also male and female), were recognized.

When they got to my age group (women 40-44), I was so thankful to accept my award for a 2nd place finish with a final time of 1:50:42 That's my personal best for a half marathon to this day! The prize was an ebony tile trophy with the race information and graphics adorning the face. What a blessing!

While in college, I took a course in Southern Imagination and was introduced to the works of many great southern writers including Eudora Welty. Long since a fan, I remembered that she lived in Jackson, Mississippi and I was eager to visit her home which I knew was just over 6 hours from my house. I decided to split the trip up and spend the first night in Canton, Mississippi approximately 24 miles north of Jackson. The next day I would drive to Jackson, tour Eudora Welty's home in the morning and drive to Baton Rouge that afternoon.

After the race, I planned to drive to Meridian, Mississippi since I had never been there before. I wanted to tour that city before driving back to Franklin the next day. However, I altered my return trip after experiencing such a great and unexpected time in Canton that first night.

The weather was ideal the entire weekend—beautiful sunshine but brisk. It was a great few days to travel and every part of the trip was wonderful.

When I first arrived at the Hampton Inn in Canton, Mississippi, I was greeted warmly by the front desk manager who told me that I picked the best time to visit Canton. When I asked why, she told me that Canton was known as the "City of Lights," because every night in December it served as host to one of the greatest Christmas celebrations in the world. It was replete with carousal rides, goodies to eat, and over 200,000 glittering lights.

She said I would probably recognize the historic courthouse square where most of the festival takes place. It had been featured in several movies including one of my favorites, A Time to Kill starring Sandra Bullock, Matthew McConaughey and Samuel L. Jackson.

I couldn't believe I didn't know about all this beforehand and was grateful for the information. That evening, I ventured out to see the "City of Lights" and it was nothing short of spectacular.

Even though it was cold, hundreds of people were milling around enjoying the carnival-like atmosphere. The Christmas light displays were the brightest and most beautiful I'd ever seen. Sure enough, the courthouse square was recognizable from the film. I absolutely LOVED it and couldn't get enough of the warmth and hospitality from citizens of Canton.

Each store I ventured into treated me like I was someone famous and they did so with everyone who entered their doors. I walked what seemed like hours and was still eager for more. It was getting late, and I knew I had a big day ahead of me, so I decided I would forego seeing Meridian, Mississippi on this trip. Instead, I wanted to return to Canton on the way home to view the "City of Lights" one more time.

The next day (Friday) I booked another night after the race to enjoy more of the Christmas celebration. I could only imagine how relaxing it would be to fully ingratiate myself in all that Canton and the festival had to offer after the race was under my belt. Until then, I was excited about visiting Eudora Welty's home and was thankful to the good Lord for such beautiful, clear skies.

Several weeks prior I had contacted the then director of education at Eudora Welty's home, Meemie Jackson, and registered for the tour scheduled for 11:00 a.m. Her warm communication acknowledged my registration, as well as providing pertinent directions and parking instructions.

Upon arrival, I discovered there were quite a few of us there for the tour from different parts of the country and world. We were all captivated by this great author and we wanted to see where she created so many of her masterpieces. There is definitely something magical about being in the place where a literary genius ate, slept and created history.

About a year later I experienced this kind of thrill again when I visited the home of my favorite author of all time, William Faulkner.

In short, there is nothing I didn't like about the Baton Rouge Beach Half Marathon. In fact, it was great in every way; great weather, great course, great race director, great finisher medal, great age group award, great PR and perhaps most importantly, great alligator piquante . It was true Louisiana cuisine at its finest!

Given this wonderful experience, I couldn't wait to tackle the remaining 37 states in my quest to see all of America.

2009: In Full Swing

At this point in my racing career, there was no doubt that I was in the best shape of my life. My body weight never exceeded 107 lbs and I maintained the lowest percentage of body fat perhaps since childhood.

My exercise regimen was strenuous but not overbearing or unmanageable. It was a comprehensive mix of resistance training and cardio (mostly running), 6-days a week without fail.

My goal was to space out the races so that my last race would serve as the long run needed to prepare for the next race, which culminated in at least one race per month.

In total, I completed 15 races in 2009, allowing me to run in every region of the country. With each race, I could sense my body and mind getting stronger and stronger as the countdown to completion got shorter and shorter.

I realized many "firsts" in 2008, but I was blessed to have a few in 2009 as well, including:

- First (and only) "Masters" Championship: Pocatello, Idaho
- Most age group awards in a calendar year: 6
- Fastest finish time of any race: Madison Quarter Marathon

- First "international" inclusion: Detroit Free Press (several miles run in Windsor, Ontario)

This marked the year that I felt like a real runner. I loved the journey I was on and in 2009, I learned to appreciate it more than ever.

Race 14

Austin Half Marathon
Austin, Texas - February 15, 2009

Magazines and Worship—
What a Blessing!

We all know that Texas is big and finding good races to run in the Lone Star state is no exception. There are literally hundreds (possibly thousands) of races offered year-round to suit every individual's running preference. Whether you prefer a small race or a large race, a challenging course or a flat course, one located in the panhandle or one just north of the Mexican border, you will find it in Texas.

Over the years I've spent significant time in both Houston and Dallas, but I wanted my race in Texas to be an opportunity to see a part of the state I hadn't yet visited. Given that criteria, a race in the capital city of Austin seemed the most ideal choice for me.

Having already gained valuable history lessons in Little Rock and Birmingham, I was eager to explore this state's capital and gain further insight into the precedent-setting governorship of Ann Richard. I also wanted to experience why Austin's official slogan is "The Live Music Capital of the World."

While there were many lodging options in downtown Austin, I decided to stay at the Hilton Garden Inn Downtown for my two nights in the city. I detest renting cars when I travel, preferring to use whatever public transportation is available and of course, my own two feet. There is so much more you can see and absorb when you are on foot as opposed to being behind the wheel of a car, especially when you are unfamiliar with the area. Staying downtown allowed me to be in the center of everything: dining, shopping, entertainment, etc. Also, this hotel was within walking distance of the race start, finish and expo, making it the ideal location for me.

Race morning started for me at 4:45 a.m. I requested a wake-up call for 4:30 and didn't get it, but I quickly shrugged it off. The one thing I learned (and would learn with races yet to come) pretty early on is that you don't want anything to disrupt your concentration the day of a race. Not getting the wake-up call could have been costly but because I woke up on time anyway, it wasn't worth dwelling upon. I quickly headed up to the 18th floor where they had some freshly brewed coffee awaiting the runners. I drank about a ½ cup and ate a few spoonfuls of goat milk yogurt before taking my time getting dressed.

Since the weather was predicted to be cold, I decided to wear a new Nike wool tech shirt that my mother had given me for Christ-

On stage to receive the Women's Masters Champion Award at the 10th Annual Idaho State Journal 10k in Pocatello, Idaho.

mas. I wore another long-sleeve shirt and new black and white shorts I purchased at a previous expo. I also wore my runners gloves and "Jesus" baseball cap. I added sweats and my jacket for the walk to the clothing drop-off at the starting area and checked my bag at about 6:35. I then found a nice spot to stretch and do my short warm-up jog before getting in line.

Just then, the race director announced over a loudspeaker that they were running about 10 minutes behind. That was music to my ears because I wanted to use the restroom one more time before starting to run. Thankfully Starbucks allowed runners to use their facilities which was surprisingly clean given the number of runners who had been in-and-out of there since about 4:00 that morning.

Unlike some of the huge 30,000 runner events, this race did not have a staggered or tiered start. Runners could line up anywhere they wanted. I decided to line up with the 3:40 pace group for the full marathon. When I crossed the start line, it was 7:16 a.m. by my watch, which was about 5 minutes after the horn sounded.

This was no easy race and I didn't expect it to be. The race director was honest in the pre-race material that this course was not an easy flat one; instead, it had quite a few hills to challenge any runner.

I prayed before I left my hotel room to just finish the race in less than 2 hours, even if my final time was 1:59:59, I just wanted to see a "1" there and not a "2".

I was a little concerned about my fitness. Although I walked a lot on Friday and Saturday, I had not run at all and I always try to do a short 2-3 mile run on Friday if I have a half marathon race on Sunday. For a full marathon, I usually bump the Friday run up to 4-5 miles. However, I was okay for the duration of the race even though the hills were no joke. It was hard to maintain my usual 8:00-8:30

minute/ mile pace, but I did so except for a couple of miles with huge inclines.

Mile 11 was perhaps the most daunting mile I've run in any race—ever. The hill was so huge that you could see it off in a distance. Try as I might, I ended up having to walk the last portion of it, which was the only time I walked, except for 30 seconds when I drank some Powerade at mile 9. Interestingly enough, I only drank once for the entire race (something I don't recommend by the way) primarily because I didn't think I'd have the energy to start up again if I stopped. I would learn how to master this without sacrificing much in time or energy.

I looked at my watch and realized that I could run the last mile in over 16 minutes and still be well within my goal of finishing the race in less than two hours. That is a great feeling when you get to that point in a race and know that if you need to, you can slow way down and still meet your timing goal.

I was surprised that mile 12 went by so quickly because when I looked up, I was at the mile 13 marker and as usual, I sprinted to the finish. My official time was 1:55:04 with a pace of 8:47 minute/mile.

Immediately after crossing the finish line, I lifted my hands to heaven and gave God the glory for the victory (something I did after every race) and spoke praises to Him aloud. I prayed a lot during this race because I needed the Lord to help me through and He certainly did. Truly I couldn't have asked for a better race or a better result. My heart was full of joy and excitement.

Typically, the bigger the race, the bigger the expo. With a total of approximately 11,500 runners (about 7,400 in the half and approximately another 4,100 running the full marathon), the Austin race was no small affair. As I've previously mentioned, expos for races this size are usually quite nice because a lot of vendors show up in hopes of showcasing their merchandise and selling a lot of product, and this one was no exception.

The best surprise was a booth for Women's Running magazine. Several months prior to the race, I had contacted the magazine in hopes of being featured in an upcoming issue in a section entitled "Women Who Move." After being interviewed, the Senior Editor notified me that I was chosen to be featured in one of the upcoming issues and I was thrilled.

About a week before the race, I tried to contact the magazine to see if they had made a decision when to run my story. I never heard back from anyone, so I told the woman manning the magazine's booth how disappointed I was that I never received a response.

Little did I know that the woman I was talking to was the Senior Editor and she gave me the good news that I was featured in the new issue that they were showcasing there at the race! What a pleasant surprise that was!

She handed me a copy and I couldn't have been more pleased with how the article turned out. She handed me 20 copies and said to come back the next day so she could give me two additional boxes of the magazine to carry home with me.

These unexpected blessings orchestrated by God at just about every race illuminate why this 50-state journey was so special for me. I could never have predicted the article would be finished and featured in that month's issue, or that copies featuring me would be given to nearly 11,000 runners who attended the expo over the weekend. Nor could I have predicted that I would receive almost 50 complimentary copies of the feature.

These unanticipated "kisses from God" showered me throughout my entire 2-1/2 year journey across this great country of ours, making this experience more special than I could have ever imagined or hoped for.

The day before the race, I went on a tour of the State Capitol Building and the LBJ Library at the University of Texas. Also, I made another visit to the expo to get the additional magazines and pick up some more free food samples at the various booths.

While I loved everything I did and experienced in Austin, the standout for me was a wonderful church service I attended the night before the race at St. David's Episcopal Church. The service was wonderful. Sadly, many missed a blessing. Out of nearly 11,000 runners, only eight people attended the service, including a non-runner and a small child. Nonetheless, I appreciated the smaller, intimate setting. It was a short service and Reverend Malcolm gave a wonderful teaching taken from the Gospel According to John.

It was a lovely service and because the pastor was a runner as well—he even wore his tennis shoes with his robe - the message had even more meaning. He noted that earlier that morning he met with the race director and prayed over the course, serving as my confirmation that it was going to be one incredible race.

Hands down, this was one of the most organized races in my journey. Good organization remains one of the key elements I use to determine if a race is for me or not, and this one certainly was.

From a logistics standpoint, everything (expo, start line, finish line, lodging, restaurants, public transportation, etc.) was within walking distance from any area of downtown, another key characteristic I look for in an out-of-town race. If the expo is 6 miles from the recommended lodging and the start line is another 5 miles away, I will quickly remove that race from contention regardless if the reviews are good and the recommendations high.

Convenience and ease of getting around trump just about everything else for me, including an easy course and low registration fees. The Austin race met all my criteria and some.

On the plane ride home, I couldn't help but reflect on how special this trip to Austin had been. I got to spend time in a Texas city I had only read about, make some new friends, enjoy a great church service, get featured in a national magazine, and pick up another beautiful medal for a hard fought race.

The Austin Half Marathon remains one of my favorite races in my 50-state quest.

Race 15

ING Georgia Half Marathon
Atlanta, Georgia - March 29, 2009

Familiar Surroundings – Familiar Friends

A lthough I mainly used this 50-state quest to visit those cities, towns, landmarks, schools, etc. unfamiliar to me, it also served as a means to return to some areas where I used to reside or had visited briefly in the past. In the late 80's and early 90's, I made my home in Atlanta and while there, I achieved many things. Most notably I earned a Master's Degree and developed some wonderful friendships with many who still live in the area.

Due to its tremendous growth over the years, I knew that Atlanta had changed dramatically from when I resided there and I was interested to see those changes, as well as visit my old stomping grounds and fellowship with old friends. Thus, deciding to run in Atlanta for my Georgia event was a no-brainer. The challenge was finding the right race to run in Atlanta and I couldn't have made a better choice than the ING Half Marathon.

Timing wise, this race kept me well within my goal of running a long distance event at least once a month so I was happy to have found it. Logistics wise, I could park my car in the hotel garage and not have to start it up again until I departed the city for home. Moreover, it was a very doable drive from my home in Franklin, Tennessee, especially since I could be in Chattanooga for my job just prior to the race, leaving a short 2 hour drive to Hotlanta. From every perspective, this was a win-win situation for me.

The expo was held at the Georgia Dome and it was a nice one. For months leading up to the race, my running shoe of choice was the Nike Pegasus and I desperately needed a new pair. So I was thrilled to discover that Nike had a huge display at the expo with just about every size and style of shoe they manufactured. I was able to get just the pair I was looking for at a major discount—yeah! This expo was big enough to where I stayed a good couple of hours before heading back to my hotel room.

Although it rained all morning on Saturday, it didn't prevent the day from being awesome. It started off with a trip to Emory University where I attended graduate school. My goal was to take a quick tour of the campus in hopes of seeing some of the new buildings erected in the past 10 years, but unfortunately, the rain was pouring and I didn't want to slosh around the whole time, so I just drove around and looked at what I could. It was just as well because I needed to get to my friend's house for lunch and I didn't want to be late.

There is no substitute for good company and good fellowship, so to say that seeing my dear friend Wanda, and later on our mutual friend Cheryl, was wonderful is an understatement.

I am so thankful that Wanda has been in my life for over 30 years.

We met when we were in undergraduate school at North Carolina State University and ended up pledging the same sorority in different years. However, it wasn't until after we graduated and both moved to Atlanta that our friendship really took off. Those early years of hanging out and enjoying the city of Atlanta as 20-somethings were very special and I was excited to catch up with my dear friend whom I hadn't seen in over a decade.

We decided to have lunch at her home that she shared with her husband and three sons and almost immediately, we fell into our old pattern of telling jokes and laughing until we could hardly breathe. Later, our friend and fellow sorority sister Cheryl joined us with her beautiful three children. As the kids went off and played, we three old friends caught up with one another and other classmates that we hadn't seen in many years.

Reminiscing with these two was fantastic. It reminded me how special friendships are in a person's life and how special this 50-state experience was to me.

Could I have seen these two ladies if I wasn't running the next day? Of course I could, but the point is I was discovering that this quest was about so much more than running. It was about meeting new people, learning new things and traveling to new places. And in places like Atlanta, it was about connecting with lifelong friends and being reminded how their presence in my life made me rich and blessed.

I could have stayed and talked all night, but I knew that I had a tough race in the morning. It was fast becoming time for me to get into "race mode." Around 7:30 p.m. I said goodnight and drove to my hotel with a full stomach and a full heart.

On race morning, I was up at 5:00 in order to be fully prepared for the 7:00 a.m. start time. Since the start line was literally right outside the door of my hotel (always the most preferable logistically), I took my time getting dressed and mentally prepared. In fact, I may have taken a little too much time because I left my room at 6:45 and had to line up in a later corral because of the number of runners. My warm-up was pretty quick and not much of one at all, but I didn't panic because I knew I was ready.

While the course was scenic and enjoyable from that standpoint, it was also very hilly. Most of the reviews I read beforehand indicated that the hills were rough, but for some reason, I had a much harder time dealing with the inclines than usual. In fact, I was tired during the bulk of this race. Maybe some of it had to do with the excitement of seeing my friends the day before but my first 10k was dismal. Thankfully, I was able to pick it up in the latter half of the race and incredibly finished with a time of 1:56:36! I was so happy but made a vow to give hilly courses a break for the time being. I needed to give my quads a rest from all the climbing and was determined to try and find a flat course for my next race no matter what.

With a total of 9,539 participants in the half marathon, I came in 2,334, beating out over 75% of all runners that day. While I certainly didn't qualify to win any awards, I couldn't have been more pleased with my result and my weekend in Atlanta. I saw some old friends, made some new friends, and picked up another beautiful finisher's medal to boot. On the drive home, I decided to reward myself with an impromptu stop in Chattanooga for a well-deserved 90- minute massage. It felt good to have State #15 in the bag!

Race 16

Madison Quarter Marathon
Madison, Wisconsin - May 24, 2009

The Record for the Fastest Time...So Far

In the early 90's after graduate school, I accepted a job located in the northwestern part of Illinois, 90 minutes south of Madison, Wisconsin. Although the job was challenging and the people were friendly, there just wasn't much to do socially as a single young person in a relatively small town. So on the weekends, several of my colleagues (also young graduates new to the area) and I would take the 90 minute drive to Madison to enjoy the college scene at the University of Wisconsin.

I fell in love with the campus and the city of Madison, not just for the diverse social outlet it provided, but also for its beauty. Situated along the southern shore of Lake Mendota, the largest of the four lakes in Madison, there was a peace and calmness there that strongly appealed to me.

The company I worked for at the time granted me permission

to participate in a three-day course conducted by the Management Institute at the School of Business at the University of Wisconsin; an incredible experience that made me long to return to that area someday. Little did I know that return would result in a quarter marathon where I would achieve my fastest time ever!

The Madison Marathon showcased four races: the marathon, the half marathon, the quarter marathon, and a kids race. By now, my preference for the quarter marathon and 10K was well established, not just because of the shorter distance (the 10k is 6.214 miles and the quarter marathon is 6.555 miles) but because I could run them the most efficiently and faster, giving me the greatest opportunity to place in my age group.

Although my 50-state journey was never based on awards, it was always a joy to earn one so the 6+ mile race became my preferred distance; however, the number of sanctioned races for this distance are few and far between. Most races focus on the marathon and half marathon which is why the majority of my races during this journey were half marathons, but whenever I found a sanctioned 10k or quarter marathon that offered a finisher's medal (one of my requirements to mark the completion of a state race), I researched that event before other distances. In this case, the quarter marathon was the clear choice.

On the flight to Madison, I sat beside a girl who asked me if I was running in the race the next day. I told her yes and we struck up a conversation that lasted the duration of the short flight. She too was a 50-stater with over 30 states completed. She was from Mobile and also participated in quite a few Ironman competitions throughout the country.

This is one of the many reasons why this experience was so special—meeting good people from all over the world who share the same joy and passion that you do. While our back stories are usually quite different, the result is the same; driven individuals striving to do our best on the race course while soaking up the many blessings accompanying our journeys.

I woke up at 5:30 on race morning and took my time getting ready. I ate my preferred pre-race meal of ½ cup of goat milk yogurt and ½ cup of coffee before taking a cab to the start line. This was atypical for me; if I can't stay in a hotel close enough to walk to the race, I try to stay at one that at least provides shuttle service to the start line—but not this time. The cab was $9.50 which I thought was reasonable, not to mention fast. Not having to rush, I took my time to stretch and get in a short warm-up jog.

The race itself was awesome. My energy level was great and I noticed early on that I was running at a much faster pace than usual, but it wasn't until the finish that I discovered just how much faster it was. My finish time was 50:47, which translates into a pace of 7:42 minutes/mile. Wow—what a surprise! I felt great afterward and surprisingly, I wasn't nearly as winded as I expected to be given that speed. So it was my fastest race to date, which normally would be cause for immediate celebration, but what followed almost tainted my achievement which you bet I addressed with the race director.

Since it was confirmed that I had indeed placed 2nd in my age group, I wanted to stick around for the awards ceremony, which was due to start at 8:45. By 9:30, it still had not begun and I knew that if I didn't leave pretty soon, I would be at risk of missing my 1:00 p.m. flight. I stood around with numerous other runners in the same boat, needing to catch planes within the next couple of hours and having no idea when this ceremony would start, or if it ever would. Although I never found out exactly what the delay was all about, it was thought to be some sort of electronic glitch in securing the official times.

Whatever the glitch might have been, I knew that I could not afford to waste any more time so I approached a group of volunteers and expressed to them my concerns. They assured me that they would mail any awards to anyone who had to leave, so I caught the hotel shuttle (it ran post-race but not before—go figure), showered, packed and grabbed a quick free breakfast at the hotel before departing for the airport. Both flights were relaxing, especially the second one from Milwaukee to Nashville where I had the entire row to myself.

Within a week or two after the race, I contacted the race director to inquire about my age group award which had not arrived yet. It wasn't until I inquired that I was told there were no awards (trophies) for age group winners in the quarter marathon, just for half marathon and full marathon age group winners. I can't tell you how disappointed I was and believe me, I voiced that loud and clear to the race director.

This race taught me a lot and I vowed that I would not enter another race if there were no awards for age group winners. Fortunately, this is rarely an issue; most race directors are all too happy to extend these type of awards because they understand how hard you have to work that day to earn one. While most age group awards go three deep (1st, 2nd and 3rd), I have participated in races that extended age group wins out to a 4th and 5th place finish. To me, that is a small thing to do given how much you sacrifice (physically, mentally, and financially) to participate in these races.

As I stated before, this journey was never about awards, but when you work hard enough to earn one, you should receive it.

Nonetheless, this race afforded me the opportunity to visit Madison again and to clock my fastest time ever in a race. Award or not, I was running quite well and I could put a check beside the state of Wisconsin, number 16 on the road to 50.

Race 17

Rocky Mountain Half Marathon
Denver, Colorado - June 14, 2009

A True Rocky Mountain High

By nature, I like to plan. For years, I've faithfully maintained a daily planner and a journal. None of this electronic junk; I'm talking good ole fashioned paper and pen. It is rare when I don't have a definitive schedule at least one month in advance. While I often admire those who "fly by the seat of their pants," that just isn't me. The random lifestyle has never been my cup of tea even though I grew up in a home where that was the norm. Perhaps that explains my almost obsessive need to plan everything well in advance, down to the most minute detail.

Given my propensity for planning, my Colorado race was a definite anomaly. I discovered the event 6 days before it took place.

Earlier in 2009, I found a 10k race in Kansas City, Missouri that seemed like it would be a good one to pursue for that state. So I booked the whole thing and thought I was set with a race for the month of June, but as the weekend for that race grew closer, re-sponsibilities at my job became a bit overwhelming and I ended up canceling my trip. That bummed me out because I was now with-out a race for June and my goal of at least one race a month was in jeopardy.

So, the Tuesday morning before the Denver race (the race was held that following Sunday), I was moved to search out a race for the month of June and discovered the Rocky Mountain ½ Mara-thon.

After perusing the race website and gathering the details, it met all of my criteria. I needed a race for the state of Colorado and June seemed like the ideal month, but would I have time to get every-thing scheduled in less than a week?

First, I checked to see if I could still register (no problem there). Then I checked the weekend forecast for Denver (clear skies expect-ed). Following that, I checked to see if I could still book a room near the start/finish area (Hilton Garden Inn still had a few rooms left). Lastly, I was able to use my credit from Southwest Airlines for the canceled Kansas City flight on the outbound leg, and a affordable fare with Frontier Airlines for the inbound portion. In less than an hour, I discovered and made all the necessary arrangements for a race that would take place in 6 days—a record for me.

Colorado is a great state for sports and running is no exception. While there are some extremely challenging courses, with more hills and inclines than you can imagine, my motivation was never to do one of those. Typically, what is considered a moderate race for Colorado is an advanced one just about anywhere else. I knew the half marathon I chose in Denver would present me with all the challenge I needed.

I was privileged to spend a couple of weeks in Denver in the mid-1990's for a job I had at the time. I enjoyed being there, so I was pleased to return.

After unpacking, I followed my somewhat normal routine of walking to the nearest Whole Foods Market or health food store in hopes of not only loading up on my food for the trip but also getting a chance to see some of the city by foot. The distance was about 1.5 miles with temperatures in the mid-70's which is my kind of weather.

On the way to Whole Foods, I passed the Capitol and several other government buildings before going through a very nice residential neighborhood consisting of mostly older homes. The day was just beautiful and somehow, it reminded me of a Saturday afternoon from my childhood where my mother and I would go to my piano teacher's house for my piano lesson and then to Hardees afterward for lunch (we were pretty into fast food in those days.) I don't know why that thought came into my mind during such a lovely walk in this interesting city but I think it had something to do with the way the sun was shining, so brightly and so beautifully. It just took me back to that really wonderful time when my study of classical music and the arts in general was in full swing. Those were good days.

The race started at 7:30 and my energy level was great right from the start, averaging just under 8 minutes/mile for the first 4 miles. Then I reached mile 6 and hit a slight wall brought on by two huge hills, costing me about 2 minutes per mile until I got past them.

While climbing those hills, I stayed true to the Word of God and kept repeating in my mind the word "endurance," thinking of the verse in Hebrews 12:2. It describes how the Lord Jesus endured the cross for the joy that was ahead. What an awesome verse of scripture for a runner. Joy is exactly what you feel when you cross that finish line, especially after a challenging course. But there was another 6.5 to 7 miles to go before I could do that.

The weather was warm, eventually reaching the high 70's before the end of the day. Typically warm weather doesn't bother me at all like it does many runners but I must admit that in this race, it was causing me to tire more quickly than usual. After my initial "hitting of the wall" in mile 6, I did so again around mile 9 & 10, and it didn't help that the Gatorade was very warm so I skipped it altogether. Thankfully, I put some jellybeans in my pocket before the race which helped me replace my electrolytes during the times I was most winded.

The course looped around a park area. It seemed like 10 miles, but it was approximately 3. They were 3 tough miles because the park was a public area so we had to contend with a large number of "idle walkers" who were understandably in no hurry. Nonetheless, it was difficult on us runners because we had to keep dodging in-and-out in order to progress, which uses up a lot of energy.

When I got to mile 10, I checked my watch and knew that I could almost run 10 minutes per mile for the rest of the race and still finish in less than 2 hours. I don't like to cut it that close, so I "pressed toward the goal of the upward call" and managed somewhere between an 8:30 to 8:45 minute/mile pace until the last full mile of the race. Unfortunately, my usual sprint to the finish was only the last 20 yards or so, but it felt much longer.

Final result: A finish time of 1:56:13! I couldn't have been more pleased.

The post-race area was nice—not very big, but nice. I grabbed a water there, a cold energy drink, a couple of small boxes of cereal, and several Larabars, for the trip home.

For a spontaneous trip, I couldn't have asked for a better experience. While the altitude took some getting used to, it didn't cause me to falter much at all. My finish time was right where I wanted it to be.

With only 1,497 runners total, it was nice running in a smaller event for a change. A year or two after I completed this race, it became a part of the Rock-n-Roll series of races, catering to a much larger number of runners. I am thankful that I participated when it was still relatively small.

Everything about this race felt right and it was good to briefly visit Denver again. Yes, it was indeed a Rocky Mountain High!

Race 18

Jokers Wild Half Marathon
St. Louis, Missouri - July 12, 2009

Great Things Come in Small Packages

The Go! St. Louis Marathon and Family Fitness Weekend attracts over 25,000 runners in 10 races, with the Half Marathon being the most popular at approximately 12,000 runners.

It is one of the largest running events in the country and usually sells out well in advance, so it was certainly a candidate for my Missouri race. Taking place in April, I seemed to always have a timing conflict and started searching for other running events in Missouri. Thankfully, my search led me to a much smaller, lesser known half marathon that had everything I was looking for: a great finisher's medal, age group award wins, great location (logistics), good organization, terrific website, and a 6.5 mile loop course that participants run twice. This ideal race was The Joker's Wild Half Marathon in St. Louis.

The drive from Franklin, Tennessee to St. Louis was approximately 5-1/2 hours, which is right on the cusp of my "one-day" driving rule, so I decided to drive and not fly. Since my job included lots of travel to Kentucky, I decided on the way back to stop in Louisville and conduct some meetings there for a couple of days. So it was all set—St. Louis, here I come.

I had a great night's sleep and woke up refreshed at 5:00 a.m. I grabbed a cup of coffee in the hotel lobby and caught the hotel shuttle to the start line, arriving at 6:15. This gave me plenty of time to stretch and do a warm-up run before getting in line at 6:41, which was 4 minutes before the start time.

As I mentioned previously, this course was a 6.5 mile loop that participants run twice in order to complete 13.1 miles. Several runner friends of mine dislike loop courses because they get bored on the second leg, having already run the route before. They prefer the scenery to change throughout the duration of the course which I can understand. While I don't necessarily have a preference, I tend to do well on loop courses because I can better control my pace since I know exactly what to expect the second time around.

As for this half marathon, the course was a tough one with a lot of uphill in miles 2, 3 and the first part of 4. The second half of mile 4 was all downhill which was a welcome change. I was able to pick up some time in mile 5, which was mostly flat, before tackling the same course all over again. Given that I knew what to expect on the return, I ran the second part of the race faster and more efficiently than the first so I knew I was doing well.

One thing I noticed with this race was the fact that I started to enjoy being on the course more. I can recall several times in past races when a fellow-runner would make a pleasant comment or observation, I would simply smile or say "yeah" to quickly end it so I could focus on my pace and energy. But having run quite a few of these by now, I recognized the need to relax more and enjoy the moment, so I made sure to observe my surroundings more and soak up the scenery, which in some cases was very beautiful.

Around mile 8, a fellow-runner started a conversation as we coasted along a flat section of the course. I don't remember exactly what we talked about, but it was something to do with the race and how smoothly it was going. This guy had long legs and could easily run right past me if he wanted to.

Sure enough, after a bit more of chit chat, he said that he was going to pick it up a bit and see me at the finish line. I told him I'd see him there and off he went. Again, what we said was nothing of importance, but it was just nice to have that moment or two of levity, something I would never have engaged in earlier in this journey. It was nice to be loosening up out there.

My official finish time was 1:57:42. I couldn't have been more pleased. Given the hills in this race, I was honored to finish with a couple of minutes to spare and still hit my mark of a sub-two hour half marathon.

After receiving my very nice finisher's medal, I decided to partake in the free pancake breakfast offered to all runners. I saturated my pancakes with real maple syrup and real butter, along with a link of pork sausage. This is a meal that I hardly ever eat but I was happy to make an exception on this day because I was famished and it smelled too good to pass up. I savored every bite!

After eating, I headed to the results area where they promptly posted the finish times. I was thrilled to discover that I had placed

2nd in my age group. They held the awards ceremony later, and I received a rather unusual but creative prize: a bottle of wine with beautiful graphics depicting a joker (Joker's Wild Half Marathon, remember), with all the key race information affixed to the label. It's a good thing that I don't drink; no chance that I'll ever open that bottle for any reason!

As an aside, it's interesting to note that some larger races equipped with the most up-to-date technology have been known to take hours and even days to post results. This race, with under 500 runners spread over 2 races, posted the results immediately. Go figure.

All in all, this was one of my favorite races. With 430 people, it wasn't too small, but small enough to capture that pure joy and excitement of just being out there doing your best. No fancy bells and whistles, just a lot of kindness and great fun. From the logistics, to the creative prizes, to the course itself, this race had it all. I was glad to let the race director know how highly I regarded their efforts to put on a first class event.

I learned a lot in Missouri, but two things stand out. First, I learned there is great joy and pleasure in relaxing on the course and engaging in a conversation or two. In fact, it might even provide you with a lift when you need it most. Secondly, great things really do come in small packages!

Race 19

Rock-N-Roll Chicago Half Marathon

Chicago, Illinois - August 2, 2009

Never Disappointed in Chicago

I mentioned in the Wisconsin chapter that I used to live in the northwestern part of Illinois. Even though I lived 2.5 hours from Chicago, that didn't stop me and several of my colleagues from making frequent trips to the Windy City on the weekends.

I've had many good times in Chicago, including Christmas shopping at Marshall Fields and ringing in the new year of 1993 overlooking Lake Michigan. That was a while ago, and after accepting a job in Baltimore, I rarely had an opportunity for a return visit. When I started researching races in Illinois, I knew that I wanted to run in Chicago.

As with any major city in this country, the number of races to choose from is exhaustive. Regardless of the race distance or time of year, there are a number of options to choose from—it is simply a matter of preference. In my case, I wanted a race primarily located in the downtown area so that I could use public transportation and my feet to get around. Moreover, I wanted a race that wasn't too big, which is a tall order to find in Chicago. It is one of the most popular running cities in the world.

The Rock-n-Roll Chicago Half Marathon, held downtown in early August , matched what I was looking for perfectly. Since my previous half marathon (St. Louis) was less than a month prior, I would maintain my goal of running at least one major event a month. In addition, having participated in a number of Rock-n-Roll sponsored events up to that point, I knew they put on a quality race. I couldn't wait to run in Chicago.

I requested a wake-up call at 4:30. I took my time getting dressed while doing a lot of stretching for a shoulder and hamstring that felt tight. In fact, my hamstring was sore, causing me to question if I could run at my full potential. I hoped so, but as I continued to get ready, the pain did not let up.

I always pray on my knees in my hotel room just before I depart for the race. Generally, I ask the Lord for protection and safety on the course, and for me to run my best. For a half marathon, my goal is always to finish in less than 2 hours, even if my time is 1:59:59; as long as it starts with a "1" and not a "2", I'm good to go. However, this morning I added a special prayer concerning my hamstring. It was really sore, and truthfully, if I couldn't lift it up to the Lord in prayer, I may not have even attempted the run. I knew that He had total control of the situation. If it was His will, I would run that race and run it well.

Enjoying one of my favorite pastimes. Here I'm hiking the famous Angel's Landing in Zion National Park in southern Utah.

I left the hotel at 6:15 and took the short walk to the starting line across the street in Grant Park for the 6:30 start time. I did a short practice run of about 100 yards and my hamstring felt okay. I found my proper corral (which was #4) just as the gun sounded. My actual start time (when I crossed the electronic mat) was 6:34 and I was off to the races—literally.

From the beginning I could feel my hamstring but it wasn't too bad. Once the crowd thinned out a bit, I was able to settle into my pace and surprisingly, the pain subsided quite a bit. When I hit the 10k mark, I remember thinking that if this was a 10k race (my favorite distance), I'd be done by now. Oh well, there was no sense thinking about that since there was another 10k and some distance left to go.

Once I reached mile marker 7, I was exactly one hour into the race. While I've been at 7.25 miles at the one hour mark several times in the past, I was definitely not complaining given how my hamstring was feeling before the race began. It was still doing okay and continued to improve with each passing mile. God had certainly answered my prayer and since my energy level was high, I felt very strong during the last half of the race.

I took my first sip of drink (Cytomax) at mile 8 or 9 (not sure which one) but it was at that point on Lakeshore drive when we turned around, so I waited to grab a cup on the way back. The drink was cold and since the temperature was climbing into the 70's, it hit the spot.

Mile 10 was tough for me, as it usually is, but my hamstring was still doing okay and by then, I was very relaxed because I was at that point where I could slow down to a 10 minute/mile pace and still finish in less than 2 hours. So I took my last sip of water at mile 11 and pushed myself for a strong finish.

After a slight hill, we turned and entered a long stretch of very enthusiastic spectators cheering us on as the theme from "Rocky" was blasting from several speakers near the finish line. With the cheers and that great theme music, I was able to sprint to the finish line and lift my hands in the air just like Rocky did. It was great! As soon as I crossed the timing mat, I lifted my hands to the Lord (a gesture that was captured on film at several races) and gave Him the glory for this victory. Then a lady came alongside me and said that she tried to catch me at the end but couldn't. I always feel good when I hear something like that.

I crossed the finish line with a time of 1:55:19 at a pace of 8:48 minutes per mile. I was very pleased with that result, especially since I wasn't sure if my hamstring would hold out for one mile, much less 13.1. After collecting my finisher's medal (the Rock-n-Roll finisher medals are always large and colorful) and some snacks, I headed back to the hotel for a free breakfast before taking a shower and catching the shuttle to the airport.

After checking into my hotel room, I enjoyed a walk around the downtown area of the city. I love Grant Park. Often referred to as "Chicago's front yard," it's over 300 acres and is home to such notable places as The Art Institute of Chicago and Buckingham Fountain, as well as many great running trails. Flanked by Michigan Avenue and Lake Michigan, I spent many fun days in this park, even having an opportunity to see an impromptu performance of the Chicago Symphony Orchestra for free. The fact that the race was starting and finishing in this park had a lot to do with why I wanted to race here.

I walked about two miles to the Gold Coast section of Chicago, which is one of my favorite downtown neighborhoods. Nestled against the Lake Michigan shoreline, this area has some of the best restaurants in the city. Although I didn't eat at any of those establishments on this trip, I've had plenty of meals there in the past to substantiate my claim.

Once I got home, my hamstring felt worse than it had all day, but I couldn't have been more thankful and joyful over the wonderful weekend visiting my beloved Chicago. It is always a pleasure to be in that city and I'm grateful for the role it played in my 50-state quest.

Race 20

10th Annual Pocatello 10k
Pocatello, Idaho - September 5, 2009

Friendship for Life, Master's Championship and Potatoes— It Doesn't Get Any Better!

O ne of the catalysts for undertaking this journey was to see those 12 or 13 states I had not been to before and Idaho was at the top of that list. I'm not sure why but Idaho was one place I just never imagined visiting. I guess because I knew so little about it, I just didn't think I'd ever have a reason or an occasion to go there, let alone what I'd do once I arrived. Oh boy was I in for one of the richest, most bless-filled stops of this journey!

I'm a bit embarrassed to say that all I knew about Idaho was a city named Boise and really delicious potatoes—that's it. Given my sad lack of knowledge about this great state, I concentrated on races in the only city I had heard of— Boise. However, it was race held in a town foreign to me that really caught my eye.

The Pocatello event was sponsored by the Idaho State Journal and consisted of four races: Marathon, Half Marathon, 10k, and 5k. They also had two children's races. It was and remains one of the premiere running events for the state of Idaho.

I was intrigued by this event and astounded by the many positive reviews from past participants. Usually, there is one bad review no matter how popular a race is with the masses. But not with this one. I combed through all the running websites looking for something negative and found nothing. Everyone spoke about a great and challenging course, A+ organization, an amazing race director (the best of any race I've ever run) and the best swag from coast to coast. I would come to discover the truth in all of these claims, and then some.

Pocatello, located in the southeastern part of the state, is the 5th largest city in Idaho and the home of Idaho State University. Although it has a regional airport, the closest international airport is Salt Lake City, which is approximately 180 miles south of Pocatello.

I took a flight to Salt Lake City and then a shuttle bus to Pocatello. The driver dropped us off at the host hotel, the Red Lion Inn.

After checking into my room, I went downstairs to the packet pickup being held in one of the ballrooms. It was easy with no vendors, just the friendliest volunteers in the business. This race wins hands down for the best swag ever, including a micro-fiber t-shirt, an incredible duffle bag that I frequently carry on trips to this day, and a large sack of real Idaho potatoes!

The pasta dinner was held in the same ballroom as the packet pickup and it was great. The food was terrific and the company even better. I met a guy named John who was 54 years old and from St. Louis. He too was a 50-stater with Idaho being number 30 for him, so we spent much of the dinner sharing stories of different races and where our journeys had taken us so far. Many of the states he had already completed were still on my list to do, so I picked up some good tips from him.

We were both a bit surprised how much we had in common regarding our 50-state quest, especially our preference for traveling to races alone and getting the maximum benefit of the experience from every perspective—not just the ability to check off another state on our list.

A couple joined us about 30 minutes later, and he was a 50-stater also. She didn't run but loved to accompany her husband. They talked about their six grown kids and how thankful they were to have weathered the storm to reach this nice place in their lives they dubbed "the good years." I thought they were so cute and it was a pleasure to share dinner with all three of them. As I've mentioned before, getting to meet great people was one of the best parts of my 50-state quest, and that was never more true than in Idaho.

I woke up at 5:00 a.m. on race morning and walked next door to the Shell station to get some coffee before getting dressed and heading to the lobby to catch the shuttle bus to the race at 6:30.

This event was different from any other I'd participated in because you had to use the provided transportation to the starting area. For those who had their own transportation, they still had to catch one of the race shuttles since no parking was available at the start line. Moreover, all four events (Marathon, Half Marathon, 10k, and 5k) started at different times in different locations, but finished at the same place.

The Marathon started first at 6:15, followed by the Half Marathon at 8:00, the 10k at 8:45 and the 5k at 9:00. Although my race, the 10k, didn't start for a while, I still had to catch the 6:30 bus since that was the only one available. It took us all to the same place, the Ross Park Aquatic Complex and from there, you had to catch another shuttle to the starting line for your particular race.

Since I was running in the 10k, my race didn't start until 8:45 and we (the 10k participants) weren't scheduled to be transported to our start line until 8:15, so I had about a 1.5 hour wait just to board the bus to get to the start.

This wait was not unexpected since the race director did an excellent job of outlining these details, but what was unexpected (at least to me) was not being able to go inside of the Aquatic facility to wait. I just assumed that we would be able to wait where it was warm and where we could use the restroom if necessary. But I was wrong. There was someone at the center who refused us entry for any reason, and that irritated me. I was cold but there was nothing I could do except stick it out. Little did I know the blessing in store for me.

I'm sure my bad mood was written all over my face. Thankfully, it didn't stop an incredibly nice person from having a conversation with me. She was participating in the Half Marathon and lived about 50 miles from Pocatello. Her warmth and kind spirit was such a blessing and I was so thankful that she wasn't put off by my awful mood. Since her race started 45 minutes before mine, she left the center before I did, but our short, meaningful conversation began what would turn out to be one of the most bless-filled experiences of my entire 50-state journey.

I was so happy when the bus arrived at 7:50 to take the 10k participants to the starting line. I boarded right away and was thankful it was much warmer than being outside had been. What happens next is nothing but a big kiss from the Lord.

When the bus dropped us off at the starting area, we only had 7 minutes before the gun was to sound. Just 7 minutes! There were two port-a-potties and it seemed like everyone made a dash for them, including me. After all, it had been quite some time since most of us had access to a bathroom at the hotel.

Just for the record, I detest port-a-potties. In fact, I can't stand public bathrooms of any kind. However, often in races you are left with no choice, especially when you are waiting in a holding area for what seemed like hours.

A girl behind me in line decided that she didn't want to wait and left to take her bag to the baggage claim area. She asked me if she could take mine which was such a blessing because we were down to just 4 minutes before starting and there were still three people ahead of me in line. I was actually in the potty when I heard someone scream, "1 minute to go." I was relieved because I knew I would make it to the start in time, and sure enough, I had about 10 seconds to stretch quickly before the gun sounded. No pre-race warm-up run, no significant stretching, no hydration, no ½ cup of yogurt; nothing of my usual routine to prep for the race ahead. All I could do was press toward that upward call and work hard out there. I felt I had already been blessed because if the lady in line had not offered to take my gear bag, I would never have made it to the start line on time.

Surprisingly, the weather warmed up by the time we started running so I was very comfortable. The course itself was flat and not very interesting to look at, which was okay by me; I wanted to concentrate on the race itself.

Within the first mile, I noticed a lady running near me that looked like she may have been in my age group. As we ran side-by-side, I did something very out-of-the-ordinary for me. I asked her how old she was. After hesitating a little, she finally replied "43." She then asked me how old I was and I replied that I was 44. Suddenly, it was game on! I can only imagine how that real-life encounter would play out on a movie screen. I mean, here are two runners going at a pretty rapid pace, discovering that they are in the same age group and just like that, each goes into overdrive in an effort to outrun the other. It was as if no one else in the race existed—it was between me and her.

Another occurrence unique to this race was the fact that I became unusually thirsty during mile 2. It was likely due to the fact that I hadn't consumed any liquid that day except the ½ cup of coffee before leaving the hotel, which was over 2.5 hours ago. I did not hydrate properly before this race and I could tell it big time, so I broke my usual routine and went for some water twice—once at mile 2 and again at mile 4. It was just a few sips both times, and I didn't even stop; I just grabbed the cup and kept going.

My pace remained steady at 8 minutes/mile, going a bit faster than that for mile 4. No doubt about it, this was turning out to be one great race. It went by rather quickly (much quicker than most races) and before I knew it, mile 6 was just steps away. I had enough energy for a quick sprint to the finish, passing my fellow age group friend. The announcer called the name of each person who crossed. They can tell who finishes by the timing device affixed to each runner. This is also how they calculate your exact finish time down to the second.

Once I crossed, I didn't hear the announcer say my name and I became nervous. This has never happened to me, but I've heard of situations where timing chips did not work and no finish time was recorded for that person. This is very rare, but it has happened. The thought of it happening to me at a race where I know I did well was devastating. However, I quickly calmed down as I realized that I was letting an unlikely scenario get the best of me without any substantiation. I totally put it out of my head. Instead, I headed to the results area and saw my recorded finish time of 50:44!

I was elated, and my fellow age grouper came up to me and stated how fast I was. Another girl asked if I was an elite runner. I told her no as I chuckled, and she said, "Well you sure look like one." Wow—what a compliment. I can't tell you how good these comments made me feel.

I had plenty of time before the awards ceremony, so I headed over to the post-race area and got a plate of barbeque, and of course, a baked potato. I'm from the south and I know good barbeque when I taste it, and this was some of the best I'd ever had. It was simply delicious! After that, I decided to get a quick massage (15 minutes for $15) which was perfect.

Soon after the massage, I ran into my new friend from the morning wait at the Aquatic Center. We picked up our conversation right where we had left off and it felt like I was talking to someone I had known for many years. Her name is Joanne and she is a practicing attorney in the area, as well as an award-winning maker of quilts, an author, and of course, a runner. In addition, she and her husband are the proud owners of four rescue dogs. It is an understatement to call this woman amazing and we continued to talk until the start of the awards ceremony, where we were both acknowledged. Joanne won 3rd place for her age group in the Half Marathon and I won the 10k Women's Masters Championship! "Huh—you have to be kidding" is all I could think of when they called my name. I was totally surprised but extremely grateful for such an honor.

In road racing, the Masters Division is for runners over a certain age, which is typically 40. This means that I was the fastest female over the age of 40 in the 10k race. While I expected to place in my age group, I had no idea that I was even in contention for a Masters Award, so it was a wonderful surprise. I happily walked on stage and accepted my awesome prize, which was a wooden plaque engraved with the event name, date and Masters insignia. In the upper right-hand corner is a clock that still works beautifully.

While I've earned several awards along this cross-country journey, none will ever be more special than this Masters win. What a great day it was in the city of Pocatello, Idaho!

Sometimes the people you meet are more important than the things you do and see. That was the case in Pocatello and I want to share that with you.

After the awards ceremony, Joanne volunteered to drive me back to my hotel which was great because I wanted to keep talking with her. We continued our great conversation and once at the hotel, we exchanged contact information and I am so thankful to this day to call Joanne my friend and sister.

This remarkable lady continues to inspire and influence me in more ways than I can describe. Her kindness is perhaps surpassed only by her humility and her love for the Lord. She will be the last person to acknowledge her amazing achievements, which now includes the publication of not one, not two, but three novels. If that's not enough, she is also a college professor, teaching in both the School of Business and the College of Law.

While her accomplishments are jaw-dropping and continue to mount with each passing year, what I find the most extraordinary about Joanne is the fact that she is my friend. It is something that I am extremely grateful for and one of the reasons why this journey has been so remarkable. Our paths would have never crossed had it not been for the desire to run in all 50 states. While the running has waned in significance (perhaps more for me than for her), our friendship continues and I pray it always will. That is the real gift of this journey; its lasting qualities that keep on giving long after the running has stopped.

Once back at the hotel, I relaxed and spent the next hour reflecting on the day with several other runners before walking across the street to Subway and getting a salad for my dinner. I was tired and knew that I had to get up at 3:45 a.m. (ouch) to catch the Express Shuttle to the Salt Lake City airport by 5:05 a.m. No problem, I thought. Getting up that early will ensure I sleep on the shuttle ride and the two flights back to Nashville.

Typically, this is where I conclude a chapter but I must add one more thing that further substantiates the exceptional quality of this stop in my journey. On the first plane of the day (Salt Lake City to Denver) I sat beside a precious older lady who told me she liked my cap. Usually when I travel on Sundays, I wear a cap that says "From the Manger to the Cross" referring to the Lord Jesus Christ.

I told her the Lord was the only One that kept me going. She replied, "Me too." We immediately bonded over our mutual love and devotion to the Lord. I needed to have that time with her because my shoulder was giving me problems that morning and bringing me down mentally. I know that God sent this lovely woman to sit beside me and minister to me.

She shared that she was on her way to visit her sister in Denver who was dying of cancer. She said her sister wasn't expected to make it through the day. She told her brother-in-law to tell her not to hang on for her because she would see her in heaven. She wanted her sister to know that if she needed to go, it was fine because they would indeed be reunited again in eternity. Wow, you could just see God all through this woman. She so beautifully illuminated the Lord in just that short time of our being together.

Just before she deplaned (I remained on the plane which was continuing to Nashville), she told me something that I will never forget. She said "When we are in trouble and need help in the world, we dial 9-1-1. Well, Psalm 91:1 is a perfect verse that reminds the believer of God's awesome protection; in fact, that entire Psalm reminds us that He is our true help in time of need." I was very familiar with Psalm 91 but had never thought of it that way before. Meeting her was God's way of sealing my Idaho experience with one great big kiss!

This race, this state, this adventure – had it all! I saw a part of the country I had never seen before, I experienced a very different start to any race in my arsenal so far, I met some wonderful people whose short season in my life was priceless (the lady who checked in my gear, my fellow age group colleague who pushed me to run my best, the woman who asked if I was an elite runner, the people I met at dinner the night before, my flying companion and fellow believer), I earned my one and only Masters Championship, and I made a friend for life.

What could be better than that? You've got me.

Race 21

ING Philadelphia Distance Run (13.1)
Philadelphia, Pennsylvania - Sept. 20, 2009

How I Love the City Of Brotherly Love

I've lived in several major cities in the United States (Atlanta—3 years, Baltimore—3 years, Los Angeles—6 years, Nashville—6 years) and I've spent significant time in many others, including Chicago, Dallas, Houston, and magnificent New York City. However, if I had to pick my favorite city of all, there is no contest: Philadelphia wins hands down.

When one of my best friends from graduate school was working on his doctorate at the University of Pennsylvania, I spent every Thanksgiving during those years in Philly and fell madly in love with the city. My friend lived in Center City so we were within walking distance of the best food, best parks, best entertainment and historical monuments of any city anywhere in the world (not to mention the Macy's Thanksgiving Day parade.)

I know that New York is considered the city that never sleeps, but Philly matches that description as well in my opinion. It has a wealth of art and culture, and there is simply no shortage of things to do. I liked exploring all that this city offers. Whether it was touring the Philadelphia Museum of Art (a must see) or relaxing in beautiful Fairmont Park, I just loved being there.

I even received a couple of unexpected surprises there, including meeting a grade school friend of mine I hadn't laid eyes on in about 20 years. One afternoon while walking along what seemed to be a deserted campus, my grad school friend and I passed a young lady who looked vaguely familiar. After continuing past her for several steps, it occurred to me who she was so I called out her first name. She kept walking, so I called out her first and last name, and she turned around. We embraced one another and took the next half hour or so catching up.

It turns out that she too was earning a doctorate at University of Pennsylvania. Seeing her again was a special treat. No wonder I associated such blessing with this city. By the way, both of these people went on to earn their doctorates and both are college professors!

You will not find friendlier people than those who reside in Philadelphia. So when it came to picking a race in the state of Pennsylvania, the only thing I had to think about was which race I wanted to do in Philadelphia. I couldn't have made a better choice than the Philadelphia Distance Run. Everything about it was just awesome!

As I've mentioned previously, one of my "must haves" for a running event is good logistics. I like to do races in a city's downtown area because typically, everything is accessible by foot or public transport. That means I can spend more time enjoying the city and activities without the added aggravation (and expense) of rental cars, parking fees, and so forth. In this regard, the Philadelphia Distance Run was perfect. It has been considered the premiere half marathon in the city since 1978.

My relatively short flight to Philadelphia departed Nashville at 9:52 a.m. which was ideal; not too early and not too late. When I left Nashville, it was drizzling and cloudy but upon arrival in Philly, the weather was gorgeous and would be all weekend long. It was 70 degrees without a cloud in the sky—wonderful!

Once in Philly, I decided to take SEPTA, Philadelphia's public transportation system, to my hotel, the Embassy Suites. At only $7.00, I boarded the train right at the airport and rode to the Suburban Station at Market and 18th, which was one block from my hotel.

I love utilizing the rapid train systems whenever it is possible. In fact, it is one of the things I research when deciding if a city is the right place for me to run or not. You can't ever beat the price and for someone who is so often behind the wheel, it is a great relief to be able to sit back, relax and enjoy the scenery without having to think. I know quite a few people who try to avoid public transit systems when they travel to a city and I don't understand why. My guess is that they harbor some kind of fear about it and if that's the case, let me assure that I have ridden trains, subways, buses, etc., both domestically and abroad, and I have found them all to be safe, reliable, and in most cases, even clean. So put your fears to rest.

The Embassy Suites turned out to be an excellent choice, especially in terms of location and since I was able to use bonus points for a free night, it was even better.

With the weather so great, I couldn't wait to get out into the city so I unpacked very quickly and with my backpack in tow, I was on my way, first to the expo.

The expo was held a mile west of my hotel at the Philadelphia Convention Center. It wasn't as big as I expected. I think I was spoiled by larger Rock-n-Roll races where it takes almost a full day to visit all the vendors. I was fine with that because I didn't want to spend too much time walking inside that day. I picked up my runner's packet and tech shirt, stopped at a couple of booths, and then headed to the start line in front of the stairs of the Philadelphia Museum of Art. These are the same stairs Sylvester Stallone ran as Rocky Balboa in the movie, Rocky. A Whole Foods Market was nearby so I stopped there for my lunch, dinner and snacks. I promptly headed back to my room to put everything in the mini fridge.

I spent the rest of the afternoon and early evening perusing the colorful neighborhoods I had come to know so well several years ago. Since the weather was so incredible, there were loads of people in the parks, sitting outside on restaurant patios, examining the goods of various street vendors and overall, just enjoying themselves. It was a great way to spend the day but with a 7:45 start time, I needed to head back to my hotel room, get into "race mode" and settle down for the evening.

Since just before the Chicago race, I had been having problems with my legs, mostly my hamstrings and knees. In Philadelphia, my left leg was giving me some trouble. Once in the hotel room, I iced it down and put some Biofreeze on it but it was still feeling very tight, so much so that I realized I might not be able to accomplish my goal of finishing in less than 2 hours. However, I prayed for God to help me through, remembering how He had done so in Chicago. I went to sleep thinking what a blessed day it had been.

My wake-up call took place promptly at 5:30 and I woke up thankful for the great night's sleep I had. I headed to the lobby for coffee they made for the runners and stuck to my regimen of ½ cup of coffee and a ½ cup of goat milk yogurt.

The weather was 50 degrees and rising with clear skies so everything was right on track. It felt so good not to have to rush to get dressed given that I was .3 miles from the start line, so I was able to take my time before leaving the hotel at 6:45. I did my stretching on the steps of the Philadelphia Museum of Art with quite a few other runners. I then turned in my bag with my sweat pants and jacket to the folks at the gear check and did a short warm-up before lining up at in my assigned corral, the number 5. I prayed for a safe race and then the gun sounded.

The race started promptly at 7:45 and my corral started at 7:52 (per my watch). My strategy for this race mirrored that of every half marathon since Virginia Beach: try to average 8:00 – 8:30 minutes/mile for as long as possible, getting to at least mile 7 by the first hour. I prayed along the way that God would keep my legs healthy and He sure did. Like Chicago, once I got going, I experienced little to no discomfort whatsoever. The only time I sensed anything unusual was around mile 9 but it quickly subsided and wasn't a hindrance at all.

Right from the start I felt great and was able to maintain my fast miles without much problem. One interesting thing in this race was that I became very thirsty in mile 3. I usually don't take my first sip of anything until mile 7 or later for a half marathon race, mostly to maintain my pace and to avoid cramping.

Once I got to mile 7, I was 58 minutes into the race and well within the 1 hour mark threshold I set for myself. I took my first swig of Cytomax at mile 8 and boy was I ready for it. Thankfully, it was good and cold which helped a lot on this day with the temperature slowly climbing into the 70 degree range.

Yes, I was running faster than normal and I think the reason was the scenic and historical quality of the course. Starting on the famous Benjamin Franklin Parkway, adorned by the beautiful fountains and public art, we gradually ran in my favorite area, Center City. We passed historical monuments like City Hall, Independence Hall, and the famous Walnut street.

We progressed along Martin Luther King Drive into the gorgeous Fairmont Park along the Schuykill River. We finished at the steps of the Museum of Art. With scenery like that it was easy to get your mind off running.

Eventually the speed would catch up to me at mile 10. I became very tired and realized for the last couple of miles, I had been running even faster than my usual 8 minute/mile pace. The fatigue caught me by surprise. That is the most winded I can remember being in a race of this distance. I mean it was a true "hitting of the wall" so I had to drink again at mile 11. The good news is that by that time, I could have slowed down to a 12 minute/mile pace and still finished in less than 2 hours, my overall timing goal.

As usual, the last two miles were tough and I barely (and I do mean barely) had the strength to carry on. I called on the Lord for strength and He was there because once I saw the finish ahead, I sprinted toward the banner! What a blessing, finishing with a time of 1:54:14.

After receiving my gorgeous finisher's medal and picking up my gear bag, I stretched on those famous steps of the museum again and drank some chocolate milk before heading back the hotel. The manager was gracious and gave me a 2:00 p.m. checkout time. I got there about 10:45, so I had time to lie down and catch a quick nap (I needed one!) before packing and departing.

On the flight to Nashville, I sat beside a lovely young lady who was completing her residency. We had a blessed conversation and it was refreshing to meet a young woman who was so poised and intelligent and being obedient to what God had called her to do.

This race and weekend was (as the Bible says) "refreshment to my bones." It had been a tough week dealing with muscle strains and discomforts in my body that were uncharacteristic, only to travel to my favorite city and run pain-free. Moreover, being able to revisit those places from many Novembers ago, added to the uniqueness of the weekend.

This 50-state journey just keeps getting better and better.

Race 22

Detroit Free Press/ Flagstar Half Marathon
Detroit, Michigan - October 18, 2009

Disappointment Lifted By Motown and a Great Race with International Charm

D etroit was one of the few big cities in the nation that I had never visited. During the time I was pursuing a race in the 50 states, it had seen better days. With the growing number of races in places like Ann Arbor and Lansing (also university towns that were high on my list), I was torn over where to run in the state of Michigan. In the end, the city of Detroit won, mostly because of a well-reviewed race spanning across two countries and the desire to see where all that great music began.

I'm just going to start by being very blunt; the city of Detroit was a disappointment. While I understand the economic decline it has experienced over the past several years, I still expected more, especially in the downtown area which to me was akin to a ghost town.

With no rapid transit system from the airport to downtown, I was forced take a cab (my least favorite form of public transportation) the 20 miles to downtown, costing me $41.90. Maybe I was just spoiled by the flourishing downtowns of Chicago and Philadelphia because almost immediately, I was dispirited.

Once at the hotel, the Doubletree Guest Suites Fort Shelby/Detroit Downtown, I checked into my suite which was just okay; certainly not the best but not the worst either. Since I was totally underwhelmed by just about everything up to this point, I thought I'd better head over to the expo where I hoped things would improve. I walked the ½ mile to the Cobo Hall Center where the expo was held and even though it wasn't that large, I was just happy to be in an environment that was uplifting because the city itself wasn't.

My wake-up call was 5:00 a.m. and I immediately went to the lobby for a cup of coffee. With the start line right across the street, I wouldn't have to leave my room early and stand in the cold waiting and I love that. The race started at 7:15 so I left the room at 7:00 sharp and did a short warm-up run down the street before finding my corral and getting in line. My energy level was high and I was ready to go.

Unlike Philadelphia and Chicago where I had leg issues that threatened to impede my running, my legs felt great. I was sure I'd have a good race. My goal was to pace myself better than I did in Philly where I started too fast and all but tanked during the final mile. I focused on starting a bit slower and clocked mile 2 at just over 9:00 minutes/mile, mostly due to overcrowding. There were over 12,000 runners in Detroit that day, with nearly 8,400 in the half marathon. While bottlenecking and overcrowding in the first few miles is not uncommon, it seemed to be more acute in this race for some reason. I had a hard time establishing some separation.

Crossing the Ambassador Bridge was challenging and involved a steady uphill climb. Surprisingly, I did the hills better in this race than most others, never getting winded like I usually do. I continued to maintain my pace as we crossed into Windsor, Canada and ran along a lovely waterfront community into some nice neighborhoods. On the way back into the U.S. we ran through the Detroit-Windsor tunnel which was very warm compared to the outside temperature. The sudden rise in temperature made it difficult to keep pace but once we came through the tunnel, we were back to 39 degrees which actually felt pretty good.

At mile 7, I was exactly at the one hour mark so I was right on target with where I like to be in a half marathon. In Philadelphia and Chicago I was closer to 7.2-7.25 miles at the one hour point in the race but by maintaining a slightly slower pace, I knew that I'd have enough left in the tank for a sprint at the end.

Miles 9 through 11.5 were tough, as usual, but not as tough as Philadelphia. Moreover, they were unusually quiet with few spectators and no music. Nonetheless, it was a pleasant couple of miles, albeit uneventful.

I only drank once in this race - a couple of sips of Gatorade at mile 8. Because the temperature was cool, I didn't get thirsty during this run although I know the importance of staying hydrated. I did have an energy gel cube in my pocket that I popped into my mouth near mile 6 and it lasted a long while due to its gooey texture.

At mile 12, I saw two people on the ground. I could tell one of the guys was very hurt with blood running down his head as several people from the medical unit were trying to help him. I had never seen anything like that before and I lifted my right hand and prayed to the Lord to help this man. It was a scene that got to me.

With that scene aside, finishing the race felt great. We separated from the people running the full marathon at mile 12.5. Because I had walked to the CVS the day before where we split, I knew exactly where we were and how much further we had to go.

As I predicted, I had enough left in the tank to sprint the last hundred feet or so for a finish time of 1:56:05. I was very pleased with this time and after the volunteers gave me my finisher's medal and Kevlar wrap (the feather-light wrapper many runners don right after a race to prevent hyperthermia by reflecting body heat), I headed over to the post-race section to grab some food and water. I was very disappointed with the meager offering I found there. Since Whole Foods Market was one of the sponsors of the race, I expected a nice post-race spread. However, once I saw what was offered, I didn't hesitate to take a pass.

They didn't even have bottled water. Instead the volunteers were handing the finishers cups of water. To me, that was just cheap and I expressed that in a review I did of the race for one of the running websites. I've participated in races much smaller than this one with much lower registration fees and a bottle of water was always available.

Touring the Motown Museum was great. I was surprised how small it was though. It's hard to imagine that all those singers and great songs were generated out of such a small house and even smaller studio. There were quite a few people there for the same tour; mostly people in town for the race. Among them were two guys, one who had participated in 165 marathons and the other in 60. They were best friends and it was great taking the tour with them. We even shared a cab on the way back to the hotel.

Fine dining was not an option on this trip. I made the best of it and decided to try the bar and grill in the hotel lobby. Two steps in the door I could smell the smoke and was appalled to learn that Michigan had yet to enact a smoke-free air law (something it did institute in May of 2010; I was just a bit too early).

"Oh boy, I thought, another negative to add to the list."

To get around sitting in a smoke-filled restaurant, I decided to get my order to go and eat in my hotel room. I chose the salad with salmon from a very limited menu, and after eating about 1/3 of it, I discovered an earring in the middle of the salad! Can you believe that? This trip was just getting worse by the minute.

The manager took off the charge and extended me a $20 credit to be used anytime during my stay, as if I would order anything else from this restaurant.

The state of Michigan could now be checked off. While this trip had its fair share of disappointments, it had some positive moments too. It provided me with my first taste of "international" running and I had the opportunity to tour a national treasure in the Motown Museum. But perhaps most importantly, this was state # 22 on this amazing journey that I was enjoying very much. While I was happy to have had this experience, I was equally glad to move on from this one.

Race 23

34th Marine Corps 10k
Washington, D.C. - October 25, 2009

Delighted In Our Nation's Capital

I typically try to space my races out with a minimum of two weeks between each one, but to run in the Marine Corps 10k, that two week minimum just wasn't possible.

The date for the 10k was Sunday, October 25, exactly one week after my half marathon race in Detroit. Having registered and planned for it nearly 2 months in advance, I knew it was going to be a quick turnaround from one race to the next. However, considering this race was a 10k and not another half marathon, I knew that my body was up to the challenge, even with the nagging injuries still lingering around.

I'm sure it has crossed the minds of some people why I would include a race in Washington, D.C. as part of my 50-state quest. After all, Washington D.C. is not a state but a federal district. I rationalized that anything involving all 50 United States should also involve the capital of those 50 states, including running.

When it comes to D.C., there is no better choice than the Marine Corps races, consisting of one of the largest marathons in the nation as well as a 10k. In 2009, over 21,000 participants ran the marathon with another 5,400 participating in the 10k. Needless to say, this is a huge event in the running world and I was determined to make it a part of my cross-country quest, even if it meant running a major race on back-to-back weekends.

From 1993 to 1996, I lived in and around Baltimore and spent a lot of time in D.C. as a result. In fact, I took a few evening courses at Georgetown University as part of a continuing education program (I just love to learn. If I could make a living at it, I'd be a professional student, no doubt about it) and just fell in love with everything Washington D.C. had to offer. Having traveled through our nation's capital on numerous occasions since that time, I was eager to get back there and spend some quality time. In other words, this race was important to me.

I debated what would be the best way to get there. I always embrace the option of flying because I love to fly and prefer doing so whenever possible. However, I needed to be in east Tennessee earlier in the week for my job, so I decided to drive from east Tennessee to my parents house in North Carolina (a 5-hour drive), spend the night with them, and drive to D.C. the next day. That was another 5-hour drive.

Since I would be staying with my parents for a night, I asked my mother if she would like to travel with me to the race, and she jumped at the chance. So, the trip to D.C. was all set and I couldn't wait.

The Thursday before the race, I attended meetings all day in Knoxville, Tennessee and then made the 5-hour drive to my parent's home that evening. On Friday, Mom and I had lunch at an outdoor eatery we like, and it was a precursor to the time of fellowship we would have in D.C. We relaxed the rest of the day to prepare for our drive the next day.

Mom and I hit the road at 5:30 Saturday morning, fueled by two cups of delicious coffee Mom made for us. We had the best time together during this drive northward. We decided to stop for breakfast at Bob Evans in Fredericksburg, Virginia, putting us 40 miles from our hotel.

We arrived in D.C. at 10:15 a.m. and stayed at one of the recommended hotels, the Doubletree in Crystal City, Virginia. It was a free stay thanks to extra points I had accumulated through the Hilton Honors Program.

The hotel was no great shakes, but it was nice and clean, and just .35 miles from the metro stop. The hotel provided shuttle service to the stop throughout the day and night, making it convenient to get around the city. Many runners stayed at the same hotel, so I was constantly meeting people participating in both the marathon and 10k.

Shortly after checking in and unpacking, Mom and I decided to take the metro to the health and fitness expo located at the Walter E. Washington Convention Center downtown. We took the hotel shuttle to the Metro station and purchased our metro tickets. We initially boarded the wrong line (green vs. yellow) but got off at the next stop and boarded the correct train. Once we did, it was smooth sailing.

The expo was big but most of the vendors were there to sell something so the free giveaways I'm used to collecting at these events was minuscule. Still, there were several food and beverage companies there who handed out nice samples of their new energy bars and shakes, both of which were quite tasty. Overall the expo was good with one exception: I always order an extra small in shirts and if they don't have an extra small option, I order a small. However, when I got to the shirt pickup area, the smallest size they had available was medium, which totally swallowed me and still does. As a result, I think I've worn it once and that was on a cold day when I needed a lot of layers. It is just too large for me to wear anywhere and that's a shame because I enjoy wearing the shirts from my running events—they are good conversation starters.

We had a great late lunch/early dinner at the Asian Spice Restaurant and Bar on H Street and the food was delicious. We returned to the metro stop just before it rained cats and dogs for nearly 3 hours. I was glad it came toward the end of the day and totally cleared out by nightfall. I went to bed feeling confident that tomorrow's race was going to be a good one.

I woke up at 5:00 in order to board the metro by 6:00. I purchased my metro ticket the day before thinking it would be crowded on race morning, but I was wrong. I walked the ½ mile to the metro station, boarded with a few other early risers, and arrived at the 10k start area (the National Mall, just outside the Smithsonian on Jefferson Drive) by 6:30.

Since the race didn't start until 8:00, I knew that I had a long and cold wait. Boy was I miserable! I simply could not get warm even though I had on gloves, toboggan, 3 layers, sweat pants, and an additional coat and jacket. However, in the midst of my misery, something wonderful happened. Inside the metro station, a group of us were led in prayer by a lovely lady, and we sang a chorus of "Amazing Grace." What a blessing from God.

Right after the chorus of "Amazing Grace" a metro cop approached and told us we had to go outside and made us clear the area. Although we were doing no harm or getting in anybody's way, he was adamant about getting us out of there, but he wasn't successful until after we praised and worshipped the Lord. What an awesome God He is!

Back outside I just could not warm up at all. Everybody was walking, jumping and running around in an effort to increase their body temperature, but in my case, it did no good.

I got in line at 7:50 and took off my gloves to discover my fingers had completely turned yellow and I had no feeling in them. I must have had a worried look on my face because a lady behind me touched my shoulder and said not to worry at all about my fingers. She told me the technical name for it (she was a nurse) and further noted that it was perfectly normal and more common in women than men. She said once I started running, I'd slowly regain feeling and she was exactly right, but I was well into mile 3 before that happened.

I am definitely a cold-natured person; I'm always cold even when most people are comfortable. I'm used to cold hands and fingers, but never to the point of having them turn yellow with no feeling. I'm thankful this woman was there to ease my concerns. Again, God is good.

Once the race started, I felt great. I maintained a pace of 8:30 minutes/mile even though I decided the day before not to push too hard in this one. I knew that with several elite runners in the mix, there was no way I could place in my age group. I wasn't planning to run my normal pace, but I just felt too good to run any other way.

The course was great, crossing the 14th Street Bridge into Crystal City and turning left on 15th Street. After arriving at the Pentagon, we ran in parallel to the marathoners until finishing at the Marine Corps War Memorial. Wow—there was just something very moving about running alongside all of that history and doing so in a race that involved so many of our men and women in uniform. You couldn't help but feel proud to be there that day.

I finished the race in 51:36, about 50 seconds slower than my run in Pocatello. Toward the end, there was a tough hill that I tried to sprint but ended up nearly breathless instead.

At the finish, we walked up a hill where we received the honor of having our finisher's medal placed around our neck by a Marine officer (awesome) and our picture taken in front of the Iwo Jima Memorial. Nowhere else can a race finish look or feel like that.

I am so glad that I ran this race because there is no feeling like running in our nation's capital. That alone makes it a unique experience unmatched by any other.

However, what really made this stop on my journey special were those moments that were totally unexpected yet filled with tremendous blessing. Moments like being comforted about my frozen fingers, joining voices in songs of praise with my fellow runners and riding the metro from stop to stop.

My cross-country journey would not have been the same without this race in Washington, D.C.

Race 24

Indianapolis Monumental Half Marathon

Indianapolis, Indiana - November 7, 2009

Still Going Strong

I was still on a high from my back-to-back races in Detroit and Washington, D.C. so I wanted to keep the momentum going. Since I needed to be in Louisville, Kentucky for 3 days the first week of November, I thought it would be ideal if I could combine that work trip with a race. While I had already completed races in most states within driving distance of Kentucky, there was still one outstanding that needed to be fulfilled: the state of Indiana.

One of my favorite films of all time is the 1979 hit Breaking Away, filmed on location at Indiana University in Bloomington. I fell in love with the scenes filmed on campus and in nearby Brown County State Park. Thus, my preference was to find a race in or near Bloomington—that is until I discovered the Monumental Half Marathon in Indianapolis.

Based on my research, this race had it all: a great downtown location, a nice finisher's medal, a decent size (nearly 3000 half marathoners) and the rare opportunity to race on a Saturday (Sunday appears to be the more prevalent day for most races).

This was the 2nd year of this event so the inevitable inaugural glitches were out of the way. From every perspective, this event seemed stress-free, which is exactly what I needed at the time so I registered right away.

After my last meeting for work, I made the easy 2 hour drive from Louisville to Indianapolis. I elected to stay at the Hampton Inn downtown on Meridian and used Hilton Honors points for a free stay. The location was ideal, putting me within walking distance to everything I needed on this short trip. The weather was great, with clear skies expected all weekend, and temperatures hovering in the high 50's/low 60's.

Up at 6:00 a.m., I walked outside to make sure my car was still there (I parked on the street) and to check the weather, which wasn't bad at all. I grabbed some coffee and juice at the hotel breakfast bar and started getting ready for the race. My energy level was good and I was itching to get started on this one.

With the start line 3 blocks from my hotel, I didn't leave my room until 7:45. It was so nice to be able to stay in a warm room until the start, unlike D.C. two weeks prior. Even though I felt good, I made up my mind that I was going to maintain a slightly slower pace than usual just because I'd spent the last week in Kentucky on meetings and my workouts weren't as in-depth as I wanted them to be. So basically, my goal was to finish in less than 2 hours but to take it easier than usual.

While in line just before the sound of the gun, a girl next to me asked what my pace time was. I told her that I normally finish a half marathon somewhere in the 1:50 to 1:55 hour range but on that day, I was anticipating a 1:58 or 1:59 finish time.

The weather was awesome with bright sunny skies and a temperature of 52 degrees. I had on one layer, a long-sleeve tech shirt and I was comfortable the entire race.

My first mile was slow at 9:30, but I picked it up as we progressed along this scenic course. We ran past several monuments and landmarks, as well as some beautiful neighborhoods, They all supported why this city makes many "best places to live" surveys.

While the course was basically flat, there were some decent sized hills also but nothing monumental, despite the name of this event.

I held to my usual routine and didn't drink anything until after the 7th mile, which I reached after running for exactly 1 hour. I drank some Gatorade at mile 8 which was a 10 minute/mile pace.

Miles 8 through 10 are usually always rough for me. The crowds are generally sparse at this part of the course and fatigue normally starts to kick in at this time. It's funny, because in the first couple of miles, you hear a lot of runners talking to one another, joking and even laughing. However, in the 8 to 10 mile range, it is as quiet as a church mouse out there, the only sound being heavy footsteps and breathing!

I drank some water at mile 10 and decided that was my final drink until I finished the race. During the last couple of miles when we got back into the downtown area, the wind was cutting through the buildings in our direction so it was terribly hard to run full throttle, but by that point, I knew that I could coast and still finish within my goal time. I even had enough to sprint my final few steps and finish with a time of 1:57:24. I was very happy with this result. Upon crossing the finish line, I lifted my hands to the Lord like I usually do after a race and thanked Him openly for allowing me to complete another race in my journey.

In the post-race area, I grabbed some bottled water, trail mix and Gatorade before jogging back to the room. I checked out by 11:45 and started my 5-hour drive to my home in Franklin, TN. It was a perfect day for driving so I relaxed behind the wheel, ever so grateful to the Lord for this great victory.

I like downtown Indianapolis and as I passed several landmarks like the Indianapolis Museum of Art and the NCAA Hall of Champions, I was a bit bummed that I hadn't planned to spend more time in this interesting city.

I did enjoy a great meal at a restaurant called the Palomino. It caught my eye almost immediately because several years prior, when I lived in Los Angeles trying to make it as a struggling actor (another story for another book), one of my many part-time jobs was as a hostess at the Palomino restaurant in Westwood. As a result, I ate there just about every day so I was intimately familiar with the menu and liked just about everything they had to offer.

I hadn't eaten at a Palomino restaurant since leaving Los Angeles, so I was happy to dine at this one, and I wasn't disappointed. My waitress was wonderful and asked me if I was in town for the marathon. I told her yes, but I was running in the half marathon, and she said I looked like a professional athlete. That caused me to smile because I was starting to get this comment often, and it never ceased to make me feel good.

I really should have stayed an additional day in Indianapolis because based on my short time there, it is a terrific city. But although I didn't get a chance to do much tourist stuff, I still received many kisses from God making this stop on my journey memorable and bless-filled. State # 23 was in the books and I couldn't wait to get to my next destination!

Race 25

51st Atlantic City 10k
Atlantic City, New Jersey
November 15, 2009

1st Place on the Boardwalk
Never Felt so Good

For years my family spent part of the holidays in Atlantic City. They would travel by bus with a group from their community and I would drive from my home in Baltimore to meet them. In those days, we mostly stayed at a casino hotel named the Claridge and the primary purpose of the trip was to gamble, plain and simple.

Once I became a Christian, gambling ceased to be a pleasure and I stopped joining them for that purpose. Nevertheless, I still enjoyed the live shows and eclectic restaurants (more so in Las Vegas than Atlantic City).

I initially looked for races in New Jersey that weren't in Atlantic City in an effort to see another area of the state. However, most of the events I found were either not a logistical fit or the timing didn't mesh with my schedule. So, when I found the Atlantic City event, I was intrigued.

The Atlantic City Marathon is the 3rd oldest running event in the country, having added a half marathon, 10k and 5k race along the way. There was something appealing about participating in an event with so much history and logistically, it couldn't have been more convenient to everything – the start, finish, expo, awards ceremony—all taking place on the famous boardwalk. Moreover, this would be the first year a new race director was taking the reins, infusing some new energy in a well-respected race. It seemed like the perfect time to participate.

Since the Atlantic City event included a 10k, and I had already demonstrated that I could handle a half marathon and a 10k back-to-back with the Detroit and D.C. races, I didn't hesitate to sign up. Doubly exciting was the opportunity to travel again with Mom. I knew she wouldn't turn down an invitation to travel to Atlantic City since she's a one-armed bandit specialist.

Usually a day or two before the race, runners can pick up their running packets, which contain the all-important timing chip and runner's bib, among other key items. However, for some reason at this event, the packets were not available for pickup until the morning of the race. On race morning, I don't like focusing on anything but the race, so I was disappointed to have to deal with this at a time I prefer to be relaxed and getting warmed up. Nonetheless, I got up an extra hour early so that I could get to the Convention Hall, pick up my packet, and still have time to stretch and mentally prepare.

About 8:15, most of the runners started lining up outside for the 8:30 start time. All four races started at the same time going in the same direction, with my race, the 10k, turning around right at the halfway mark at Melbourne Avenue and heading back to the Convention Center. The weather was great for running and while in line, I felt incredible.

Still moving around to stay loose, a young man and I struck up a wonderful conversation. He was in high school and I could tell that he was very intelligent by the way he spoke. He was in his senior year and had earned both athletic and academic scholarships to several noted universities including Duke and Cornell. He was a track champion and held several state titles but clearly his education was important to him. This young man was impressive and it was evident he had an amazing future. He ran in the 5k, and as I expected, he placed in his age group and was one of the top finishers in the entire event.

This race couldn't have gone any better for me. In fact, I can't think of a time when I felt more relaxed and settled on a race course. Being perhaps the most fit in my life, I remember just gliding along, running well within my normal pace without the threat of fatigue at any part of the course. I just loved every minute of it.

After crossing the finish line, I knew I had placed and even if I hadn't, I wanted to see the awards ceremony. I headed back to the hotel room where Mom was already up and ready to go. I showered and dressed quickly so that we could attend the awards ceremony where I was blessed to win 1st place in my age group. Technically this was a Masters win because I had the fastest time of all women over the age of 40. I was the 3rd female overall and 12th finisher overall (out of 88 total finishers.)

As a result, I was awarded a beautiful glass trophy from Crown denoting I was the top female for the 40-49 age group in the 10k, with the event name and date. In addition, I was given a certificate valued at $50 for dinner for two at Harrah's Resort, Caesars, Bally's or Showboat, good through June 30, 2010.

I can't remember why Mom and I didn't use it for dinner that night. I guess the theory was to hold onto it for a while since it was good for a whole year. However, I never made it back to Atlantic City within that time frame, which I'm happy about now. I still have the certificate prominently on display among my most treasured awards from this amazing journey!

It had been a while since my last trip to Atlantic City before this race, so I knew much had changed. I was used to an "old" city with older buildings and facilities, lacking any kind of a modern feel. I was pleasantly surprised how much "younger" the city seemed to me at the time of this event.

I really enjoyed this race very much and I'm thankful for the role it played in my 50-state journey. A true blessing.

Race 26

Rock-n-Roll Las Vegas
Half Marathon
Las Vegas, Nevada - December 6, 2009

Ending the Year on a Beautiful Note

It's a pity that December races are few and far between because I love running in that month. With the wonderful memory of last December's race in Baton Rouge still fresh in my mind and heart, I wanted to try and duplicate that blessing and joy. Having already participated in several Rock-n-Roll events, I was all too familiar with their great organization, classy finisher medals, and good logistics, so I didn't delay registering for their half marathon in Las Vegas. In fact, I registered in May to ensure I got a spot in one of the largest races in the country.

First, I will state for the record that I love the city of Las Vegas, although not for the reasons of most people. My enjoyment is relegated around the almost year-round great weather, fantastic food, and wonderful concerts - not the gambling and other shenanigans most folks partake in while there.

The list of celebrities I've seen perform in Las Vegas is exhaustive, including Gladys Knight (whom I saw perform twice and is one of my all-time favorites), Charo, Olivia Newton John, Clint Black, Lorrie Morgan, Clint Holmes, Siegfried and Roy (I was privileged to catch their show 4 months before Roy's accident), and Wayne Newton, to just name a few. Other shows include most of the Cirque de Soleil performances and the Blue Men Group.

As for the weather, I get some of the best exercise in my life when I visit Las Vegas. Most mornings very early before the sidewalks become too crowded, I run the Las Vegas Strip, usually getting in 5-6 miles at a minimum. My favorite route is from the Vdara (my preferred hotel because it is non-smoking and non-gaming) down to the Stratosphere at the end of the strip and back, or sometimes I will go in the other direction, turning around at Mandalay Bay. Regardless of the route, the strip is flat and makes for an easy run that many runners take advantage of while there on vacation. I also enjoy running along the strip to Town Square where Whole Foods Market is located, as well as many other shops, restaurants and movie theater.

And when it comes to well-prepared, great tasting meals, Las Vegas is second to none in my book, and that is saying something since I don't eat that much on a daily basis. However, when I go Vegas, I engage in eating more than anywhere else in the country (no wonder I run so much when I'm there.)

When I lived in Los Angeles, I can't recall the number of times I made the journey across the desert to Las Vegas, especially when friends from the east coast would visit. I got to know that stretch of road very well in those days. So for me, visiting Las Vegas is like seeing an old friend. I know the city very well and find it extremely easy to get around in. It was a given that I had to include it in my journey.

Since I registered for this event seven months in advance, I had no idea that just 3 weeks prior to the race, I would have completed one of my most successful 10k races in its cousin town, Atlantic City. Given that it was Las Vegas, I invited Mom to attend with me knowing the answer would be yes before I even asked.

We decided to make a vacation out of it, arriving the Friday before the race and departing the Wednesday after (the race was on a Sunday.) I used vacation days the entire week so that it could be a true vacation with my cell phone off the whole time.

Since the race started and ended at the Mandalay Bay Resort, I decided to stay there. I had enough points to get our room free all three nights. On Monday after the race, we checked into the Flamingo Hotel and stayed there (free also) two additional nights before flying back east on Wednesday.

A bonus to this trip was that my friends from the Corinth, Mississippi race, Barbara and Tall, were coming as well with Barbara participating in the half marathon. We planned to have dinner the night of the race and I was so looking forward to seeing them again. I just knew this was going to be a great way to end the year.

I attended the expo held at Mandalay Bay on Saturday and true to form, it was spectacular. Since the total number of runners for both the full and half marathon exceeded 25,000, the expo was no small potatoes. Exhibitors from every company you could imagine, small and large, were there in abundance and the free goodies were in large supply. I enjoyed taking my time, stopping at each booth and learning what I could about the latest products, foods, gadgets, etc. specific to the running industry. It was quite a day and made me even more excited about the race.

The race started at 6:15 a.m. which is earlier than most but I was glad to be starting early. Due to the number of runners, it was a wave start to reduce overcrowding although it was after mile 3 before we got some good separation.

The temperature was in the high 30's but there was plenty of sun so I was comfortable for the most part. This race felt good to me from the start to the finish. It was one of the only times I knew the course in advance, having run it so many times on my own over the years. The familiarity with knowing where I was going had its advantage and I knew that I was going to finish this race with one of the fastest half marathon times ever. Crossing the finish line in 1:53:35, it would end up being the 3rd fastest half marathon in my 50-state journey.

I spent the rest of my vacation in Las Vegas dining with my friends, seeing several shows, and just having a good time. There was no better way to end the amazing running year of 2009.

2010: The Fullest Race Schedule So Far

It was hard to imagine topping the year I had in 2009. I was blessed with wonderful new friendships, visits to new cities and states, several wins and age group placements. I had thousands of short unique experiences I call "kisses from God." With all that, there didn't seem to be much to look forward to in 2010. Was I wrong!

The year started off with quite a few changes for me, the most prominent being a new job in a new state. Just after the Vegas race last year, I was presented a promotional opportunity with a new company. The catch was that I had to agree to relocate to North Carolina before accepting the position. This was a hard decision for me because I loved living in Nashville and my house of 6 years had been a real home. The thought of selling it was heartbreaking, but this promotion was too good to pass up.

The responsibilities of the position were similar to my previous job in that I would be required to travel a great deal, except instead of traveling throughout Tennessee and Kentucky, the bulk of the travel would be in North and South Carolina. Having grown up in North Carolina, the area was familiar to me. In addition, the increase of salary made it easier to make the decision to move.

With all the details involved with moving, selling one house, buying a new one, starting a new job with a new company, etc., there wasn't much time or energy to devote to my running or my 50-state quest. I gave myself the month of January and most of February to concentrate on getting settled. Even though there was still much to do in that regard, I was determined not to let any more time pass before getting back in the saddle and seeing more of our beautiful nation via the road races of life. I was eager to get back out there, unsure of how the year would unfold. Nevertheless, I looked forward to every detail of discovery.

Little did I know I would run more races this year than ever before (16), and see parts of the country that had been on my wish list for years, including Wyoming, New Hampshire, Nebraska and the beautiful Dakotas. I would also learn a very valuable lesson that continues to guide my footsteps in all aspects of life.

Race 27

Columbia Half Marathon
Columbia, South Carolina - February 27, 2010

A Last Minute Replacement that Turned Out Well

Having grown up in North Carolina, one might think that I had spent a lot of time in South Carolina but such was not the case. Although I drove through South Carolina on many occasions as I traveled from my home in Atlanta to visit my parents, I never spent any "quality time" there, although I certainly had my chances.

Just before I graduated from North Carolina State University in Electrical Engineering, one of the seven jobs I was offered was with DuPont's Atomic Energy Division at the Savannah River Plant in Aiken, South Carolina. They sponsored me on a plant visit so that I could visit the community. I liked that part of the state. Being close

183

to the Georgia border and the historic city of Savannah, it would have been an excellent opportunity for me. However, being 21 and without much discernment, my focus was on too many of the wrong things. I turned down the offer and accepted a position in Atlanta instead. So, I blew an opportunity to be a resident of South Carolina, a state I would in later years explore extensively.

My new job required me to be in South Carolina quite often so I was getting a second chance to learn more about it. Like many people, my favorite areas are along the coast, specifically Hilton Head Island and the Myrtle Beach communities. It is hard to beat the serenity and beauty of these towns, not to mention the historic charm of cities like Charleston and Columbia.

After taking off the month of January from road racing, I was ready to restart my 50-state journey. I decided there was no better place to start 2010 off than with one of the largest and most popular events in the state, the Bi-Lo Myrtle Beach Marathon. I'd heard about this event for years. I had several friends who participated and said good things about it. I coordinated some meetings for my job around the February 13 race date and registered for the half marathon as soon as possible.

Everything was all set until a severe winter storm arrived that Friday. I was in Charlotte with plans to leave early that morning for Myrtle Beach when I noticed the road conditions starting to change. After checking the weather forecasts and learning that the threat of icy conditions was inevitable, I canceled the trip and returned home

Later that evening (Friday) the race director decided to cancel the event for the weekend. There was a lot of buzz about this in the running community. Many were upset with the decision to cancel the race. Most wanted the right to run even if the conditions were less than favorable. I thought the cancellation was warranted, given the severity of the weather, although I understood the frustration the protesters. It is a hard pill to swallow when you've spent time and money on airfare, lodging and food with nothing to show for it.

In my case it wasn't so bad since I was able to cancel my hotel reservation without penalty and take the short 2-hour drive back to my house. All I was out was my registration fee. Most events state clearly up front that all registration fees are "nonrefundable" regardless of circumstances.

Although this race was a no-go, I was still ready to get back in the game and immediately started researching other races in South Carolina. I was hoping to find one I could enter before the end of February. I found a good one!

The Columbia Half Marathon was an inaugural event taking place on the last Saturday of the month. It appeared to meet most of my criteria for races: decent logistics, good tech shirt, nice medal, and in this case, not too large an event. With time left to register, the only slight glitch was that the host hotel downtown was sold out; I stayed in a different part of the city and drove to the start line. While Columbia is the capital of South Carolina, its downtown area is seldom overcrowded and I knew that parking would be plentiful. Even without my preference for being able to walk to the start from my hotel, I felt this race was still worth doing.

Since Columbia, South Carolina was a 3-1/2 hour drive from where I was staying in North Carolina, I decided to make it a one-day trip. I arrived late afternoon on Friday, and returned Saturday afternoon after the race.

I started the drive at 10:00 a.m. with a quick stop in Rock Hill, South Carolina. I wanted to get some healthy food at Earth Fare, similar to Whole Foods Market. I arrived at my hotel about 2:30 p.m. After checking in I drove to the Hilton downtown where the packet pickup was being held and was not pleased to discover we had to pick up our timing chip in the morning before the start of the race.

I was already a bit bummed there were no hotel vacancies within walking distance of the start/finish (although that was my fault for registering so late), so this added news didn't put a smile on my face.

Since I had to get to the starting area early to get my timing chip, I couldn't follow my established routine. It was no deal breaker, just inconvenient. I expected some bumps along the way. I returned to my hotel and settled into race mode knowing I had to be up by 5:30 a.m. because my morning was going to be more complex than normal.

I had a nice start, pacing myself in the first few miles somewhere between 8:15 to 8:45 minutes per mile. The first half was pretty easy although this race had a lot more hills than I expected.

Between miles 4 and 5, I audibly expressed my disgust over the excessive number of inclines. A runner near me exclaimed, "I know it is a lot of hills but unfortunately, it is going to get worse." He was right. He had obviously studied the course map closer than I did (in fact I didn't look at it at all) because the hills kept coming and going for the remainder of the race.

Even with the hills I was running well, reaching mile 7 in 58 minutes, which was 2 minutes faster than my normal pace. I kept this good pace until around mile 9 when I began slowing down significantly and "hitting the wall."

Enjoying tennis at the U.S. Open in the amazing Arthur Ashe Stadium.

The last 5 miles or so of this race were just plain boring from my perspective. There were no bands, no spectators, and just a few volunteers at this point in the race. It was obvious that I had been spoiled by some of the larger events where a new band played music at almost every mile.

I was still doing okay until something totally unexpected happened at mile 11. My left IT band began acting badly. I couldn't believe it. This was an injury that had been under control for over a year, and now suddenly it was back. It got so bad that at one point I started praying fervently for the Lord to relieve the pain so that I could accomplish my goal of finishing the race in less than 2 hours.

Thank God for answered prayer. At mile 12, the pain began to subside and I was able to forge ahead although most of mile 12 was one large hill and I slowed down to what could barely be considered a jog.

I asked a guy next to me where the finish line was since it was obvious I had not studied the course at all. He enthusiastically replied "At Taylor Avenue. From there it is all downhill baby."

His use of the word "baby" made us both laugh even though I was too exhausted to be wasting that kind of energy. It turns out he was exactly right as Taylor Avenue was so drastically downhill that, in a way, it was just as hard to run as the uphill portions.

Finally, I crossed the finish line at 1:58:49. I was very pleased with that time given the fact that my training had been limited. I had no runs past 6 miles since the half marathon ran in Las Vegas almost 3 months prior. With the lack of training, relocation, and all those hills, I was achy and tired after this race.

I made my way to the post-race area. The food did not look appealing, so I grabbed some water and Gatorade before heading back to my hotel to shower and change.

This race was no great shakes, especially when you compare it to others on this journey. I wish the weather had held up two weeks earlier so that I could have participated in the Myrtle Beach half marathon.

However, I can't complain too much about this race. I didn't see much of the city, although I would come to know Columbia quite well over the next 3 years thanks to my job.

Although it wasn't pretty, I did accomplish my goal of finishing another half marathon in less than 2 hours and declaring state # 26 as a done deal!

Race 28

Caesar Rodney Half Marathon
Wilmington, Delaware - March 21, 2010

You're Never Too Old to Learn

This journey was always about more than running long distance events or visiting all the states in this country. It was also about being open to learn new things about life. Most importantly, I was learning about myself. Since I love being a student, I looked forward to whatever new lessons I was destined to learn.

Thankfully, most of the lessons came easily and wrapped in nice packages. But the lesson associated with the Delaware event was not so pretty. Sadly, it was delivered at the hands of a family member. God is good, however, and although the devil used this person to derail me, in the end it made me stronger and smarter, both on the race course and off.

I was familiar with the state of Delaware because I lived in Columbia, Maryland for a number of years in the mid-1990s. I drove through it countless times en route to New Jersey and other northern states. However, to say that I had spent any significant time there would be a gross exaggeration. I was looking forward to changing that on this 50-state journey.

Unlike larger states like Florida, California, Texas and several others, distance running events matching my criteria were few and far between in the state of Delaware. Thus, I was thrilled when I discovered a relatively small half marathon in its largest city and economic hub, Wilmington.

This half marathon was named after the American Revolutionary leader Caesar Rodney. It is referred to as "the granddaddy of Delaware road races" because it has been in existence for over 50 years. From a logistical standpoint, it more than matched my requirements. It started and finished in downtown Wilmington near Rodney Square. It had lovely scenic stretches along Brandywine Creek and Rockford Parks. Given the convenient downtown location, I decided to stay at the Doubletree on North King Street and it was an excellent choice.

Although the drive to Wilmington would have been 5.5 hours (right at my 5 hour rule), I decided to fly instead. The flight to Philadelphia was right at an hour. In Philly, I rented a car and drove the 32 miles to Wilmington, giving me the opportunity to explore the area more.

Everything about this race seemed positive. Since I did well in my first half marathon of the year, I was ready to tackle another one—or so I thought.

Without going into much detail, the eve before I departed for Delaware, a member of my family (usually I refer to family as my family in Christ, but in this case I'm referring to a blood relative) started a horrible argument with me in front of my mother. That left both my mother and I devastated and saddened. At the time it happened, I was angrier with this person than I ever imagined I could be. My mother and I decided to go out to dinner after that episode, but we were both upset by what had taken place. We agreed that my going to Delaware would be a great way to forget the whole ugly mess.

The next morning I was up at 4:30 to get to the airport on time for my 8:30 flight. I was so thankful to be getting away from the mayhem. With the most gorgeous weather I could hope for (low 70's the entire weekend), my enthusiasm to get there was greater than ever. Because I fly so much, the girl who worked at the newsstand in the Southwest terminal recognized me and inquired where I was off to this time. That small acknowledgment made me feel good.

I arrived safely and on time in Philadelphia. I rented a car at the airport and felt blessed driving along I-95. The sun was shining brightly and I listened to a man on the radio discussing the first round of the NCAA tournament taking place that weekend. I felt such a lightness and joy in my heart as I drove along. It illuminated so much about me as a person. I was a woman who loved to travel, run, meet new people, see new things, and give God the honor and glory for it all. I was thankful to be right where I was at that moment.

While on the way to the packet pickup, I passed the University of Delaware campus. I felt a joy that always exists when I'm near a college campus. That was something that became prominent in future races.

The packet pickup was held at the Delaware Running Club in Greenville. Located in an eclectic shopping village, it reminded me of Town Square in Las Vegas. It was very trendy and sophisticated.

It felt like a home to me and I was loving every minute of it. The second I walked in the door, I was met with so much warmth and care, and interestingly enough, I was told twice to, "make sure I hydrated well before tomorrow morning." You would think that I would have heeded that message especially since it was stated twice, wouldn't you?

Just beyond the running company was a place called Janssen's Market, where I picked up some healthy snacks for later in the day. Along the way I noticed the upscale homes in this area, and it just felt nice to be there. I also passed a school where several students were practicing on the track, getting ready for the upcoming track season no doubt.

I drove to my hotel—the Doubletree Downtown on N. King Street—and was fortunate to find a parking space on Market Street, just one block from the hotel. They offered free parking all weekend.

I checked into a nice room and rested while watching parts of the NCAA tournament. After printing out my boarding pass for my return flight, I decided to set out on foot to explore downtown Wilmington. I asked the man at the front desk about a good place to grab dinner, and he told me to head toward Market Street where I'd find many dining options.

Off I went, but was surprised to find no restaurants. I did find a large contingency of homeless people. It was heartbreaking to see so many people living on the streets. It reminded me of the days when I briefly served in the homeless ministry at my church in Los Angeles, The Church on the Way. Every Saturday a group of us would travel to the downtown area of Los Angeles where we would hold church service and minister to those without a home. After service, we would serve food and pray with the people. It was a moving time in my life.

Eventually I discovered two nice restaurants on 11th Street, opting for the one named Deep Blue since they specialized in seafood which I had a taste for that evening. They had a television so I, along with quite a few others, watched coverage of the NCAA tournament. I ordered the salmon with tossed greens and it was delicious. What a fun way to spend the evening, eating good food and watching my favorite thing on television—sports.

The race didn't start until 9:30 so I was up quite a while before the race started. I finished the salmon I ordered the previous night, along with some coffee and ½ of an energy bar. This was quite a departure from my usual pre-race meal of a ½ cup of goat milk yogurt and come coffee. This brings me to one of the lessons I learned from this stop of my journey: Don't vary from your usual diet the day of the race.

The temperature was already in the low 70's and climbing by 9:30. An earlier start would have ensured lower temperatures, but it was too late to make any changes at that point.

In the beginning of the race, I felt comfortable and was maintaining my pace goal of 8:15-8:45 minutes/mile up to the mile 6 area. I reached mile 7 in 1:02, just two minutes over my goal time of 1 hour, so I was pretty satisfied.

Then something went drastically wrong. The first 5 miles were basically flat, but from miles 5 to about 8, it was only uphill. By the end of that stretch, I was totally wiped out. I didn't just hit the wall, I slammed right in the middle of it! Unlike every race I had run up to that point, I was unable to get it back together. I thought if I drank a bit more than usual, that would help, so I stopped at just about every water station from that point until the end. But it didn't help. In fact, I think the water and Gatorade was more of a hindrance than a help since my body wasn't used to that much liquid consumption in a race.

By the time the course flattened out again, I was too out of it mentally to regain my normal pace. I spent the last 4 miles of the race in a run/walk scenario, realizing that my goal of finishing in less than 2 hours was an impossibility.

As I climbed the final hill (this race finishes uphill), I was devastated. For the first time since August 2008, I did not finish a half marathon in less than 2 hours. My final time was 2:09:45. I was crushed.

I limped back to my hotel room (not literally, but figuratively) in utter disgust with myself. I contemplated what went wrong. How could I have run so poorly? My mind was twirling like a pinwheel in disappointment, shame and concern. However, once I checked out of the hotel and began the drive to the Philadelphia airport, I started to get some clarity on the situation.

First, I recognized what a blessing it was to have completed a run in Delaware on such a gorgeous day. I thanked the Lord for His mercy in allowing me to do so. I also realized how wonderful this trip had been with the time spent in Greenville the day before and the nice walk and meal in downtown Wilmington that evening. I didn't run well but that didn't take away from how blessed I had been otherwise.

It was clear that I was not performing up to my capability and unless I addressed what the problems were, I would be powerless to institute measures to guard against them from happening again. Thus, I identified the following:

Stay Mentally Strong

The verbal attack I received the day before I left for Delaware took more out of me than I initially thought. I acknowledged that mental exhaustion is related to physical performance. The more I reflected on that ugly episode, the more physically drained I became. I did not fully recognize that before.

No Diet Changes on Race Day

I ate much more the morning of the race than I do even for a long practice run. Moreover, what I ate (salmon) was foreign to my body prior to a race. This combination proved to be destructive to my overall performance. I learned the hard way that if you are going to make changes to your diet, don't do it the day of the race.

Review the course beforehand

While I've never been too concerned about the elevation of a course, I learned from this race that it is a good idea to be familiar with topography. I needed to better prepare my body for the rigors of each particular course.

Fitness

With all the moving details and responsibilities associated with starting a new job, my fitness took a big hit. I was about 5 lbs. heavier than I was when I ran Las Vegas the previous December. With such a small body frame, that additional 5 lbs. over a distance of 13.1 miles was a noticeable impediment.

It was obvious what I needed to do in order to be better prepared for my next race. It seems odd that it would take me almost 3 years into this journey for these issues to surface, but in retrospect, the timing was perfect. I was just a little more than halfway through this quest, and by addressing these issues now, I was ensuring that the second half of my journey would be even more excellent than the first had been.

I finished well off my mark in this race. Yet, it gave me some powerful insights. Victories come in many forms. This race turned out to be one of great blessing even though that blessing came in a different form than I was expecting. It is amazing how God uses "all things to work together for good to those who love Him and are called according to His purposes."

Race 29

Charlotte Racefest 10k
Charlotte, North Carolina - April 10, 2010

The Redemption Race

Upon my return to North Carolina., I went to work addressing the four areas of improvement I identified after my Delaware debacle. I registered for the Charlotte Racefest 10k in late February, so I had about 3 weeks to prepare for this race. I was determined to get back to my desired level of performance at all costs.

My level of fitness was of primary interest to me. I returned to the clean diet that defined my eating habits for more than two years and I stepped up my exercise regimen to include an additional 10 miles of running a week. I also expanded an already exhaustive core routine I completed 3 times a week. I even managed two workouts on most days.

No doubt about it—my fire was back! I knew from a mental

standpoint that it was critical for me to stay focused and away from anything and anyone that would weaken my resolve to be my best. Unfortunately, this meant I had to distance myself from a few people. Nevertheless, I remained prayerful that they would understand my values and goals, and if they didn't, oh well.

I was thankful that my first race on the "road to renewal" was a 10k and was in the city of Charlotte, North Carolina. While the half marathon was my most frequent race along this journey, and in a lot ways the most gratifying distance, the 6+ mile races (10k and quarter marathon) remained my favorite distance, and history shows this is the distance where I've had the most success. Naturally, it is easier to maintain a faster pace with a distance of 6 miles versus 13 or 26 miles, and I could scale down my training (once I returned to top form) for the shorter distance races. Also, since Charlotte was barely a 2-hour drive for me, I could get there quickly without much effort and remain focused on nothing but the race itself.

Because of my job, I made frequent trips to Charlotte and knew the city well. It is considered a mid-sized city with some very desirable areas, my favorite being the SouthPark neighborhood where the race was taking place.

Since I always stayed in the that area when I visited for business, I did a lot of practice runs on just about every street in the lovely residential communities nearby, so I was more familiar with the route of this race than any I had ever participated in before, except for perhaps Las Vegas. Logistically, it couldn't have been a better choice for convenience to and from the race, as well as numerous choices for dining, lodging and even health foods.

The stage was set and I was raring to go.

The race fell on a Saturday, which I always prefer over Sunday. The weather was great with sunny skies and rising temperatures starting in the mid-40s. I was up at 5:30 and consumed my normal breakfast of ½ cup of yogurt and ½ cup of coffee (no more salmon.) I felt energized and strong and stayed in my room warming up and stretching before walking to the starting line outside my hotel . I just love staying in a hotel close enough to walk to the starting line. You just can't beat the convenience.

Since this was my first race after stumbling in Delaware, my primary goal was to return to the level of performance that characterized my races of the past 1.5 years. I wouldn't be truthful if I claimed that placing 1st, 2nd, or 3rd in my age group wasn't in the back of my mind, especially since this was a 10k event where I tended to do well. I knew I was ready, having returned to my preferred run weight of 107 lbs. and feeling stronger than ever, but the proof would be in the pudding.

From the first step, I felt great and pushed myself knowing I had to go 6.21 miles. The weather was a big help with the cool breeze keeping my thirst level from going through the roof. I decided not to drink anything along the way which is my usual pattern for the 10k and quarter marathon distance, except for Pocatello.

Thankfully, the course was relatively flat (no hills to climb like in Wilmington) although there was a steady incline at the very end of the race. Several runners passed me at that point but they were mostly men. The few women I saw looked to be much younger than me and not in my age group, Thus, I thought a podium finish was still intact and I had enough in the tank to comfortably sprint to the finish. I immediately lifted my hands to the Lord and gave Him the glory for the victory whether I got to stand on the podium or not. I was already a winner in more ways than one!

As I collected my finisher's medal with the biggest grin on my face, a girl approached me and said that she had been trailing me for most of the race. She said she read my shirt from Detroit that stated "half marathon" and thought that if I had run that distance in the past, she would not be able to catch up to me.

As she talked I remembered seeing her on the course and thought she was ahead of me the whole time, but at some point, I must have passed her. Either way, it is funny how I had similar conversations after races in Virginia Beach and Pocatello, which serves as a reminder that runners really do watch one another in races.

Eager to find out my official finish time, I was disappointed to discover that there was no results table and none of the volunteers seemed to know when or where the results would be posted. A lady from the packet pickup the day before told me that the awards ceremony would take place around 9:30. Since it wasn't even 8:30 yet, I had time to shower and pack before returning to see the ceremony.

I returned to the post-race area right at 9:30 where they started posting the final times. I knew from my watch that I did well but rarely was I so excited to find out my official time. I found my name and discovered that I finished 5th in my age group and I was elated! No, I wouldn't be standing on the podium or receiving an age group award, but that was okay with me because I had a victory far greater than a trophy or plaque could represent. I fought and clawed my way back to the level I knew was in me all along. At that moment, all I felt was joy—unspeakable joy!

My official time was 51:01, meaning that I had run only two 10k races faster; Corinth 2009 and Pocatello. Now that does spell victory! State #29 was in the books and I was forever changed. My heart was very full.

You see why the title of this chapter is aptly named. This 10k was truly my "redemption race" because I regained my fitness and confidence in exchange for a lot of hard work and determination to stay the course. I needed to prove to myself that I could do it and now that I had, I would remain focused and approach each new race and adventure of this journey with the same fervency and commitment.

Race 30

3rd Annual Papillion 10k
Papillion, Nebraska - May 16, 2010

A Good Time in The Cornhusker State

It was a little over a month since my last race in Charlotte and a lot took place during that time away from the world of road running. I purchased and moved into my second home (I still owned the one in Franklin, Tennessee at the time of this race) located in Mebane, North Carolina, approximately 8 miles from my parent's home.

It was good to be settled in my own place again, and I was ready to continue my 50-state quest. To stay competitive, I participated in a small local 5k and placed 1st in my age group. My Mom was the real hero of the event. She did the 1 mile race and won the award for the oldest competitor on the course that day. I was so proud of her.

The state of Nebraska was one of the 11 states I had never visited when my journey began. My limited knowledge of it was based on Lincoln since it was the capital. I also knew about the Cornhuskers since that was the name of the athletic program at the University of Nebraska.

I initially set my sights on Lincoln, but quickly shifted gears when I discovered a small racing event in a town whose name I love saying—Papillion, Nebraska. It is a southern suburb of Omaha and often makes "the best small community" lists due to its stable economy and good schools. Their annual running event, which also includes a half marathon, was on its 3rd year. Based on the reviews I read from other runners, it was definitely worth considering.

This was a small race in a small community so my usual logistics criteria were not a fit. However, the opportunity to leave the big city and meet people in neighborhoods where the term "hustle and bustle" is unnecessary, appealed to me. Moreover, I was already registered for a half marathon in nearby Council Bluffs, Iowa the following weekend. The race in Papillion would give me the opportunity to learn the lay of the land before returning in less than a week. So Papillion, here I come!

Since the race was on a Sunday, I decided to spend two nights. I arrived on Saturday and planned to depart early Monday morning. After changing planes in Chicago, I arrived in Omaha around 4 p.m. and immediately rented a car so that I could get this show on the road.

As usual, one of my first stops was to the Whole Foods Market in Omaha where I stocked up on my staples: yogurt, cantaloupe, watermelon, fiber bars, and Kombucha. I also prepared a small plate from their hot bar and ate it outside in their patio area. It was nice and peaceful, but I cut it short because I needed to pick up my packet before they closed for the day.

Traveling about 22 miles south of Omaha, I easily found the packet pickup location. The volunteers were very friendly. They were happy to know that someone traveled all the way from North Carolina to participate in their event and they made sure they answered all my questions, especially regarding the best place to park on race day. After I left the packet pickup, I drove to the start/finish area to avoid the dreaded "getting lost" scenario the morning of the race. Along the way I enjoyed the look and feel of Papillion. It was easy to see why its residents adored living there and everywhere I went—the park, the mall—I was met with kindness and warmth.

I elected to stay at a Hampton Inn & Suites in Omaha using points for two free nights through my Honors program. I was tired and ready to settle into race mode for the evening. Arriving at the hotel near 8:00 p.m., I laid out my race clothes and read 2 Timothy before saying my prayers and going to bed. I was looking forward to tomorrow's race.

I was up at 5:30 and felt energized. The temperature outside was a pleasant 50 degrees so I knew I'd have no hydration problems. I left the hotel at 6:30 and had no trouble finding a parking space upon arrival at 7:00. I stayed in the car with the heat on until close to 7:20 before venturing to find a restroom.

The race started and finished at Papillion-La Vista South High School, one of two high schools in their public school district. Thankfully, since the school was open for the race, we had access to the restrooms in the football stadium. They were surprisingly clean. Most races have port-a-potties but they are seldom clean. That's why I prefer staying in my hotel room as close to the start of the race as possible.

The half marathon started promptly at 7:30 and my race, the 10k, started shortly thereafter at 7:40. The course for this race was one of the most unusual I had ever run due to the combination of hard surface trails, normal streets, and several blocks of gravel. Since I only had experience running on a hard road surface, I wasn't sure what to expect. Moreover, it was not the flattest course either, with a decent sized hill right out of the chute, which I was glad to get out of the way early, but there would be more later on.

Even though the temperature was great and the skies overcast, I still thought it prudent to have a sip of water at mile 2 (just a quick swallow without stopping.) I was feeling good and maintaining an early pace of 8:15-8:20 minutes/mile.

Just past the mile 2 mark, a man running near me asked if I had run that course before. Preferring not to talk much during a race, but remembering how much I enjoyed doing so in St. Louis and Pocatello, I told him I had not. He then said he ran it last year and that a hill was coming up almost 3 times larger than the ones we had already encountered. I thanked him for the heads up as he ran ahead of me.

Because the course was an out-and-back, a turnaround occurred at the 3.5 mile mark where the huge hill he described stood. Since he was ahead of me, we faced each other as I was ascending and he was descending. Happily, the climb was not as taxing as I expected it to be. In fact, I ended up passing him once I cleared the hill and stayed ahead of him until the finish.

By the final mile, the course was once again flat and I had a strong finish with a time of 51:53. I was thankful for that considering the hills and frequent change in terrain.

Once I received my finisher's medal and grabbed a bottle of Gatorade, I saw the gentlemen whom I conversed with on the course.

He told me that he didn't mean to throw me off my pace or get into my head with the hill comments. I told him it was no problem and that I appreciated the information. I enjoyed our little exchanges and would continue to open myself up for more of them in future races.

The race staff did a great job of posting the results quickly and I saw I came in 4th in my age group, but not the way I anticipated. In most races, the age group categories are broken into 5-year increments—age group 40-44 or 45-49. However, for this event, the age group categories were divided into 10-year increments, making my category 40-49. I bring this up because if the groupings had been in the more common 5-year increments, I would have placed 3rd and received a trophy. Don't get me wrong, this journey was never about awards and trophies, but when I ran fast enough to earn an award, I'm always happy and thankful to receive it.

Course officials can define the age group categories in whatever increments they choose, but personally speaking, my preference is the way it's done in the vast majority of races, which is by 5-year increments. In fact, only in Atlantic City had I ever encountered anything but 5-year age group categories.

Nonetheless, it was a great race and I was very pleased with my performance. I hung around talking to other runners and snacking on some of the post-race food before driving back to my hotel. I rested before doing a bit of sightseeing.

I enjoyed the Heartland of America Park situated along the Missouri River with gorgeous fountain displays and a nice walking trail surrounding a lovely lake. Although the sky remained overcast, there was no rain so it was serene.

Later that evening, I discovered another walking trail in a quaint residential lake community. Intrigued, I walked the trail and then branched off into the neighborhood sidewalks for several miles, taking in the sights and understanding why this was such a desired area to call home. I enjoyed my conversations with the people who lived there and I think the feeling was mutual. I wanted to see more of this Midwestern city but I had to be up at 3:30 in order to catch my flight the next morning so I cut it off just as dawn drew near.

I'm glad that I chose to do this race in Papillion. It wasn't very large and it didn't have a lot of bells and whistles, but it had what was most important - a good race with good people.

Race 31

Council Bluffs Half Marathon
Council Bluffs, Iowa - May 23, 2010

A Welcome Return to
a Different Part Of Iowa

When I lived in western Illinois in the early 90's, every few months a group of my friends and I would drive to Dubuque, Iowa and have dinner on one of the riverboat cruises that traveled along the Mississippi River. I really enjoyed those evenings and hoped to get to see more of Iowa someday. That day came in May of 2010.

Located on the opposite side of the state from Dubuque, Council Bluffs is on the east bank of the Missouri River, less than 8 miles from Omaha, Nebraska where I ran just 5 days earlier.

With races from last year in Detroit & D.C. and Indianapolis & Atlantic City, I knew that participating in events on back-to-back weekends would not be a problem as long as the combination was a half marathon and a 10k or quarter marathon. I had no reservations about the timing of these two events. In fact, I was looking forward to running another half marathon, my first since faltering in Delaware. I was ready to test myself at this distance again.

Logistically this race met my criteria with a start and finish at the riverfront Council Bluffs Harrah's Casino. For someone who prefers not to gamble, I sure have run my fair share of races near casinos. Following the same pattern as Las Vegas and Atlantic City, I asked Mom if she wanted to go, knowing the answer would be yes if there was a casino involved.

Due to severe weather on our second flight from Chicago to Nebraska, we had to sit on the tarmac for nearly 2 hours waiting for the storm to subside. We did not get to Council Bluffs until after 9 on Friday night. Since the race did not take place until Sunday, I had time on Saturday to attend the expo, sightsee, and get ready to run.

The hotel provided shuttle service to and from the Omaha airport, as well as areas of interest in and around Council Bluffs, so renting a car was not necessary. Not having to drive is always a welcome plus for me. However, I wanted to go to Whole Foods Market, but it was outside the shuttle's travel parameter, so I had an expensive cab ride to get my staples. The only upside was the good conversation I had with the driver. His sister was a graduate of UNC and lived in the same community I did until she accepted a position in Kansas. Before dropping me off, he said that it was a blessing talking to me and all I could do was thank God because He is so good about sending small subtle blessings my way just like that short but fruitful conversation with the cab driver. I guess that's why I love the scripture in 1 Kings which states that God often speaks to us in a "still small voice." How true that verse is.

After putting my groceries away, I found Mom and we attended the expo which was just a packet pickup. Then we caught the shuttle to the Horseshoe to explore that part of the area. I left Mom there to enjoy the casino while I went back to Harrah's to print out our boarding passes for the next day. I also took a short run on the golf path near the hotel to make sure I was ready for the race.

The weather was windy but otherwise great so I headed back to the Horseshoe to meet Mom for dinner. On the shuttle ride back, Mom and I met several people there for the race, including a very nice couple from Kansas. Meeting new people is always fun.

Mom returned to the casino and I retired and began preparing for the race. I knew I had to be up by 5:30 and I really wanted and needed to be well rested for those 13.1 miles.

I had some nagging discomfort in my shoulder when I awoke. Fortunately, it felt better as the morning progressed. After my usual breakfast of ½ cup of goat milk yogurt and a few sips of coffee, I dressed and started some light stretches about 6:30. From the hotel window, I could see several runners taking their warm-up run and stretching in the pre-race area. After saying my prayers and making one last restroom visit, I headed to the start line at 6:45.

The weather was 73 degrees with cloudy skies. Many of my runner friends prefer it much cooler, but the higher temperatures have never really bothered me. Since I live in the south, I'm used to training in high humidity and heat.

The gun sounded at 7:01 by my watch and from the start I was pacing well, finishing mile 1 in 8 minutes flat and mile 2 in 8:45 minutes.

The course was relatively flat which enabled me to reach mile 7 in 57 minutes, 3 minutes faster than my normal pace.

All of a sudden I started to panic because it was at this point in the Delaware race where I began to stumble. I quieted those fears by staying focused on the race at hand and reminding myself that I had put in the work to correct what went wrong then. In addition, I felt too good to buy into any negative self-talk.

It started to get hot out there. It seemed like I couldn't stop sweating, and that was usual because I tend to sweat very little, even when I'm running at full throttle. In a half marathon, I consume a liquid at least twice; usually the first is between miles 7 and 8, then again between miles 9 and 10. However, on this day, I stopped to drink at least four times. Once I just threw the water over my face and chest to combat the ever mounting heat. It was that hot, but it didn't seem to stop people from having conversations.

A man running behind me noticed the back of my shirt. I wore my short-sleeve tech shirt from the Denver race I did last year—still one of my favorite tech shirts from a race. He commented, "This is a lot more humid than Denver, isn't it?" All I could do was respond with, "Way more humid."

Shortly after that brief conversation, another man ran up

beside me and I immediately noticed how good-looking he was. The visual was enhanced because he had his shirt off. You may get tired on the race course, but that doesn't stop you from noticing handsome members of the opposite sex. He asked me how I was doing and I told him I was already tired. He said, "Me too" and we both remarked about the humidity. Then he wished me a successful finish and ran ahead of me. I would end up passing him close to mile 11 and stayed ahead of him to the end.

The last couple of miles were not as difficult as some have been in the past. I stayed relaxed and coasted along knowing that my pace up to that point assured me a finish time of less than 2 hours, unless something totally unexpected took place.

Hands lifted unto the Lord, I collected my medal and went straight to the results booth after downing two cold bottles of water to discover my finish time of 1:57:44. That put me 4th in my age group.

First I jumped for joy over my official return to a sub-2 hour half marathon. Then I had to chuckle over finishing in 4th place for the second time in 2 weeks. Why was I just missing the podium? The previous week I could use the excuse of the 10-increment age group categories, but I had no such argument this time. The age groupings were in the usual 5-year increment; there just were three ladies between the ages of 45 to 49 who ran faster than me, plain and simple.

The third place winner finished in 1:57:19, a whopping 25 seconds faster than me. Oh well, there was no room for complaints. I was thrilled with my finish time and thrilled with the race in general. It felt good to be back at the performance level I was used to and expected of myself.

This race was special for me in two ways. First, it gave me an opportunity to return to a state that played a part in my young adult life as I was starting my career. Second, it marked my return to a sub 2-hour half marathon.

It felt great to be back, and now that I was, I knew I would never regress again.

Run 32

Minneapolis Half Marathon
Minneapolis, Minnesota - June 6, 2010

Adding Another Great Memory
in Minneapolis

One of my favorite recording artists and performers of all time is the great Miss Tina Turner. I love the sound of this woman's voice and the integrity she infuses into her music and live shows.

I was fortunate to see her perform live at a concert in Chapel Hill, North Carolina in the late 80's and when she had embarked on another U.S. tour in the mid-90's, I wanted to go see her again. Unfortunately, none of my friends wanted to make the 6-hour drive from Illinois (where I lived at the time) to Minneapolis, where she was performing at the Target Center. I decided to make the trip by myself, unaware that I was helping in a small way to birth my 50-state quest. The weekend I spent in Minneapolis almost 20 years prior to running was one of the best experiences of my life. Now, I was going to realize another amazing experience in Minneapolis - not in a sold-out stadium, but in a 13.1 mile road race.

Logistically, this race was perfect with everything being held downtown, thus, planning for this trip was a breeze. Since I had enough bonus points for a one-way ticket with Southwest, I decided to mix-and-match carriers, flying to Minneapolis via Southwest and returning to N.C. via US Airways. With the race taking place on Sunday, I figured that as long as I arrived by noon on Saturday in Minneapolis, I would have all day to attend the expo and refamiliarize myself with the downtown area.

While waiting for the train from the airport to my hotel, I met a nice lady who was in town from Baltimore for her nephew's high school graduation. We kind of helped each other figure out the payment system for the tickets and boarded the half-empty train. I love riding at a higher elevation and overlooking the environment. It is something I get to do all too seldom so when I have the opportunity, I really try to take full advantage of it.

We were barely 5 minutes into the ride before it started pouring down rain, and I do mean pouring! Oh well, I thought, there was nothing I could do about it at that point so I pulled out my rain jacket from my suitcase and prepared to get wet.

The packet pickup was scheduled to take place in The Depot Hotel, which I happened upon while heading to my hotel so I decided to stop there first. It proved to be a good move because when I asked the man at the front desk which street to take to get to the Renaissance, he told me it was connected to The Depot (both Marriott properties), so I wouldn't need to go back outside. Bingo! That was news to my ears since the rain was even heavier at that time.

After the weather cleared, I was able to see some of the city.

Returning to my hotel room, I thought about the race the next day. Having regained my form and performance level two weeks prior in Council Bluffs, I knew I was ready for this race. In fact, preparing to return to Minneapolis was the most excited I had been about an event in a long time.

I scheduled a wake-up call for 5:15 a.m. When I woke up, the first thing I noticed was the unusually bright sun. As I rolled over I thought that surely it was 5:15 by now so I took a quick look at the clock and saw it was 5:42. I couldn't believe it! I sprang out of bed and immediately went downstairs to the front desk where I found the night clerk who was 15 minutes from getting off work and could have cared less about my lost wake-up call. I decided at that point to focus on getting to the race on time and address the calling debacle later.

Thankfully, The Depot next door had some hot coffee prepared for the runners who stayed there. I grabbed a cup and ran back to my room to get ready for the race.

Usually I take care of things like affixing my race bib to my shirt and attaching my timing chip to my shoe the night before. For some strange reason, I didn't do either of these things this time. So on top of running late, I still had those tasks to complete in addition to eating some yogurt.

The weather was great. There was a slight cool breeze and plenty of sunshine. I dressed lightly with a short-sleeve tech shirt from my Indianapolis race, pink shorts, and Jesus cap.

Speaking of Jesus, he was definitely with me because despite the poor preparation and late start to the day, I made it to the start line (right outside the hotel door) by 6:45.

There were several pace runners with signs so I decided to line up with the one holding the 8:47 pace sign. I thought that would be a good pace to start with and, depending on my energy level, I could either speed up or slow down as the race progressed. I prayed for a safe sub-2 hour race just before leaving my room so I was ready to run!

This race started slowly for me due to the number of walkers and slow runners near the front. In large races, they have a staggered start so that the slower runners are near the back preventing bottlenecking in the early miles. However, it took nearly 3 miles before the crowd started thinning out. Once it did, I knew it was going to be a good race for me.

The hills were more of a problem for some of the runners than for me. I handled them pretty well and was thankful that for every serious uphill, there was a nice downhill section.

By mile 7, I was exactly one hour in. I couldn't have been more pleased because I was right where I wanted to be time-wise.

At mile 8, I took my first drink of Gatorade and it hit the spot.

We made a loop near the mile 9 mark to turn around and head back toward downtown. With much of the race along the Mississippi River, the views were interesting and pleasing.

The final mile before the finish was just about all uphill. Uphill finishes are tough. When I reached that point, I remembered the verses I read that week in several epistles by Paul using words like "press on" and "fight." I did just that and finished strong. I was thankful for the completion of this race and lifted my hands to the Lord in thanksgiving for another wonderful half marathon.

Just before leaving the race grounds, I discovered that my finish time was 1:56:18 and I couldn't have been happier with my result.

Minneapolis is a beautiful city situated along the Mississippi River. There are pockets of the downtown area that are just gorgeous. One of the men at the hotel suggested going to the waterfront about two blocks away, dominated by a row of nice restaurants.

I started walking in the other direction and crossed the Stone Arch Bridge, the only arched bridge made of stone along the Mississippi River.

I avoided most of the usual tourist stuff on this trip because it wasn't my first time to Minneapolis. Also, there was only about an hour of sunlight left once the rain subsided. So I simply chose to walk the downtown neighborhoods for a few miles, soaking up the culture of this diverse city.

The only negative thing I can say about this race was the lack of post-race food and drink. I was ready for a cold bottle of water but couldn't find any, which is rare. Usually, right after you collect your medal, the post-race food table is a few short steps ahead. However, for this event, you had to go quite a distance to reach that area. In fact, I found out later that several finishers never even found the post-race area. When I did get there, several volunteers were handing out water in paper cups like in Detroit, which was disappointing.

I'm okay with a lack of post-race food, but at the very least, every race should have plenty of bottled water on hand for people who just conquered 13.1 miles. In reading several reviews the following week, I found I wasn't alone in this regard.

Returning to Minneapolis was wonderful. I really like this city and with each visit, the blessings continue to mount. This time, the blessing was wrapped in a gorgeous finisher's medal denoting another state that was in the books.

Race 33

Rock-n-Roll Seattle Half Marathon
Seattle, Washington - June 26, 2010

New City, Old Friends

E ven though I had never been to the state of Washington before, it wasn't hard for me to decide where I wanted to run. For years I wanted to visit Seattle and when I discovered the Rock-n-Roll series held an event there, I registered without hesitation.

As I've mentioned previously, the Rock-n-Roll races are very well-organized and always well attended. The Seattle event was scheduled to host 27,000 runners participating in both the marathon and half marathon. If large races are not your thing, you will probably want to skip this one.

The staff that organizes the Rock-n-Roll events do an outstanding job. Their websites are the best and most informative making it much easier to plan, especially when you are traveling from a long distance. As far as I was concerned, this was the perfect choice for my race in the state of Washington.

The race took place on a Saturday and since I had to travel across country, it made sense to spend the entire weekend in Seattle, arriving Friday and leaving Sunday. I was looking forward to being in the state of Washington for the first time and as an added treat—I would get to see my dear running pals Barbara and Tall again. Barbara was participating in the full marathon. We decided to meet for dinner on Saturday after both races to recoup with some good food and great fellowship.

Traveling across country is a bear primarily because of the change in time zones. I was up at 3:30 on Friday morning for my first of two flights departing from Raleigh-Durham at 6:35 and arriving in Seattle at 10:35 a.m. PST (1:35 EST). After over 7 hours in the air and another 2-3 hours in airports, I was just thankful to finally get there.

Logistically, this race wasn't my ideal because the start and finish line were not in the same area. The start line was not near any of the lodging options. Nevertheless, the Rock-n-Roll staff does a good job of arranging shuttle services and transportation schedules to get everyone where they need to be on time.

I decided to stay at the Doubletree Guest Suites in Southcenter, which provided shuttle service to and from the airport. Upon landing, I called the hotel for the shuttle and they picked up myself and another runner by the name of Bill. He was 74 years young from Los Angeles and runs full marathons all along the west coast. Originally from Holland, he's made the U.S. his home since 1953. We talked non-stop until we reached the hotel. Once each of us checked in, we agreed to meet at noon and travel to the expo together.

The expo was located downtown at the Qwest Event Center so

we took the hotel shuttle back to the airport where we caught the Central Link light rail for $5.00 roundtrip.

As usual with the Rock-n-Roll events, the expo was great. Bill and I agreed to check back in with each other after an hour so we went our separate ways to explore the many vendor booths.

I was starving since I had not eaten a thing since 3:30 a.m. EST, so all the free food and drink samples they were distributing at the expo were great. I enjoyed mixing and mingling with other runners and vendors, talking about our expectations for the race.

Eventually, Bill and I caught up with each other at one of the lectures. At the larger expos, there are usually several guest speakers, typically former and current elite runners or other industry professionals, who discuss a variety of subjects relating to the world of running.

After 15 minutes or so, I left Bill in search of directions at the information booth. I decided I wanted to explore downtown Seattle and pickup dinner at whatever health foods store I could find.

The sun was out more by this time and the temperatures where warming up. Outside the Qwest Center, I took a free bus to Westlake, where I walked five blocks to a Whole Foods Market.

The Westlake stop was in the same building as Nordstrom and as I walked along I realized how much I liked downtown Seattle. It seemed much cleaner than most of the other downtown areas of large metropolitan cities I frequented.

I scheduled a wake-up call for 5:00 but I was up by 4:00 since I was still operating under Eastern Standard Time where it was 7:00. I ate my usual ½ cup of goat milk yogurt and some water—no coffee that morning.

I went downstairs to catch the shuttle bus by 6:00. Before I left my room, I prayed my usual prayer on my knees—that God would bless me with a safe and healthy race in less than 2 hours.

The shuttle driver dropped us off about ½ mile from the start area due to the heavy traffic. None of us minded the walk and since I had not stretched or conducted any kind of a warm-up, I needed that time to get my blood flowing and my body in motion. Once I found the gear check trucks, I did two very short practice runs before checking my jacket and sweatpants at 6:45.

With 27,000 runners, a wave start was necessary. I started making my way up to my corral (#4) and was thankful to find that it was not overly crowded.

The race started promptly at 7:00 with my corral starting at 7:02. Right away, the cool air felt good and I was comfortable. I decided to wear blue shorts and my pink tech shirt from the Detroit race because the sleeves were mid-length. However, by mile 3, I rolled them up. Before I left the hotel, I put three sports beans in my pocket and ate all three by the midpoint of the race.

The wave start helped to thin out the crowd by mile 2. From there I was able to maintain my 8:30-8:40 minute/mile pace successfully.

By mile 7, I had a little more than 30 seconds to spare before hitting the 1 hour mark, so I was on target to have a sub 2-hour finish. However, there were hills in this race and by mile 8, I was starting to slow down, so I decided to drink some Cytomax (an energy drink similar to Gatorade) at the next stop.

Then, just before going into a tunnel at mile 9, there was a very steep hill that wasn't very long but I ended up walking most of it.

That led me to do something I never do—grab a GU packet at mile 10. GU Energy Gel is an endurance sports nutrition product popular with athletes. Although GU has been distributed at several prior races, I've always abstained from consuming it, but since I was running out of steam with more than 3 miles to go, I decided to take a small taste of the grape flavor. I must say it did help me energy-wise.

One of the main characteristics of the Rock-n-Roll events is the music, of course. Normally, a different band or DJ performs at each mile, providing a big boost when you need it most. In this race, however, some of the music played was unsuitably slow. The best musician all day was a DJ inside the tunnel at mile 9. He was jamming and I had to give him "a big thumbs up" when I passed because that was the perfect spot in the race for a pick-me-up.

With one last drink of water at mile 12, I finished the race strong with a time of 1:54:02. I was so thankful!

After the race, I looked to the sky, lifting my hands in thanksgiving to the Lord for the blessing and privilege to have yet another wonderful half marathon completed in less than 2 hours. Although I was struggling in the last couple of miles, I felt energized when I crossed that finish line!

After receiving my beautiful medal, I downed a bottle of water right away. I grabbed a bag of chips from the post-race area, and picked up my gear. I put on my Louisville Running Club pullover I received at the Louisville race, and my jacket, because it was cold due to my soaking wet clothes.

Since my hotel was directly across the street from the largest shopping center in Washington and the Pacific Northwest, my friends Barbara and Tall and I decided to eat at one of the restaurants there. The food was good and the company was even better.

As we fellowshipped together, I was reminded of how special this 50-state quest really is. While running and seeing the country are at the center, the blessing of establishing lifelong friendships is the icing on the cake. You can't plan or prepare for; it is just a gift from God.

I'm glad that my first time to the state of Washington was such a positive one. I couldn't have asked for a better way to put a check mark beside state #32.

Run 34

Freedom Half Marathon
Salt Lake City, Utah - July 3, 2010

A Second Place Finish With a First Place Dear Friend

Things were going well in my life at this time. I was settled in my new house, the sale of my home in Tennessee was finalized at a price that was pleasing to me, and, I never felt better physically. My running form was better than ever and I was performing in races more efficiently and at a faster pace than I thought possible. As a result, I did not want to lose any of this renewed momentum so I scheduled races as often as I could, hoping to go no more than a month in between events.

Earlier in the year, I registered for the Salt Lake City Half Marathon. It had good reviews and I wanted the opportunity to visit Salt Lake City, a city I had never been to and was eager to see.

The year before, I spent several days in St. George, Utah at the Red Mountain Resort. I fell in love with the beauty of red cliffs and canyons. Also, it was there that I developed my love for hiking when I climbed the 1,488 foot tall rock formation known as Angels Landing in Zion National Park. So I had already developed a love for southwestern Utah and wanted to explore a different part of the state, specifically its capital and most populous city.

The Salt Lake City Half Marathon was scheduled to take place in mid-April. However, at that time, I was heavy into the negotiations to buy my new house and travel for my job was at an all-time high, so I had to cancel my plans to attend.

My thirst to see Salt Lake City had not diminished so I stayed on the lookout for another event there, and stumbled upon a much smaller race called the Freedom Half Marathon. Right away, there were things that made me question if this would be a good race for me, such as dubious logistics, an okay website, and the fact that it was an inaugural event. After I emailed the race director a few questions and found his responses were clear, timely and informative, I felt better about it.

The deciding factor was that my friend Joanne, whom I met at the Pocatello race, was planning to attend. I figured it was worth it if I got a chance to see her and run in a Utah event, even if the race was less than stellar in some ways.

Having made my plans well in advance, I knew that participating in this race would mean running two events on back-to-back weekends. Having done so several times already, I knew I could do it but in the past, the two events involved a half marathon on one weekend and a 10K on the other. This time, it would involve two half marathons. Still, I felt stronger than ever and didn't expect it to pose a problem, so I proceeded with plans to participate. Since this race took place during the July 4th weekend (hence the name Freedom Half Marathon), I could factor in some vacation time and extend my time there a few extra days.

Once I started researching flights, I noticed that most connections from RDU (Raleigh-Durham) to Salt Lake City took place in Las Vegas. Since it was a holiday weekend, I asked my mother if she'd like to visit Salt Lake City and then spend a few days in Las Vegas. You know from previous chapters how my Mom answered that question. So, I planned our trip to both Salt Lake City and Las Vegas.

We landed in Salt Lake at 3:30 p.m. and took the Valley Shuttle for $8 per person to our hotel, the Hilton Salt Lake City Center. After checking in, I grabbed my backpack and set off for the packet pickup at Dick's Sporting Goods in a shopping district called the Gateway, approximately four blocks away.

Our shuttle driver told me about TRAX, Salt Lake City's light rail system that would take me from the packet pickup to the Whole Foods Market I wanted to visit, and then back to the hotel. With a map from the front desk, I started my walk. I liked Salt Lake's downtown right away. It is a very clean city with a simple design, but far from boring.

Once I got to the Gateway, I was impressed with the nearly 100 stores catering to everything from retail to fine dining. The packet pickup was held at Dick's Sporting Goods.

All packets were arranged in alphabetical order using the participant's last name, so my packet would have been filed under the letter "S." When I stated my last name, the person behind the table slowly looked up at me with disappointment. I couldn't imagine what was wrong, Finally, he told me the packets under the letter "S" were not ready in time for the pickup and would be available tomorrow morning before the race.

I thought this must be a joke. How is it that this mishap occurred with only one letter, and that letter happened to include my packet? All I could do was laugh because it was so preposterous.

I talked to the race director who assured me that he would personally have my packet with him in the morning before the start of the race. His words provided little comfort but there was nothing I could do. Thankfully, the packet for my friend Joanne was available so I picked up hers and caught the train to Whole Foods. Since Mom and I were planning to have dinner that evening, I didn't load up on my usual items, opting just to get some yogurt and watermelon for the morning.

When I returned to the hotel just before dusk. Since it was getting late, we decided to have dinner across the street at the Macaroni Grill for the sake of convenience. I stuck to what I knew my stomach could handle the night before a race and got the salmon. By the time I returned to the hotel room, I was exhausted and knew that I needed to settle into race mode. That wasn't a time because by 10:30, I was deep in dream land.

My wake-up call sounded promptly at 4:15. I was up, dressed and downstairs by 5:15 to meet my friend Joanne.

I was so happy to see her. Even though we had communicated often via email and snail mail, there is nothing like being able to see your friends face-to-face, especially when they live so far away. We met another lady in the lobby from Pennsylvania and the three of us

Just a few of my medals from my 50-state distance running adventure.

rode together to the Utah State Capitol Building. I can't remember if I got my packet there or where the race started, but it was not a problem getting it that morning.

Buses transported us from the Capitol Building, where the race would end, to the start line on Emigration Canyon Road. It seemed like it was a long ride and if Joanne had not been there to talk to, it would have been miserable. The race was to begin at 7:00 and it was only 6:30, so I decided I had better use the port-a-potty, which was more gross than usual.

The start line was pretty much in the middle of nowhere. It was a canyon road with no gear check, no area for water or food, no nothing. All we could do was stand around on this road trying our best to stay warm, which for me was practically impossible because it was so cold out there. I did everything I could to warm up but to no avail. I even made up my mind that I was going to run in my jacket since there was no gear check. Running 13.1 miles in a wool jacket—that would certainly be a first.

My cold fingers turned yellow like they did in Washington, D.C. However, it was getting close to 7:00 and we would be starting soon, or so I thought. As if everything else wasn't bad enough, this race did not get underway until 7:27. I was so annoyed, and if my friend Joanne had not been there, I'm afraid of how I might have reacted. Thankfully, through her kindness and gentle spirit, all of the negatives were minimized and I was filled with blessing in our conversation and fellowship.

Just before the race was finally set to begin, I saw the race director and asked him if he could take my jacket to the finish area. I wasn't alone in that request. He took quite a few jackets, sweatshirts, and sweatpants in his car, teaching him that you always offer a gear check service, especially when you start the race out in the middle of nowhere on a cold morning.

I didn't take a warm-up run like I usually do, but I wasn't worried about trying to finish fast in this one. Since I had just run a half marathon the weekend before, I was dubious as to how I'd feel in this race. My goal was to enjoy the sights of Salt Lake City and have fun.

Once we finally got under way, Joanne and I ran the first 3-4 miles together, which was pleasant because they were just about all downhill.

Around mile 4, Joanne stopped to get a drink and I kept going thinking that I probably should abstain from liquids until I was a little farther along. Thankfully, my body temperature was rising. I felt much more comfortable than I thought I would considering the cold temperatures earlier. There is no way I could have run the entire way in my jacket.

By mile 7, I was 2 minutes over my target of 1 hour. I wasn't upset because after the initial downhill, we had some serious hills to climb, not to mention that the road surface kept changing from concrete to dirt to gravel. This was no surprise as the race director described the course well in the pre-race literature, but it was hard to maintain a specific pace with all the variations in surface and elevation. Nonetheless, I did my best and stopped for liquids at miles 8 and 10.

I noticed that I talked more in this race than usual. For the first few miles, Joanne and I talked periodically and then I had a nice exchange with a man who passed me at one of the first hills. Then, as we were descending on one of the gravel sections of the course, I said to a girl running beside me that I was getting sick of those hills, which prompted us to have a short conversation. She said she was from San Francisco and she and her husband was moving to Denver. They stopped in Salt Lake to run this race before arriving in Denver the next day. We talked a bit more and eventually I pulled ahead but I would meet up with both of these runners again at the finish.

Shortly into mile 12, I looked at my watch and noticed that I had roughly 9 minutes to get to the finish to achieve a sub 2-hour race. I was surprised because I had not been watching my pace as closely as usual. With all the variations, I assumed I was too far off my mark to finish in less than 2 hours. However, when I saw that it was still possible, I dug in deep and pushed myself at the end, which thankfully was all downhill.

The finish line crept up on me. When I crossed, I thought I finished near the 1:57 mark but set out in search of an official time. At the table where the times were being posted, I was told by one of the workers that I came in 4th in my age group, but it would be several days before everything was finalized and officially posted on the website.

What was it about this year and finishing in 4th place? I came in 4th in Papillion and again the very next week in Council Bluffs, and now, 4th place again. Oh well, what can you do?

I picked up my jacket and Joanne and I hung around a bit before heading back to the hotel to shower and dress. While we ran, Mom decided to tour the Mormon Tabernacle and enjoyed it very much.

We met up with Mom and the three of us had a lovely lunch. It was wonderful and such a special way to celebrate completing another race on this 50-state journey.

After lunch, Joanne had to start her drive back to her home in Idaho. Once Mom and I checked out of the hotel, we flew to Las Vegas for a couple of days before returning to the east coast.

A week after the race, the official finish times were posted and I ended up finishing 2nd, not 4th, in my age group with a time of 1:57:19. I was happy and called the race director at the number listed on the website.

We talked and he said that he would send out the trophies to the winners sometime that next week. So I waited and never received anything. When I tried to call him back, the number no longer accepted messages.

To make a long story short, I contacted the USATF, the organization who sanctioned the race, who also tried to contact him with no success. Eventually, in early November, the race director finally responded and sent me a link to order my plaque, which I did. It was a laminated picture of me taken by the race photographer with all the pertinent information of the race printed in the corner. It was well done but should never have taken 4 months to receive.

In all honesty, this race had many more downs than ups as far as I'm concerned. That is the chance you take with new events where there is no proven history to gauge it by.

Thankfully in my case, most inaugural events I've participated in were well-organized and successful so the cliché is true that, "one bad apple don't spoil the whole bunch." For all the misgivings concerning the race, the total experience was a blessing because it gave me the opportunity to spend some time with my dear friend and sister Joanne, giving it value beyond measure. Also, the state of Utah gets a check by its name and the journey continues.

Race 35

Green River Run
With The Horses 10k
Green River, Wyoming - August 21, 2010

A Challenging Race in
Breathtaking Country

Wyoming is one of those states that I never imagined I would visit. All I knew of the state was what I saw of it in movies, mostly westerns, and it always appeared scenic and peaceful. I would come to realize the truth in that impression during a challenging run on the high country of southwestern Wyoming.

Still relishing the surprise of a 2nd place age group finish in Utah, I wanted to schedule another race as soon as possible and I wanted that race to be located somewhere in the west. While Salt Lake City was great, there was so much more of the western U.S. I wanted to see and since most of those states were still on my "need to run" list, I had to get on it.

Although Wyoming is not a state known for a ton of long distance running events, it has more to offer in that regard than one might initially think. While several caught my eye, there was one event that seemed to stand out from the rest, although it was in a city I had never heard of before.

Green River, Wyoming is located in the southwest corner of the state and serves as the host city to one of the most respected and well-received running events of the state. It is appropriately named the "Run with the Horses" Marathon, Half Marathon and 10k.

In addition to wild horses, runners are guaranteed to see some of the most breathtaking views in the entire country, but at a price, because the out-and-back course is a series of hills on graded dirt roads, which makes it unusually challenging.

While I read the reviews concerning the hills, I was not deterred because my main focus was a chance to see those beautiful wide open spaces surrounded by mountain ranges and to soak up some of the culture in this unfamiliar part of the country. So from that perspective, this race was ideal and given that it was about 5 weeks after my last race, the timing was a total match.

Located 175 miles east of Salt Lake City, I decided to fly there and rent a car so that I could enjoy the scenic drive to Green River. Although my flight landed about 1.5 hours behind schedule, I still had time to rent the car and pick up my dinner and breakfast from Whole Foods Market before driving to Wyoming.

The route to Green River (mostly I-80E) has some of the most breathtaking views I've ever seen. So spectacular were the views that I had to pull the car over and videotape several sections of it for posterity. The mountains had a golden brown color to them and the road between them was completely flat. It reminded me of New Mexico when I drove across the country in 1998. There would be nothing but flat beautiful land for miles and miles, and then suddenly, a cluster of homes and buildings would appear before giving way to more flat unpopulated land.

I stopped at two rest areas and was surprised how sparse both were. We're talking a couple of toilets and a couple of sinks—that's it. I must say that the simplicity of this part of the country impressed me. It had a feel of being totally unmanaged, vibrant and spectacular in the purest form. I loved it.

The running event was part of a 2-day festival sponsored by the city's Chamber of Commerce, complete with games, concerts and even fireworks in a park named Expedition Island. Although Green River is home to approximately 15,000 people, the festival was far from crowded. I stopped by the booths of several artists and vendors showcasing their goods and services and it put me in mind of hundreds of similar events I've attended throughout the south; nice food, nice vendors, and very nice people.

As the day progressed, I could feel the fatigue coming upon me so I found the trailer for the packet pickup and was impressed with the variety of mementos they gave us specific to Green River and Wyoming. One of the ladies working in the pickup area gave me directions to the Hampton Inn, which was less than a mile away and reminded me and several other runners to make sure we arrived before 6:00 race day morning in order to find a decent parking space. I took several more pictures of the festival and of the real "green river" before driving to the hotel.

I was up the next morning at 4:30 and felt good. I ate my goat milk yogurt and starting moving around slowly. At 5:00, I stepped outside to check the temperature. There was a slight breeze, but I knew I'd be fine with a short-sleeve tech shirt. I wore the one I got while racing in Indianapolis, some black running shorts, and a blue tech cap I received at the Minneapolis race.

I arrived at the park close to 5:50 and found a great parking space on one of the side streets. It was still dark so I stayed in the car where it was warm. At 6:15 I walked to the starting area and stretched along the way. I had time to use the restroom prior to the start (not a port-a-potty thank the good Lord.) While standing in line waiting for the gun to sound, I heard someone call my name.

I was sure they were referring to another Bridget, but when I turned around, it was my friend Paula from the Jackson, Mississippi race. We embraced and were very happy to see one another. We both indicated through various correspondence that we might do this race, but at the time, neither one of us had finalized our plans. That was good because the spontaneity of the moment made it more special. She was participating in the half marathon and since it was so close to the starting time, we couldn't talk very long. It was just so good to see her.

From the first step, the two words that best categorized this race are "hilly" and "difficult." No doubt about it, this was by far the hardest race for me up to that point in my journey. As I was continuously climbing well above sea level, I kept saying "thank you" in my spirit that I only had to run a 10k that day.

Since the course was an out-and-back, I was able to pick up some speed after the turnaround point. As I was descending the hill on the way to the park, Paula and I gave each other a high-five as she continued to climb even higher for the half marathon.

Had I studied the elevation map more closely, I would have

known how steep the hills were in the first part of the race. Since I didn't, I just had to wing it as best I could, even walking the last big hill before the turnaround. While taking that uphill walk, a man asked me if I wanted one of his energy blocks. I told him, "No, but thanks anyway."

He was super nice and told me he was from Sioux Falls, South Dakota. I told him that I was scheduled to participate in a race there next month and he assured me that it was much flatter than the race we were tackling that day. We ran together and talked up to the point of the turnaround where we separated since he was running the full marathon. As we parted, he said that he would see me in Sioux Falls—and he did.

On the way downhill, I passed quite a few folks who shouted out encouragement like, "good job" and "keep it up." Runners are the friendliest people in the world.

What happened next is still a bit disturbing to me to this day. Once we reached the Hampton Inn where I stayed, the course got confusing and suddenly, there were no more signs outlining the route. It was the strangest thing because, by that time, I had run past several runners and found myself on the course completely by myself. I had never been in a situation like that before in my running life. There is usually always another runner or volunteer or spectator near you on every inch of the course, but not in Green River.

With only 48 people in the 10k race, almost the entire second half was me running alone. For the first time since embarking on this 50-state journey, I had to break stride and literally wait for another runner to come along, hoping that he or she knew the route to take. Thankfully, within a couple of minutes, a guy came along and I was able to follow him to the finish. Without the guidance from this anonymous runner, I don't know how I would have finished this race.

My unofficial time was 57:32, by far the slowest 10k I've ever run. Considering the hills and the getting lost factor, I was okay with it.

Since they did not use timing chips or any modern technology in this race, we were clocked the good ole fashioned way - by someone holding a stopwatch at the finish. By the stopwatch, my official time was 58:10. I knew from the day before that they were not giving out awards of any kind for the 10k race, so I didn't have to worry about sticking around for the awards ceremony. Had they issued awards, I would have earned a 2nd place finish.

I didn't get a trophy, but the finisher's medal was quite nice— very colorful with several images of horses carved into the middle with the event name and date embossed on the outer ring. The uniqueness of the design makes it stand out from some of the other medals I've received.

The drive to Salt Lake was even better than the drive to Green River, mostly due to the amazing sunshine and clear skies. Once again, I had to pull over to the side and film the beauty of that amazing land. As I stood there, peaceful and quiet, I felt like I was the only person on the earth, a feeling that will forever remind me how blessed we are to live in a country where views like that can be experienced for free. I a.m. so thankful to have spent this part of my journey in Green River, Wyoming.

Race 36

Sioux Falls Half Marathon
Sioux Falls, South Dakota
September 12, 2010

The Nicest People, Don't Cha Know

I knew nothing about South Dakota. Truly. I mean nothing. So when it came time to find a race in the state, I worked from a blank slate. In this case, ignorance was bliss because I found the perfect race that blessed me far beyond what I accomplished on the race course that day.

Sioux Falls, I would later find out, is the largest city in South Dakota. Located in the eastern part of the state, it is only 15 miles from the Minnesota border. This running event included both a full and a half marathon, and by being held in mid-September, the temperatures would likely be favorable, so I was sold. Since the race occurred on a Sunday, I arranged to fly into Sioux Falls early on Saturday in order to see as much of the city as possible.

My day on Saturday started at 3:30 a.m. in order to catch my first of two flights to Sioux Falls. Being a small airport, there were not an abundance of flights going into the city but I was fortunate to find one with Delta that arrived in Sioux Falls close to 10:30. Once there, a shuttle from the hotel picked up me and two other runners.

Since I knew nothing about the city and always try to stay in hotels within walking distance to as much as possible (especially the start line), I relied on the race director for lodging recommendations. She suggested two hotels that would provide shuttle service before and after the race, as well as reduced rates to race participants. Since neither recommendation was a Hilton property, I chose the Sheraton. It was two blocks from the starting line and provided shuttle service to and from the airport.

The room was very nice and clean so I was thankful for that. However, on the ride from the airport, the shuttle driver told us that the packet pickup (held at Scheels All Sports) was almost 6 miles from the hotel. Although 6 miles is never too far for me to walk, there were other things I wanted to do besides walk 12 miles (back and forth) and I needed to save my legs for the race the next day.

So one of the other runners and I decided to share a cab for $10.00 to go to the packet pickup, which was exactly that - a packet pickup. There was no expo of any kind, just a table with our packets laid out in alphabetical order.

Since the weather was absolutely gorgeous (clear skies and 71 degrees), and I was already on that side of town, I decided to walk to the mall. The lady distributing the packets told me it was 1-2 miles away.

I started walking and decided to ask a man coming toward me how much farther did I have to go before reaching the mall. At the time, I didn't know why I asked him since I had only walked a short distance. But later, I would come to understand exactly why I asked him that question.

He replied that he was on his way to the mall via the bus and that the stop was a couple of blocks away. He added that the fare was only $1.00 and I was welcome to walk with him to the stop. I gladly accepted his invitation, unaware of how monumental my hour with him would be.

His name was John and he spoke exactly the way the characters did in the movie Fargo. I'm talking accent, expressions —everything. It almost seemed like we were rehearsing for one of the scenes in the movie. I loved how so many of his sentences ended in "don't cha know," and how unassuming his voice was, regardless of the subject matter. His tone never changed and I couldn't get enough. He was a talker. I prefer not to talk if I can help it, so I couldn't have asked for a better companion.

We reached the stop and waited for about 25 minutes for the bus to arrive. John was a native of Aberdeen, South Dakota and moved to Sioux Falls for his work. He was knowledgeable about his adopted city and knew everything from its actual population to the number of schools it had and other statistics.

Once on the bus, we continued talking, with him pointing out various landmarks along the way. Upon arrival at the mall, I thanked him and expressed how much I enjoyed our time together, to which he replied "likewise." We parted ways—or so I thought.

Empire Mall is said to be the largest shopping complex between Minneapolis and Denver, and I could certainly see why. It took a while to go from one end to the other and because it was a Saturday, I think the entire city was there.

I was hungry so I grabbed a 6-inch sub from Subway before eventually making my way to the bus stop, only to find John seated near the front of the bus. I was happy to see him again and he told me that he boarded from a bus stop located behind the mall. So, along with another guy sitting next to John, our conversation picked up where we left off. They told me about good restaurants, but none of them were close to the hotel.

They also told me about several parks in the area, including Falls Park and Sertoma Park, which were both included on the course route so I was happy I'd get a chance to see them.

If I liked listening to John by himself, I loved listening to him speak in tandem with his friend. At times, it was as if I wasn't even there. Their banter back and forth with those unmistakable northwestern accents peppered frequently with the catch phrase "don't cha know" was just priceless. Whenever I think of those guys, especially John, I can't help but smile heartily.

Once the bus arrived downtown, they instructed me to transfer to the #6 bus to get back to my hotel. I thanked them both with a hug and left them knowing that whatever happened on the race course, this trip was already memorable.

I got back to the hotel later than I had hoped, so I ended up eating dinner at the restaurant in the hotel. I couldn't find any health foods stores in the area but I had enough energy bars and non-perishable goods to sustain me for the weekend. By 8:30, I was in my room settling into race mode. I watched about an hour of the U.S. Open tennis matches before drifting off to sleep, knowing that tomorrow it was back to business on the race course.

The race started at 7:30 so I woke up at 6:00. I walked outside to test the temperature and was happy it wasn't too cold. I decided on my mid-length tech shirt from Detroit and matching pink shorts. I started my walk to the starting area at 7:10 and found it easy to stretch and take a couple of warm-up runs.

With approximately 1200 runners participating in the half marathon, this was not exactly a small race, but certainly nothing like the Rock-n-Roll events. It was nice to participate in one that was in between the two extremes.

After checking my bag with the gear check folks, I secured a place in line and was ready to go. Right from the start, I felt very relaxed in this race, finishing the first mile in exactly 8 minutes flat. By mile 7, I was 59:20 in the race, giving me a 40 second cushion to play with. Continuing to stay true to form, I took my first sip of Gatorade at mile 8 and couldn't have been more pleased with how I was doing up to that point.

The course itself was quite nice. After passing Covell Lake and the lovely St. Joseph's Cathedral, we entered the downtown area where I was the day before. Later, we entered Falls Park and ran along a paved bike trail that was part of the Greenway along the Big Sioux River, before finishing the race in Sertoma Park.

For some reason, my right lower knee (just below the knee-cap) really tightened up at mile 12.5 rendering me unable to finish with my usual sprint but that was okay. I knew my time was good on this one so I could afford to take it a bit easy at the end.

Once I crossed, I lifted my hands to the Lord in thanksgiving for the safe and healthy completion of another half marathon. Almost like God was responding to my praise, the man I talked to on the course in Green River, Wyoming a month previously came up and said, "Hey, remember me?"

I did, of course, and was so happy to see him. We hugged and I noticed he was dressed in street clothes. He told me that he did not run but because he lived there, he wanted to come out and support his friends who did participate.

After introducing me to his son who was with him, we talked some more about Green River before they were approached by several of their friends who had just crossed the finish line. As I parted to get some water and food in the post-race area, I was reminded yet again how wonderful the running community is. It brings people together from every walk of life and provides us with this wonderful platform with which to share kindness and goodness with one another. There are very few things in life you can say that about and mean it.

I slowly made my way over to the results table and discovered my time was 1:54:47. I was very pleased to have accomplished it. Being different from the vast majority of events, the officials for this race distributed trophies only to the 1st place age group finisher as opposed to the top 3 in each age group. Even still, I had to smile when I noticed that I had finished 4th in my age group yet again. I have no idea what it was with me and 4th place since the Papillion race, and little did I know it wouldn't be the last time.

South Dakota was the 35th state in my 50-state journey and one of my favorites for reasons that had nothing to do with running. Don't get me wrong, the course was beautiful and a pleasure to run, but when I reflect on this race, I'm reminded of the people I met.

The conversation with John and his unique use of the English language was charming and intriguing all at the same time. The reunion with my friend from the Green River race, whose warmth was such a blessing invigorated me. Countless others, from the shuttle drivers to the race director, turned what could have been an ordinary experience into an extraordinary one. For someone with no clue about South Dakota, I reaped a beautiful blessing by being there.

Run 37

Kroll's Diner Bismarck
Half Marathon
Bismarck, North Dakota
September 18, 2010

A Little Bit of Snow
Doesn't Stop the Show

I discovered the races for North and South Dakota at the same time, so I was acutely aware of the fact that they were one week apart. But after running half marathons on back-to-back weekends almost 2-1/2 months prior in Seattle and Salt Lake City, I knew that I could handle it, even if it wasn't the optimal option.

Also, knowing how adverse the weather gets in that part of the country during the winter months, I knew that mid-September might be the last opportunity to get in a good race before the snow and ice took over for the next 4-5 months.

Surprisingly, I knew more about North Dakota than South Dakota, but only by a hair. Certainly the movie Fargo helped in that regard. More than that, one of the largest running events in the country is held every May in Fargo. I was very interested in participating but I could never get it to fit in my schedule.

So, I began researching other events in the state and stumbled upon the half marathon in Bismarck. I found Bismarck interesting because it is the capital of the state and the 2nd largest city, just behind Fargo. Moreover, the reviews of the race were mostly positive, emphasizing its great organization, friendly race staff, and a relatively flat and scenic course. With just under 500 participants in the half marathon, it was a small race with few frills but an excellent option for seeing this part of the country in a way unique to the racing world. I was sold wholeheartedly.

I knew from the outset that this race was going to be challenging, and not just in the ways one would expect. First was the challenge of getting there since there aren't an abundance of flight options to Bismarck. For the few that are offered, the cost is above average—to put it mildly.

In addition, with connections, I was facing an average travel time of approximately 7 hours, which is never desirable when you have to run 13.1 miles the next day. My choice of lodging was dependent on hotels that were providing transportation to the airport as well as the race, which left few to choose from.

Finally, I couldn't find any health food stores via the Internet prior to making the trip. I took as many non-perishable items as I could, but I realized I might have to compromise my clean diet more than I desired.

Despite all these possible concessions, I was looking forward to seeing North Dakota for the first time.

Bismarck's airport is small, and understandably so. As soon as we entered the terminal, it seemed like the temperature dropped

30 degrees. It was so cold and cloudy that I began dreading the weather we might be facing on race day, although the forecast called for clear but cool skies. Rain and possible sleet was in the forecast for the evening until approximately 2:00 a.m. on race morning. Oh well, at least it was going to be interesting, I thought.

I called the hotel for the shuttle to pick me up, and within 20 minutes, I was riding along the streets of Bismarck in the back seat of a van. I chose to stay at the Best Western Ramkota (the other two choices were Expressway properties) primarily because they offered a discount to people participating in the race. They were providing shuttle service to the airport and the race start/finish area, and that was a big plus.

Except for the heater being exceptionally loud (at least it worked), the room was fine for just one night. I was surprised that some of the hotel staff knew very little about the race considering they were one of the host hotels, but I continued to stay optimistic.

The packet pickup was located right across the street in a place called Kirkwood Mall. While getting my packet, one of the volunteers told me that the start line was going to be about a mile from my hotel so I would definitely want to catch a ride in the morning. Thankfully, I had already talked to our hotel shuttle driver about that. He confirmed that he would start transporting all runners at 7:00 in the morning for the 7:30 start time.

It was starting to get dark so I headed back to the hotel when I noticed some drops from the sky. At first, I assumed it was rain until I paid closer attention and saw that it was sleet and snow. I couldn't believe it. In all the weather reports I scanned before making the trip, not one of them called for snow. Cold weather, yes but not snow. Nonetheless, it was coming down pretty hard and it was sticking.

I gathered with several other runners in the lobby questioning whether or not the race would take place if it continued snowing like this. Several people had already talked to the race director who made it clear that come rain or shine, the race would go on. There is nothing I can do about it now, I thought. I paid over $500 for my plane ticket, another $98 for the hotel, $24 in airport parking, and money for food and incidentals, so there was no way I was going to turn back even if they did stop the race.

I said goodnight to my fellow running buddies and retired into race mode. Thankfully, I was tired due to starting my travel so early in the morning. I was ready to settle down and prepare my heart and mind for what I expected would be a very challenging half marathon.

My wake-up call sounded promptly at 5:45. I dreamed that night that I woke up at 7:20 and missed the race. I was relieved to know that it was just a dream.

I went downstairs to check the weather. Although there was still some snow on the ground, it had stopped, and in some places it looked like nothing more than a dusting. That was a good sign.

I caught the shuttle at 7:00 with two other runners from Fargo and found a spot near the gear check area to stretch. It was super cold to me but I was prepared with three layers on top, cap and toboggan, and gloves. Someone stretching near me said that it was 32 degrees and I think it stayed that way until I finished the race.

I turned in my gear and took my place in line beside a very nice lady who asked me where I was from. She said that she and her husband were from Bismarck, but due to his job with the Army, they traveled all over the world and all her children were born in other countries. After he finished his final tour, they decided to return to Bismarck because they were so homesick. "Homesick for this weather," I thought. "It takes all kinds."

She introduced me to her son who was a few rows behind us, and I told her she looked too young to have a son that old. It was clear that she was in good shape, and once the horn sounded, she took off and I didn't see her again until the finish. She was an amazing runner.

The course was relatively flat and fast, although coming out of a tunnel near mile 11 was a hill that I had to walk. Other than that, there were no real surprises in this race. I enjoyed the scenic parts of the course, especially along the Missouri River.

The weather kept away spectators (I'm guessing) because there were few except at the end, which is usual. I expected there to be some slick spots from the night snowfall, but thankfully, the road was free from ice and snow. I was able to run at my full capacity in the first half.

By mile 7, I had nearly 1.5 minutes to go before reaching the one hour mark, so I was more than satisfied with my time. However, shortly after that point in the race, I began slowing down considerably. My guess for the slowdown was a combination of having run a fast half marathon the week before and not being able to maintain my normal diet on this trip.

I drank some Gatorade at mile 8.5 and mile 10.5 which helped, but fatigue was setting in toward the end of this race. All I could do was remember what I read in the Bible to "press" forward no matter how tired I became.

I crossed the finish line in 1:54:27, thirty seconds faster than the previous week in Sioux Falls. I was more than satisfied and very grateful. Seeing little that was appetizing in the post-race area, I decided to walk back to the hotel and passed a McDonalds where I ordered an Egg McMuffin and coffee. I ate half the sandwich and kept sipping the coffee until I reached the hotel. By now, the sun was shining brightly although the temperatures stayed very cool.

While I wouldn't call this stop of my journey spectacular, it certainly was interesting and one I'm glad to have made. With an outstanding finisher's medal, v-neck tech shirt and mesh cap, it ranks in my top 5 of best race swag, behind Pocatello and several yet to come. While I remain curious about Fargo and still plan to visit someday, I'm glad that Bismarck was the destination for this leg of my 50-state journey.

Run 38

Maine Half Marathon
Portland, Maine - October 3, 2010

My Favorite State with a
Touch of Amazing Grace

Without question, the state of Maine is my favorite state in our entire nation and has been since my first visit there at the age of 12. A couple close to my parents decided to spend a week driving up the east coast from North Carolina to Maine, and we ended up tagging along. Every part of that trip was notable including stops in Washington, D.C., New York City and Providence, Rhode Island. However, the most memorable time for me was our 2-night stay in Bar Harbor, Maine.

It was this quaint town where I caught my dinner, a 1-1/4 pound Maine lobster, and where I developed a love for the richness of land and ocean that defines so much of Maine. Nearly 10 years later, I would get to visit another part of this great state when a boyfriend I was visiting in Boston suggested we drive up the coast to Kittery,

Maine, where we spent the day perusing the notorious shopping outlets. Then, we spontaneously decided to drive an additional 30 miles north to Kennebunkport, where we posed for several pictures outside the Bush compound. It was a most memorable day and further cemented my love for this beautiful state.

I'm not the only person who feels this way about the state of Maine, at least not in the running world. How do I know that? Because the races held there throughout the year are outstanding. Being the home state of Joan Benoit Samuelson (gold medalist in the women's marathon at the 1984 Olympic Games and someone I had the privilege of meeting at a race in Tampa), I'm sure has something to do with Maine's devotion to running community. Whatever the reason, it was good to know I had a host of events from which to choose. Based on my criteria, and what I deem important in a race, the Maine Half Marathon seemed ideal. Logistically it was perfectly positioned; the time of year couldn't have been better, and it was located in Portland, a city I had never visited but desperately wanted to.

This was one of the most organized races I've ever had the privilege of being a part of. With a very thorough and detailed website, there was no guess work left for the participants. I love it when I know exactly how to plan my weekend due to great information by the race director from the outset. When you need to book airfare, lodging, etc., attention to detail to that degree is so appreciated.

Once at the Hilton Garden Inn, a very nice young lady checked me in and gave me a map to the city and directions to the Whole Foods Market and the University of Southern Maine, where the expo was being held. I was in my room long enough to dump everything out of my backpack except my registration materials and wallet before heading out to enjoy this beautiful city.

I decided to stop at Whole Foods first because I was starving. I had some watermelon, cantaloupe, and oranges on the way to the airport that morning, but it was now 2:30. The only way to describe the weather was beautiful—no clouds, just a slight cool breeze and sunshine as far as the eye could see.

Without question, this was the best Whole Foods Market yet and I certainly patronized enough of them across the country from which to substantiate this claim. The hot bar was not the usual 3 rows, but a total of 5, with everything looking and smelling good. I filled a small container with just about everything I saw and ate it in the dining area off to the side.

Totally satisfied with my meal, I walked for another mile or so until I reached the Sullivan gym on the campus of the University of Southern Maine where the expo was being held.

For a relatively small race (2,039 in the half marathon; 992 in the full marathon) this was a nice expo and some of the friendliest volunteers on the planet.

The lady who gave me my packet said that she named her daughter Bridget with the same spelling as mine (usually people add another "te" at the end), so the blessings continued to mount even before the running began.

The goody bag was one of the best yet, including a box of Wheaties, several granola bars, several Larabars, Biofreeze samples (excellent for aching joints and muscles), package of Wheat Thins, some corn wafers, an ink pen, a bag of Cheetos, a package of natural shampoo, a roll of KT tape, a $500 gift certificate to Red Star Worldwear, and best of all, a DVD of the movie Marley & Me with Jennifer Aniston. It was a movie I actually liked so I was thrilled to have my own copy.

With one of my favorite long-sleeve tech shirts displaying the state of Maine outlined on the front, this is by far the most plentiful gift bag I've ever received. Overall, it is in a close tie with the Pocatello race for the best swag ever and that's because of the carrying bag and sack of potatoes they provided!

I stopped to take several pictures of the campus of the University of Southern Maine. There is no way I could have ever attend this school because I'd never go to class, opting instead to just gaze at that amazing water views.

After touring the rest of the campus, I walked back to Whole Foods to pick up dinner and yogurt for the morning. With my newly acquired swag from the expo, my backpack was pretty heavy, but it was only a minor hindrance. Given the spectacular views and weather, there was no way I was going to ride anywhere!

Once I got back to my hotel room, I relaxed just long enough to lay out my race clothes for the next day and affix my running bib and timing chip.

With a much lighter backpack, I set out on foot again, this time to explore all the waterfront properties along the Portland Harbor, particularly the historic areas of the Old Port neighborhoods.

With over 3000 runners in town, as well as all the tourists not affiliated with the race, the waterfront and side streets were filled with people. I liked everything I saw that evening. Most of the restaurants were packed and the food looked delicious, especially a place called Walter's. I had no room for more food, but it was going to be the first place on my list to visit during my next trip to Portland.

Even though it was dark at this point, I just had to keep walking. I was too comfortable and too happy where I was to call it a night. So I continued along the waterfront until I reached an area on Commercial Street far from the busyness of the tourists and shops.

It was a very quiet area with no street lights so it was quite dark. As I turned to ascend a hill, I began singing the hymn, "Amazing Grace." It just came out. I had no plans to sing aloud, but I was deeply moved in my spirit to sing this song.

I sang two verses and as I did, my heart filled with tremendous comfort and peace. It was one of the most special moments I've had in my entire life, not just on this 50-state journey. It was clear that I had been in the presence of the Lord all day and night in Portland, Maine. As a Christian who loves the Lord, it is the only place of true joy for me. I felt blessed in that moment.

Eventually, it was necessary for me to return to my hotel room and settle into race mode even though I didn't really want to. As I started laying out my race clothes, I just couldn't stop thanking God for the privilege of being in Portland and preparing for the 37th state of my journey. I can't remember being more full of His love.

My wake-up call arrived promptly at 5:30 and I couldn't have been more energized and excited about a race to come. I slowly ate my yogurt and sipped on some of the Kombucha I purchased the day before as I began getting ready. I went downstairs at 6:30 to get some coffee and check the temperature outside.

I made arrangements with the front desk for a cab to pick me up and take me to the race since it was slightly more than 2 miles away. That was a little beyond my pre-race distance criteria and I needed my legs to be fresh for the upcoming 13.1 miles, so a cab was necessary.

The driver was at the hotel promptly at 7:00 and I had him drop me off at Hannaford Market, very near the start line. The fare was $6.10 which I thought was more than reasonable. Since it was a bit cool that early in the morning, I walked around in Hannaford to keep warm. I wasn't alone; there were quite a few runners walking up and down the aisles for the same purpose. I'm surprised the store management allowed it but then again, I think they realized some pretty good purchases in the process.

Eventually, I made my way over to the baggage check area where I used two bags since I had my sweatpants and my bulky Alaska jacket to check. It was cool but not cold, so I found a nice, sunny spot to warm up before getting in line around 7:40 for the 7:45 start time.

By my watch, I started the race at 7:48 and was relaxed from the first step to the last. Usually I start with a faster pace on purpose so that I can afford to slow down later in the race if fatigue tries to get the best of me. However, I didn't use that strategy in this race. As I prayed over the run before leaving my hotel room, I experienced the same peace I've had the whole time in Portland, so I just felt comfortable running whatever pace felt right at any given moment. Thus, the first mile was slower than usual at just over 9:00 minutes, which was perfectly fine with me.

The course for the Maine Half Marathon was beautiful and scenic, with the water playing a big role. The first mile and the last 3 ran along the Back Cove without a cloud in the sky. It was just a beautiful day, although I was glad that I had on two tech shirts because of the breeze.

Miles 3, 4 & 5 were along the shoreline and I could tell that the water was relaxing me because I wasn't checking my pace. It was as if I was "gliding" along so I had no idea how far on or off pace I might have been at that point.

Just before the turnaround point at mile 7, I checked my watch to see where I was with respect to the 1 hour mark, and I was pleasantly surprised that I had 20 seconds to spare. I thought I was running much slower than usual, but I guess the relaxed feeling I was experiencing made me think I wasn't working as hard as I usually do. It was nice to discover that I was.

As I've mentioned before, I love races that are out-and-back because on the way back, you know what to expect, just in reverse. So I knew there were some nice downhill areas to look forward to since I had walked a bit in mile 5 where a hill caught me off guard.

I stopped to drink twice—once at mile 8.1 and again at mile 10—and no doubt about it, that Gatorade does the trick. Like clockwork, I take two gulps, walk for about 20 seconds, and then pick up my speed.

The last 5k of any half or full marathon is tough and this race was no exception. Somewhere around mile 10, I started remembering my walk last night and before I knew it, I began humming Amazing Grace in my head. What a beautiful moment. In fact, there was no end to beautiful moments on this trip.

For the last little stretch, I had enough energy to sprint to the finish with a time of 1:56:40. Yeah! Goal accomplished and state #37 on this journey was completed! Once I crossed the finish line, I gave the Lord thanks and received my finisher's medal carved in the shape of the state of Maine. How awesome.

I dreaded leaving Portland because I had bonded so deeply with this great town of lobsters and lighthouses. However, my sadness was supplanted with a big smile from a conversation I had with a man on the first flight from Portland to LaGuardia. He was a handsome gentleman who worked for Pratt Whitney for 22 years and had just participated in an event where the fathers were the date for their daughters. As he described it, you could see how much this man loved his 12-year old daughter and it gave me great joy to listen to his story.

My 50-state quest yielded some great highs but none greater than what I experienced in Portland at the Maine Half Marathon. I look forward to visiting this beautiful city again, and again, and again— and I suspect that when I do, I'll still be singing.

My journal entry for that Saturday night (10/2/10) says it best. In all caps, I wrote "I LOVE PORTLAND MAINE!" What more can you add to that?

Race 39

ING Hartford Half Marathon
Hartford, Connecticut - October 9, 2010

Two Races – One Weekend: PART I

The weekend of October 8-10, 2010 was by far the most rewarding, adventurous, educational, and fun weekend of my 50-state quest. While the reasons are numerous, primarily it's because I ran two races in two states in one weekend, and in the process, I got to see parts of Connecticut and New York that will forever change my life. This chapter focuses on the first race of the weekend in Hartford, Connecticut.

Transportation for the weekend was easy since I decided to fly in and out of Hartford, renting a car for the drive to New York and the other stops I had on my agenda. While I try to avoid driving as much as possible, I actually looked forward to it on this trip so that I could take my time and really absorb the fall foliage along those scenic country roads. I can't express how much I was looking forward to the weekend.

The ING Hartford Marathon and Half Marathon is one of the most popular and well-organized races in the United States. This race came highly recommended and since I had never been to Hartford, it was an obvious choice for me. Moreover, I longed to see the beauty of the northeast in the fall, so I began making my plans in early June for this race. Somehow I knew it was going to be quite special.

The word "superb" comes to mind when describing the distribution of information for this race. I've participated in many running events with good websites and pre-race literature, but none hold a candle to the staff of the ING Hartford Marathon and Half Marathon. Every detail essential to a race—logistics, in-depth description of host hotels, schedule of events, transportation and parking information, precise course maps and other details - were professionally addressed on the website and in pre-race literature.

As a runner, especially one traveling a long distance and unfamiliar with the area, this attention to detail is appreciated. It is always a pleasure when I don't have to contact the race director in a separate communication about something because it wasn't properly addressed on the website.

In addition, the race staff put together an amazing "insider's guide" that outlined everything you needed to know, whether you were a runner, an observer, or a volunteer. This one-of-a-kind guide stayed with me the entire time and helped me maneuver my way through all the race activities and the city of Hartford. All of this detail helped send my enthusiasm for this race through the roof. I couldn't wait to get there!

I was up before my 6:00 wake-up call the morning of the race. I went downstairs to get a cup of coffee and they tried to charge me $2.00. Are you kidding me? When the waitress went to seat somebody, I got a cup and was done with it.

The weather was terrific and all I needed were two long-sleeve tech shirts to stave off the morning chill. I left the hotel at 7:30 and was in line by 7:50, a little farther back then I expected to be, but I was not dismayed. My strategy for this race was totally different from half marathons I'd run in the past, simply because I had another race the next day.

Having never run two events in the same weekend, I had no way to gauge my energy level on day 2 of this adventure. So my goal for the race in Hartford was to run at a slightly slower pace than usual, still striving for a finish time in less than 2 hours. I wanted to be closer to 1:59 than 1:53. You may be thinking, "What's the difference in 5 or 10 minutes?" Anyone who has run a long distance event will tell you that there is a difference. Nevertheless, I knew that I wanted to preserve as much energy as possible for the next day. Moreover, it felt good not to put so much pressure on myself. I wanted to relax in this one and really soak up the experience since I knew I'd be going slower.

The gun sounded at 8:05 and I crossed the start mat at exactly 8:08:09. This race was very crowded for the first 1.5 miles due to that fact that the full marathon and half marathon runners shared the same route up to that point. Just past the one mile mark, the half marathon runners veered in a different direction, allowing for better spacing. Since I decided to run slower in this race, I didn't check my watch at each mile like I normally do, so I had no idea what my pace was. I noticed by mile 5, I wasn't very winded so I took that as a sign that I was staying true to my plan of running slower.

I loved the course of this half marathon. Taking Park Street through downtown, we weaved in-and-out of town streets through West Hartford that were quaint and peaceful.

By mile 7, we passed the campus of St. Josephs College and I recognized where I had journeyed yesterday after having lunch. This was also the first time in the race I decided to look at my watch. Usually by mile 7, I try to be right at or slightly under the 1-hour mark, but this time, I was 3 minutes over an hour! Wow, I was surely following my plan of running more slowly; however, I had no idea I was running that much slowly. I was curious if I could still finish in less than 2 hours at that pace,. I was determined not to check my watch again until mile 11.5 or 12—I was enjoying the scenery too much to alter what I was doing up to that point.

I got some Gatorade at the 8.5 mile mark, and again at mile 10.5. By mile 8, we entered the beautiful Elizabeth Park, which is on the national register of historic places and showcases over 100 acres of the some of the loveliest gardens on the planet. I loved running in this serene section of the city and was thankful it made up nearly 2 miles in the second half of the race, when a lift was definitely needed. Just outside the park at mile 11, I decided to check my watch to see how I was doing and recognized that I needed to maintain a 10 minute/mile pace the rest of the way to finish in the 1:59 range.

The miles in the park were very quiet with little to no spectators and I slowed down even more without realizing it, so I knew I had to push in the last mile. Thankfully, the finish was downhill as we turned into Bushnell Park and I crossed the finish line at the Soldiers and Sailors Memorial Arch in 1:59:25! I just did make it across in less than 2 hours. I was elated and thanked God right then and there; not just for a great finish time, but for a beautiful day and a scenic course. I felt fantastic!

Once I received my medal (a very classy design of the Soldiers Memorial Arch), I walked over to the post-race area and got some water. Then I headed back to the hotel since I had nice drive ahead of me and another city and state to focus on the next day.

When I arrived the day before the race, I decided to take some additional turns while in route to my hotel in order to see some of the Hartford. I loved the tree-lined streets of this part of the city as I passed the campuses of the University of Hartford, Saint Joseph's College, and the University of Connecticut-Hartford.

I began the "walking" part of my exploration (something I commonly do on the eve of a race) in Bushnell Park, the setting for the start and finish of the race. It is the oldest publicly funded park in the United States. There was a lot of activity that Friday within the 50 acres comprising the park, mostly from volunteers putting up booths and tables in preparation for all the post-race festivities. I enjoyed the green space and pond area, as well as the historic monuments and statues.

From there, I walked across the street to the State Capitol Building and all the other municipal structures, before continuing down the streets of downtown Hartford. While the downtown area was no Philadelphia or New York, it certainly was no Detroit either. There was much to enjoy as far as I was concerned. I was looking forward to the race where I'd get to see additional sights like the Elizabeth Park and Old Main Street.

Although this walk was far from what I experienced in Portland, Maine the week before, I still enjoyed it and was able to get in a good 5-6 miles before needing to call it a night and getting into race mode. The day had been wonderful and somehow I knew, it was just the beginning of more good stuff ahead.

The first leg of my "two races in one weekend" adventure could not have gone smoother or been more fulfilling. With a nice breeze and plenty of sunshine, I was looking forward to my drive through more of Connecticut and eventually New York. If the second leg of this adventure was anything like the first, I was in for one amazing treat!

Race 40

Westchester Medical Center Running Festival Quarter Marathon
White Plains, New York - October 10, 2010

Two Races – One Weekend - PART II

L et me preface this chapter with the following statement: I love New York! There is no question the important role New York City plays in my life, and has for quite some time. As a huge tennis fan, I attend the U.S. Open tournament in Queens during the last week of August as often as possible, and make it a point to get to the city an additional 4-5 times a year.

New York is like a second home to me and when I'm there, I live like I reside there full-time. Always preferring to stay near the Columbus Circle area, I run in Central Park every day, eat a lot of meals at the Whole Foods Market, attend my home church in the city (Calvary Baptist on 57th Street), shop, socialize, and patronize the theater community by attending every play I can.

It is my kind of city with my kind of interests, so it makes sense to assume that I would choose a race in NYC to run as part of my 50-state quest, but that would be inaccurate. As I've mentioned previously, one of my goals for this quest was to see parts of the country foreign to me, and since there is so much more to the state of New York than NYC, I desperately wanted to explore those regions as part of this journey. I considered races in Buffalo, Rochester, Albany, and the Hamptons, but it was a small race in White Plains that received the final vote, and I'm very glad it did.

The only association I had to White Plains is that a friend of mine from college was raised there; otherwise, I had no knowledge of it or interest in it. But once I happened upon literature for a race held there every October, I was immediately intrigued.

The Westchester Running Festival features three primary races: a half marathon, a quarter- marathon, and a half marathon for walkers only. With just over 1,000 participants total (274 in the quarter marathon), the course for all three races takes place along the historical and scenic Bronx River Parkway in Westchester County. Starting in White Plains, you run south toward the Bronx before turning around and finishing where the race began. Having the opportunity to run along this famous closed parkway parallel to the Bronx River was too good to pass up, especially since I was curious to see up close and personal the differences and comparisons of an area so close to Manhattan in proximity but so far away in many other ways.

However, the real selling point of this race for me was the date. Since I had scheduled my race in Hartford many months in advance, I knew that I'd already be in that part of the country so the timing couldn't have been better. Moreover, since I chose to participate in the quarter marathon (my favorite distance at

6.55 miles), I felt confident that I could handle both races the same weekend.

I hopped back on Interstate 91S and was cruising along nicely until encountering a wreck that reduced us to a standstill for about 30 minutes. Finally I hit the White Plains city limits and decided to go straight to the expo at the Westchester Medical Center, the sponsor of the festival. I got there close to 4:30 and discovered it was not an expo but simply a packet pickup. Once I got my packet, I realized I was hungry so I drove to you know where? The Whole Foods Market is connected to the Westchester Mall, an upscale shopping mall in downtown White Plains with Nordstrom and Neiman Marcus being two of the anchor stores. They had a nice hot bar so I had my usual dinner before picking up my yogurt and fruit for race morning.

I wrote the race director several weeks before the race for hotel suggestions close by the event and he recommended the Residence Inn in White Plains. This was perfect since I had enough points to use for a free night, so I drove there from Whole Foods and checked in. This hotel was a great choice. The lady at the front desk was exceptional and the room was clean and large.

Although it was getting late, I wanted to walk around some and see what I could of White Plains on foot. Though kind of in a commercial area, I liked this city and its layout. It put me more in mind of a mid-sized city in the south than one less than 30 minutes from New York City.

Finally, I returned to my hotel room to settle into race mode. It had been a glorious day and one that I thanked God for before drifting off to a wonderful sleep.

The next morning, I felt fantastic. Since the race did not start until 9:00, I had plenty of time to get ready, although since I had to drive to the start line and I wasn't entirely sure where to park once I got there, I didn't want to dawdle too much. I had time to listen to Dr. Charles Stanley deliver an incredible message on forgiveness, leading me to include prayers for forgiveness for two lost family members, along with my prayer for a safe race before leaving the hotel at 8:15.

The weather was terrific just as it had been the day before in Hartford, with temperatures starting in the low 50's and plenty of sunshine, so I went with two long-sleeve tech shirts – one from yesterday and one from the Maine race – along with my mesh cap from the Minneapolis race and my gray racing gloves.

Now normally I don't carry any money with me to a race basically because there is no need to do so. However, just as I was heading out the door, I grabbed a $5.00 bill and wasn't even sure why. Well, the answer is simply the Lord because when I arrived at the Westchester County Center, it cost $4.00 to park in their lot. There may have been some mention of this in the literature but if there was, I sure didn't see it. Had I not taken that money with me, I would have really been in a pickle because all free parking on the streets had been secured well before I arrived and there was only 20 minutes before the race was due to start. No doubt about it, the impulse to take that $5.00 bill with me was a blessing from the Lord.

With the car safely parked (and with an extra dollar in change),

I was ready to get started with my New York state race. Since it was pretty cool, I stayed in the car with the heat until about 8:45 and began stretching before slowly making my way to the starting area.

As I put my key and license in the zippered back pocket of my shorts, a guy looked at me and said "4 minutes to go. Start following the crowd to the balloons." Well, when I spotted the balloons he was referring to, they looked to be farther away than I expected, so me and quite a few other runners, started picking up the pace and got there just as everyone else was singing the last line of the National Anthem. Talk about cutting it close! In 30 more seconds, the horn sounded and we were off.

Without question, the Bronx River Parkway is beautiful. Its scenic views of the Bronx River and stone arch bridges made it feel like we were thousands of miles away from civilization. With the exception of runner's footsteps, the parkway was quiet and peaceful, and I found it very easy to relax in this race. The feeling that best describes my heart during this race is "carefree." I know several runners who've told me that they feel carefree in every race, and while that has always been my goal, I can't honestly say that has been my experience. However, it was in White Plains and it felt terrific.

Adding to the natural beauty of the parkway were the gorgeous houses that adorned our path. As I observed how large, spacious and well-kept they all were, I wondered what one would cost. Given that view and proximity to NYC, I'm sure the price tag was well out of my range.

The course was an out-and-back for both the half and the quarter marathon, and though there were some pretty respectable hills, it was a very doable course. I was enjoying myself and although I wasn't following my watch at all, I knew in the closing quarter mile or so that I was running at a good pace. However, right at the end, there was a sharp left we had to take with another 20 steps or so before crossing the finish line. I wasn't aware of that little "hook" and so as I was running full throttle straight ahead, I had to make a sudden shift and slowed down tremendously, causing me to lose some valuable time. I would find out how valuable a little later in the day.

Feeling great once I crossed the finish line, I grabbed some water before returning to my car to get my jacket. As I got back to the finish area, they began posting the results and I earned a 4th place finish, but only because of the way the age groups were categorized. Just like the Papillion, Nebraska race, the racing staff in White Plains elected to go with 10-year age groupings instead of the more commonly accepted 5-year increments. Had the age grouping been in 5-year increments, I would have finished 2nd. However, what hurt most was that I missed getting the 3rd place spot by 5 seconds. Moreover, when I originally missed the sharp hook turn at the end, the girl who was behind me moved ahead and she was the one who finished 5 seconds faster.

I say it hurts, but truthfully I didn't go there expecting to win a trophy. What I received from the entire weekend experience far exceeded anything you can put on a shelf. Nonetheless, it would have been nice to add it to my collection. Now I know how LoLo Jones felt in the 2008 Olympic Games when she lost the gold medal by mere seconds due to a misstep on the last hurdle. Okay, so maybe my 5 seconds is not on the same scale as an Olympic competition, but a girl can dream can't she?

There are many wonderful things to see in this region. On my way to White Plains, I was determined to visit New Haven and spend some time on the Yale University campus. Rarely that spontaneous, I was excited for the quick change of plans so I got on Interstate 91S and began the drive to school, so to speak. The weather was just amazing and since the rental car came with Sirius Radio (something I can't justify paying for on my own but will surely listen to if it comes with a rental), I found a good house music station and felt like a college student again. It was fabulous.

A short drive from Hartford, I reached New Haven pretty quickly and since I had no idea what the layout of the city was, I found a side street to park the car and do what I do best—take off on foot with my backpack. I found a parking spot across from what they call "The Green" and set out from there.

Yale is a beautiful campus. The architecture of the older buildings and the air of sophistication that engulfs the campus truly set it apart. While walking along and taking a ton of pictures, I noticed a tour group a few feet ahead so I caught up with them and joined right in. The meter where I parked charged a quarter for 10 minutes and I only had about 36 minutes to spare, so I kept an eye on my watch.

Our tour guide was great. He was junior and it was clear to see how much he loved his school. Quite knowledgeable, he talked to us about everything associated with Yale, from the history of the buildings architecture to its system of residential colleges. He showed us how each college has its own library, dining hall, dorms, etc. as we sat in one of the common areas of Calhoun College. For someone who did her undergraduate work at a public university, I found all this fascinating and wondered how my life might be different had I attended a school like Yale. Although I'll never know, a part of me will always feel like I may have missed the boat in that regard.

Just as our guide was wrapping up the tour, I noticed that I had about 5 minutes left on the meter so I starting heading back to the car before I got totally lost. I was surprised because I usually have a great sense of direction but not this time. For some reason, I didn't look at one street sign as I wondered onto campus and all I could remember was the sign I saw that said "The Green." I saw a police officer and described to him the area where I parked and he gave me perfect directions back to my car. As it turns out, I was nearly 5 blocks from where I parked so I covered some ground, but the tour was absolutely fabulous. I loved every minute of it.

I adore colleges and college towns and look forward to touring them whenever I can. While I've toured most of the renowned campuses in the south (Ole Miss is by far my favorite), I've had yet to do so with many schools in the northeast. Thankfully, that would change over the next several years.

The weekend was incredible and in some ways the most adventurous part of my 50-state journey. Seeing parts of these states from the road, by foot and by car, allowed me for the first time to experience total freedom and do so without even being aware of it. And the unexpected excursion to New Haven added a distinction to the weekend that would be paralleled by no other.

States #38 and #39 were now completed and I couldn't have anticipated the joy and blessing I would receive in doing so.

Race 41

Baltimore Running Festival Half Marathon

Baltimore, Maryland - October 16, 2010

Good to Be Back in a Place
I Once Called Home

As I mentioned earlier, I lived in the Baltimore area for nearly 3 years in the mid-1990s. Specifically, I lived in the planned community of Columbia, Maryland and I've often wondered how my life would be different today if I had remained there. It was a time of tremendous growth for me in just about every aspect but especially spiritually because while living in Columbia, I awakened to the things of God and would truly hear the gospel of Jesus Christ for the first time. There will always be a special place in my heart for this city, compounded by one of the most memorable races of my journey.

Since everything associated with this half marathon takes place downtown, with the start, finish and expo all happening at the M&T Bank Stadium (home to the Baltimore Ravens), it more than fulfilled my logistics requirement. Moreover, when I lived in the area, I frequented downtown Baltimore and was looking forward to seeing it again. Past participants gave the race good reviews so there was nothing left for me to do but register and plan my trip.

Having long since realized that running races on back-to-back weekends was not an issue for me, the fact that I'd be participating in a 13.1 mile race 6 days after my previous race didn't phase me a bit. In fact, it made me even more excited for the challenge it would present.

Traveling to Baltimore was easier than my last 7 or 8 races with a 10:40 a.m. non-stop flight from Raleigh-Durham. What a nice change of pace to leave my house at 9:00 a.m. for the airport and not 5:00 a.m. as I did on so many occasions. The short 1-hour flight was another welcome change of pace from all the layovers and plane changes of past races.

I took an airport shuttle to my hotel, the Hampton Inn & Suites Inner Harbor, which I chose mostly because it was .2 miles from the start line. It was a nice hotel and many runners stayed there for the weekend.

As usual, I set out on foot with my trusted backpack to the Whole Foods Market for lunch. Then I walked approximately 2 miles to the expo at the stadium and was a bit disappointed with it. I knew it wasn't going to be as grand as the Rock-n-Roll events, but with over 8000 participants in the half marathon alone, I expected more. While there were a fair number of vendors in attendance, few were giving out free samples (something I had come to expect at expos). Nevertheless, I stopped at each table and talked a while with various volunteers and staff officials before leaving around 4:30.

The weather was great, although a bit breezy in the evening. I just wanted to take it as easy as possible and enjoy the festivities of the Inner Harbor, the popular waterfront development and home to some of the best restaurants and shops you will find in any city.

Having spent many an evening at the Inner Harbor when I was a resident, I always enjoyed its entertainment aspects like the live bands and street performers. It was always a great way to spend an evening and I could see that it still was. I stopped to listen to one of the bands who was pretty good and continued walking toward the Fells Point area.

In August 1995, I starred in a play at the Fells Point Corner Theater entitled "Canada". I spent many days and evenings in that part of the city rehearsing, socializing and performing. It was a grand time in my life and one that I miss a great deal, so being able to revisit the "old neighborhood" was refreshment to my bones.

The peace of that evening was wonderful and just what I needed. Once I reached my hotel room, I felt a strong prompting to pray over my health and future medical examinations. This is something that had been stirring in my heart for some time and on my walk in downtown Baltimore that evening, I received the clarity that I needed. In short, I made the decision that evening to no longer engage in the traditional practice of western medicine. I'm not saying that I will never visit a doctor's office again, but the practice of arbitrary annual tests administered whether necessary or unnecessary would no longer be a part of my health regimen.

While I have no aversion to those who engage in these practices, I realized that for me at this time in my life, daily exercise and a clean diet were how I planned to stay healthy and strong and it continues to serve me very well all these years later. So I equate the turnaround in my health practices to my race in Baltimore, causing its significance on this 50-state journey to go far beyond that of running.

The morning of the race, I woke up full of vim and vigor. At the breakfast bar, I got some coffee and a small box of Cheerios to add to my goat milk yogurt for a hearty breakfast. Unfortunately, the half marathon didn't start until 9:45, which is the only thing I didn't like about this race. The vast majority of running events start between 6:30 to 8:00 which is preferable.

Most runners will tell you that the earlier the start time, the better. Typically, we are early risers so to have to wait around until 9:45 tends to throw a lot of people off. I just tried to stay relaxed and loose until 9:30, when I left the hotel for the start line. Since I was so close, I was in line by 9:33 and of course, the crowd had already formed with the vast majority of participants already in place. The weather was ideal with loads of sunshine and a slight cool breeze. I wore 2 long-sleeve tech shirts and was comfortable but I could have gotten away with only wearing one.

I started this race rather sluggishly, not because I was tired but because the start time was later than my body was used to, so it took the first mile to get me into gear. After that, I was back at my usual pace of 8:30 to 8:45 minute/mile, even though this course was pretty hilly throughout. In the back of my mind, I was concerned how I would hold up during this race since it was my 4th event in 3 consecutive weekends, but God is good. I felt fine the entire time.

I was hoping to return to my normal plan of finishing 7 miles by the first hour of the race and I hit that mark exactly in Baltimore, almost down to the very second. Last week in Hartford, I hit the 7 mile mark in 63 minutes so I knew I was back to my usual form. If I continued with my normal race plan, I would have no problem in finishing this event in less than 2 hours, but you never know what the second half of a race will yield.

The course was interesting and took us on a big tour of the downtown area and several of the smaller more quaint neighborhoods. As we ran out of Clifton Park, we entered a 1.3 mile loop around the beautiful Lake Montebello. It was fun to look across the water at the runners making the circle ahead and behind me. I always enjoy that aspect of looped courses.

At mile 10, a guy beside me said that the remaining 3 miles were all downhill. Typically, such news thrills me, and it was good to hear this time. However, I didn't have any trouble with the hills in this race and was able to run them all without walking, so either way, I was performing well and having a good time in the process.

I didn't take my first sip of water until mile 9, which is a little later than normal, but again, I was kind of in rare form for some reason. I followed that up with some Gatorade at mile 11 and things were going so well that I didn't even realize when we passed the mile 12 marker. When I did, I looked at my watch and it was 11:30, meaning that I had over 15 minutes to run 1.1 miles and still accomplish my goal of finishing in less than 2 hours. What a great feeling that was.

During the final mile downtown heading to Camden Yards (where the Baltimore Orioles play and where the race finished), the streets were filled with spectators yelling and supporting us as we made that final turn. I was particularly invigorated when a group of African-Americans started cheering me on and yelling "Go Sista. You got this. You look great. Keep it up baby girl!" It made me feel good.

I talked to God a lot during this race and by that last quarter of a

mile, I was flying as we entered the Camden Field gates and sprinted to a finish time of 1:54:06. I just kept thanking God and lifting
my hands to Him when I finished. I don't ever remember crossing a
finish line and feeling so good. It was such a blessing!

I received my gorgeous finisher's medal with the number 10
prominently featured to denote the 10th anniversary of this event.

The cool breeze was going all through me since I was sweating
from the race so I wrapped up in one of the Kevlar blankets the
volunteers handed out, and proceeded to the post-race food table to
grab a bag of Wheat Thins, potato chips and water.

I slowly made my way back to the hotel and showered and
dressed by the checkout time of 1:00 p.m. The shuttle to the airport
wasn't due to pick me up until 1:45 so I sat in the lobby with several
other runners and watched some of the college football games.

A guy sitting across from me said that he was in Baltimore for
business. He ran marathons although he didn't participate on that
day. It was easy to tell from his body frame and structure that he
was in great shape. We talked about the various races we had participated in over the past several years. He was from San Francisco
so he had run many races on the west coast. This is typical of the
kind of conversations I have with runners nearly every day.

Participating in running events throughout the country make
you a member of a very prestigious yet informal club and it's one
that we are very humble and thankful to be a part of.

The shuttle stopped and picked up 2 additional runners at other
hotels; a guy from Boston and a girl from Birmingham. All three
of us were in the middle of our 50-state quest, although the two of
them were running full marathons to complete their journeys (God
bless 'em).

We shared stories of events we had completed so far and I asked the guy about a race I was eyeing in Hyannis, Massachusetts. Since he was from Boston, I thought he might be familiar with it and could share his opinion. He told me that he had participated in that event for the past two years and loved it. The race wasn't scheduled to take place until February, but due to his endorsement, I registered as soon as I got home.

This trip to Baltimore wrapped up a very active October that included four races in 4 states in 3 consecutive weeks. Amazingly, I couldn't have been more energized. It had been an immensely bless-filled ride that enhanced my 50-state quest to a new level.

Thanksgiving to God filled my heart and my mind as I prepared to continue the journey. Although I felt good, I was looking forward to a weekend at home for a change before I started on the road again.

Race 42

Manchester City Half Marathon
Manchester, New Hampshire
November 7, 2010

Why Did It Take Me So Long To Get To New Hampshire?

For as long as I can remember, I've held a fascination with New England and specifically, the state of New Hampshire. I'm not sure why because my knowledge of that region was never very extensive, and while I had been to other parts of New England, visiting New Hampshire always seemed to escape me. I looked forward to my first visit there as part of my 50-state quest and now that I've had an opportunity to taste the beauty of this great state, I wonder what took me so long to get there.

When I discovered the Manchester City Half Marathon, I must admit that I'd never heard of the city of Manchester, which is embarrassing considering that it is the largest city in the state. However, after reading only positive reviews, I knew this race had all that I was looking for and I registered as soon as I could, which was early July.

With several months to plan for this race, I spent a lot of time learning as much as possible about Manchester and was surprised by what I uncovered. Manchester is not only the largest city in New Hampshire, but it is the largest city in northern New England, which encompasses Maine and Vermont as well as New Hampshire. With several postsecondary institutions, a vibrant downtown, and an abundance of venues for the arts, I already knew that I would love being in Manchester. The race couldn't have come soon enough for me.

Well rested from my two weeks of not participating in a running event, I was happy to be traveling again. My flight was early Saturday morning so I was up at 4:20 in order to catch my 7:35 flight to Baltimore before arriving in Manchester. Both flights were short and smooth and as we began our descent into New Hampshire, the sun was shining beautifully although the flight attendant announced that the temperature was 41 degrees. I checked the weather report and knew that the high for Saturday and Sunday was not expected to exceed the mid-40s, so I was prepared for the colder weather in this race.

I arrived in Manchester at 11:00 and called my hotel, The Hilton Garden Inn, to be picked up from the airport. My shuttle driver was a wonderful guy named Fred who was 74 years old and an absolute hoot. His son taught at M.I.T. and lived on Cape Cod. I told him I was going to run in Hyannis in February and was concerned about the weather. He replied that the Cape didn't get much snow and ice so I should be fine even in February.

The Hilton Garden Inn in downtown Manchester is a great hotel. Located along the Merrimack River and adjacent to the baseball field where the farm team for the Toronto Blue Jays hosts their games, its location is hard to beat. I was happy I made the choice to stay there.

I walked the half mile to the expo located in the Radisson Hotel and was impressed with the size and quality of the expo. Since this was technically a "sports and health expo," there were several healthcare professionals offering free cholesterol, blood sugar and body fat readings. While healthcare facilities and individuals are pretty common fixtures at expos, free screenings are not although I have seen a few here and there. I decided to check my body fat percentage and discovered it was right around 12-13% in the athletic category, which pleased me a great deal.

From the expo, I walked through the streets of downtown Manchester and was very impressed with this city. To me, it was the perfect combination of vintage sophistication and modern charm. I found it to be a very warm and inviting place with some of the friendliest people on the planet.

I returned to the hotel to drop off my bag from the expo and checked to see if Fred could take me to a place I had researched called "The A Market." Similar to Whole Foods Market, it showcases organic foods, most of which are grown in the state of New Hampshire. He was available and waited for me to get all my shopping completed. I was able to get all my normal foods, including goat milk yogurt, energy bars, and Kombucha to drink. They didn't have a hot bar but that was okay; food wise I was doing fine. Once we returned to the hotel, I put my food in the refrigerator and then Fred took me to "The Mall of New Hampshire", one of the largest shopping centers in that part of New England. It was lovely. Even Santa Claus was already there and it was just the first week of November!

Fred gave me 2-1/2 hours before he would return so I could really take my time in the 125 store structure. Since there is no sales tax in New Hampshire, I thought I might find some good deals even though I am no shopper. How some people spend an entire day in a mall is beyond me but being that this was a new part of the country for me, I wanted to observe the people here and the mall is probably one of the best places to do just that. Getting hungry, I decided to have dinner at Ruby Tuesdays mostly because they had several big screen televisions and I wanted to see some of the college football games. I had the salmon and some vegetables and while it was not bad, I only ate about 1/3 of it.

While at the mall, I found out from some girls who were also there for the race that Carrie Underwood was performing that night at the stadium next to my hotel. Her concert had been sold out for weeks so there was a lot happening in Manchester that weekend.

Fred picked me up promptly at 6:00 and we continued our hearty conversation about everything from health foods to his grandchildren. Since he was off the next day I knew I wouldn't see him again so I gave him a nice hug when I departed and he blew me a kiss. What a lovely man and another example of the blessings you receive on a quest like this—they just keep coming.

I called Mom from my room overlooking the city lights and told her how much I loved it there, to which she broke out in laughter because she said that I've made that same remark about every place I've visited on my 50-state journey, except for Detroit. When she reminded me of that, I had to laugh too, but there was something extra special about Manchester. It was so diverse and the level of comfort I experienced touched me deeply. I just felt very blessed to be there.

That night while settling into race mode, I studied the Word of

God and focused on three verses that were speaking to my heart: Exodus 15:26, Exodus 25:25, and Hebrews 11:6. As I fell on my knees and prayed, giving God thanks for such a great day and the blessed conversation I had with my Mom, I fully recognized the privilege it was to be on such an amazing journey.

Due to Daylight Savings Time, we turned our clocks back one hour and I was looking forward to the extra sleep.

The morning started nicely. I was up before my appointed wake-up call at 6:45. The time change really helped and I was totally energized. I went to the lobby to get coffee and ran into quite a few runners for the full marathon. There was an early start for those expecting to take a longer time to finish so many of them were up to take advantage of that early start. Thankfully, I was starting with the majority of participants at 8:50 so I had plenty of time to get ready.

Although the start line was close enough to walk, I decided to take advantage of the hotel shuttle that was driving anyone to the start that wanted a ride. I caught the 8:15 shuttle along with four other runners, one being a nice lady who was there to accompany her husband who was the one running. They reminded me of Dr. Rick and his wife from the Little Rock race.

Race morning was COLD. Just before I left the hotel, the news stated it was 38 degrees but it felt a lot colder than that to me. The good news was that the sun was out and would remain that way throughout the race. The shuttle driver dropped us off at 8:20, 30 minutes before the start of the race. I had on two pairs of shorts and three tops including a white high top non-tech sweater and a Nike double thick mesh shirt. With my black toboggan and two pairs of racing gloves, I was still cold. I walked over to the baggage claim area to get a bag-tag when I stumbled into the office that was heated. What a blessing! Two other runners and I found refuge in there until about 8:38.

Finally, I took off my jacket and sweatpants, bagged and turned them into the baggage claim window. I stretched just a bit and did a warm up run to the start line just before we sang the National Anthem. We started the race at 8:50 on the nose.

I knew from the literature that this was a challenging and hilly course. The race director did not try to fool anybody, so I knew I had to dig deep on this one. My goal was to do my best but if I needed to walk, I was definitely going to walk without guilt or disappointment. Because I was up so early, I was able to hydrate quite a bit so I felt strong. Above all, I wanted to enjoy myself out there.

The first mile wasn't bad at all. I was relaxed and ran it at an 8:30 minute/mile pace. Mile 2 had a hill but I still maintained a 8:45 minute/mile pace; however, I had to walk about 15 seconds of the hill in mile 4, but that would be the last time I walked in this race.

By the time I got to mile 7, I was just 30 seconds over the 1-hour mark which was fine with me. At mile 7 I drank some Gatorade, but I was getting pretty tired by then. I panted more than usual in this race and I knew it was because of the hills compounded by the cold. However, every time I thought I had hit the wall, the Lord gave me a boost and I was able to run another mile rather easily. I definitely had a couple of 10 minute/mile segments but toward the end, I was back on pace at 8:45 minutes/mile.

By mile 10, a girl who knew the course told me and another runner that we had one more hill to climb and then it was all downhill. I asked her where the hill was and she replied that it was about a ½ mile ahead. She was right, and when we got there I did not have to walk any of it. I think knowing that was the last big incline before the end of the race gave me extra motivation.

Once we got to the end, I couldn't sprint but I pushed as hard as I could those final few yards and received an unexpected treat at the end. Before I crossed the finish mat, my timing chip denoted who I was and the announcer said "Here comes Bridget Simpson all the way from North Carolina." It felt good to be announced and I came in by myself which rarely happens.

I thanked the good Lord for an amazing race and after putting my finisher's medal around my neck, I quickly grabbed one of the Kevlar blankets because I was really freezing now that I had stopped running.

The Athlete's Village in Veterans Park was where the post-race food was being served. It was quite a selection—everything from vegetarian soup, chili, rolls, butter, coffee, hot chocolate, fruit and water was available. After those hilly 13.1 miles, I was super hungry. The chili looked good. I couldn't wait to try it and found a nice spot near one of the statues so I could put my gear down and focus on eating. Without question, that was some of the best chili I have ever had. It wasn't quite a good as the alligator gumbo I had in Baton Rouge, but it hit the spot, especially given how cold it was.

I picked up another cup of yogurt before wrapping up and walking back to the hotel. The walk seemed much longer than it actually was because I was wet from sweating and the cold air was cutting through the Kevlar blanket and my jacket.

I finally reached the hotel and immediately got a cup of hot coffee to keep warming me up. Since I wasn't due to leave for the airport until 1:00, I had over 1-1/2 hours to get dressed and packed. So I took my time and was able to get my final finish time before leaving. My official time was 1:56:58 and I was ecstatic.

As I was on the plane returning to North Carolina, all I could think about was how much I enjoyed being in the state of New Hampshire. It was a blessing and I had already made up my mind that it would be a place I would visit many more times in the future.

Race 43

Gobbler Grind Half Marathon
Overland Park, Kansas - November 21, 2010

A Not-So-Great Race to Finish
Out-A-Very Great Year

As the calendar year comes to a close, so do the number of races. While there are still a few out there, you have to be diligent and willing to work a little harder to find them. Thus was the case with the race I chose for Kansas.

Having never been to Kansas and not really interested in visiting, I didn't have a preference where to race. So when I found the Gobbler Grind event, I decided to participate because it allowed me to complete another race before the end of the year and check off the state of Kansas.

Aptly named for taking place so close to Thanksgiving, the Gobbler Grind was a relatively small event (1,323 half marathon participants; 241 full marathon participants) in Overland Park, a suburb of Kansas City.

A far cry from the downtown location of the bigger city races, the start and finish were about a mile from the host hotel. That was more or less within walking distance to most of what I was interested in, so I didn't have to rent a car.

Traveling the day before the race was more hectic than usual because for some reason, I did not pack the night before. That is unusual for me because I can't stand to be rushed on the day of travel, but there I was, up at 5:00 for a 9:10 flight, packing, dressing, etc. to get to the airport on time. Although I cut it way too close for comfort, I made it in time and after a short layover in Nashville, we landed safely in Kansas City, Missouri.

Since the airport is in Missouri, not Kansas, the hotel did not provide shuttle service to the airport, which was about 35 minutes away. So I pre-paid for a round trip ticket with the Super Shuttle, and within 10 minutes of landing, me and one other passenger were driven across the Missouri border into Kansas and then to the Doubletree Hotel in Overland Park.

It was about 1:30 when we arrived and my room still was not ready, so I went straight to the packet pickup area located in the lobby and was disappointed. There was no expo, just a packet pickup. However, the real disappointment was how unorganized it was. This probably shouldn't have been a big surprise considering that I sent an email to the race director in July and didn't receive a response until the week before the race.

Moreover, one of the volunteers told me there would be no gear check area in the morning. Are you kidding me, I thought?

The forecast was calling for starting temperatures in the low 40's and the walk to the start line was just over a mile. Naturally, we would need to check at the very least a jacket or coat of some kind. It was becoming clear to me that this was not going to be one of my better race experiences. At this point, I was just hoping to get through it successfully and check Kansas off the list.

If the lack of a gear check wasn't enough, I discovered that I forgot to pack a sports bra in my haste to pack that morning. That is why I always try to care of that task the night before—it is just too much going on the day of travel to add packing to the list. So, I put it on my list to pick up a sports bra while on my usual walk in the neighborhoods the day before the race.

Knowing there was a Whole Foods Market about 4 miles from the hotel, I asked the girls at the front desk if the route I planned to take had sidewalks. They said they weren't sure, and added that they couldn't believe that I was planning to walk 4 miles. When I reminded them that I was runner and there for the race the next day, they laughed and said "Oh yeah. That walk won't be anything for you but it is way too far for me to walk." People have got to get in better shape.

I started on my way with my trusted backpack, and as I walked through the various neighborhoods before turning into a commercial district, I was reminded of how different certain parts of our nation are from others. Simple and lacking fanfare, I detected no pretense here; it was "what you see is what you get."

The walk was great and just what I needed on such a beautiful day. Near Whole Foods was a New Balance store, a perfect place to pick up a sports bra.

The young lady waiting on me said that she was running in the 5k the next day and really admired the fact that I was on a 50-state quest. We had a nice conversation about health and fitness, and she said she was going to be more dedicated to improving in that area. It is always nice when you can influence someone in a positive manner. I purchased the sports bra without needing to try it on and it remains my favorite one to this day.

From there I went to Whole Foods and was disappointed with the selection at the hot bar. Moreover, they didn't carry several of my staple goodies like glee gum or the brand of fiber bars I like. I was able to get enough for dinner, as well as my yogurt and fruit for in the morning.

I ate my dinner in their dining room before calling the hotel for a limo service they used. It cost me $12 to get back to the hotel but with a couple of bags of groceries, walking an additional 4 miles wasn't too realistic. The limo picked me up and the driver was incredibly nice. We talked about the race and my 50-state quest (it seems like I was telling everyone about it on this trip), and when we got to the hotel, he said, "You have a great personality." His comments made me feel good.

Once in my room, I put away my groceries and began prepping for race mode. I laid out my running clothes and began preparing myself mentally for the race ahead. This was going to be an important run because it would be my final race of the year—and what a year it had been. I really wanted to finish well so I prayed for a good night's sleep and a safe and healthy half marathon.

I woke up before my 6:00 wake-up call and felt pretty good. I ate my goat milk yogurt and some Kombucha but was careful because I had a bit of an upset stomach the night before. I'm not sure if it was something I ate or just nerves considering that this would be my final race of the year. Either way, I wanted to be careful with my stomach before starting the race.

I went downstairs to check the temperature and it felt great. Not too cold with just a slight breeze. Another runner was checking the temperature too and she asked me if I was planning to wear shorts and I told her that I always do, even when it is super cold. I further stated that I need several layers on my upper body but when it comes to my legs, unless it is blistering cold, (like in Little Rock and Birmingham) I prefer to wear shorts. We kept talking and it turns out, she runs events all over the country as well and she was as surprised as I was to know that they didn't provide a gear check at this race. We laughed it off and wished each other a great race.

Since there was no gear check, I wore 3 tech shirts including the one they gave me. I knew that I wouldn't need that many once the race began, but I get so cold before the race starts. Since I couldn't stay in the hotel right up to the start time, I knew that I needed to have enough clothing to keep me warm before the race began.

The 1-mile walk to the start wasn't bad and I was comfortable even with the breeze. I got to the starting area about 15 minutes before the race began so I continued to stretch before lining up.

I must have been excited because I ran the first two miles at a 7:30 minute pace. I knew that there was no way I could keep that up for 13.1 miles so I immediately slowed down and by mile 3, I was back at my usual 8:30-8:45 minute/mile pace.

I was doing well until mile 5 and then boom; I got really tired. In other words, I hit the wall big time and that is unusual for me so early in the race. Although not sure why, I think it had to do with my upset stomach the night before. I didn't have my natural energy from fuel because my stomach was totally empty except for the ½ cup of yogurt I had about 2 hours before the start.

The constant hills didn't help. Most of the course was a series of up and down. It never really flattened out, but somehow, I found another gear and by mile 7, I had about 20 seconds to the good before reaching the 1-hour mark. So I was where I wanted to be half way through the race, but I was dog tired. I just couldn't get my breath and by now, my legs had gotten very heavy. This was unusual territory for me and I wasn't sure how to turn it around. To help, I stopped for Gatorade at every water station from mile 7 until the end of the race.

Miles 8, 9 & 10, were boring and so tough. By the start of mile 10, I needed to finish the race in the next 32 minutes in order to complete it in less than 2 hours. Thus, I had to maintain a 10 minute/mile pace until the end. That was fine until the last 1.5 miles which were the hardest I can ever remember in any race I had completed up to that point. I don't remember longing for the finish line more than I did in Kansas. Everything just kind of shut down and all I could do was just put one foot in front of the other. I didn't hear anything around me and I didn't see anyone near me. I was just so tired.

Although I don't know how except just sheer adrenaline, I managed to sprint the final .1 miles to a finish time of 1:57:46! To me, that was like winning the gold medal given how exhausted I was.

The reviews for this race weren't that favorable and I could see why. The one I wrote wasn't favorable either.

Totally exhausted and desperately needing water, I was shocked to find that they had no bottled water at the finish. There were just two women dunking cups with their bare hands into a water bin. How nasty I thought—and the only food I saw was sliced oranges.

Even more disappointing than the lack of post-race food and water was the finisher's medal. Small and plain, it didn't denote the city, state, date—nothing really. It just says Gobbler Grind with the year on the back. For the registration fee alone, a better medal is the least they can do here. Needless to say that I wasted no time returning to the hotel, where I quickly showered and dressed. I was ready to leave Kansas and return home to a good meal and my own comfortable bed.

Although this was one of my least favorite races and destinations on my 50-state journey, it yielded two very important things. One, it allowed me to check state #42 off the list. Two, it enabled me to have a successful finish to one of the greatest years of the journey so far.

With just eight states left on my quest, I was in rare form and looking forward to a restful December to prepare for the home stretch of this amazing expedition.

2011: The Home Stretch

It seemed almost impossible to imagine that I had only eight states to go to complete my 50-state quest. In some ways, it seemed like it had just begun, and in other ways, I could feel every bit of the nearly 3-year journey.

Of the eight remaining events, four occurred in states I had never been to before and seven occurred in cities I'd only read about and was on fire to see and explore. Moreover, these final 8 races were a mixture of just about every long distance, with five half marathons, two 10ks, and one full marathon. Albeit unplanned, this mix of distances helped to provide the perfect summary to an amazing 3-1/2 year quest.

If I could use one word to sum up the last leg of this journey, it would be "excitement." From finding the races to making the arrangements to actually being there, the entire process generated more passion and joy than ever before. I loved every minute of it.

So onward and upward with the final 8; may the vicarious ride be as grand as the actual one.

Race 44

P.F. Chang's Rock-n-Roll Arizona Half Marathon

Phoenix, Arizona - January 16, 2011

Starting the Year Off Right

I couldn't have picked a better event to start the year than a half marathon with the always reliable Rock-n-Roll organization. Given that I had never spent any significant time in Phoenix, I knew that by participating in another Rock-n-Roll race, I could really focus on seeing the city and being back on the race course. Moreover, this race provided the opportunity to run in not one, but three cities. The race began in Phoenix, then went into Scottsdale, and concluded in Tempe. With all these pluses, I couldn't wait to get to Arizona.

I wanted to take my time exploring this cluster of cities so I decided to make it a mini-vacation of sorts, arriving on Friday and not departing until early Monday morning. This way, I could be assured of seeing everything I wanted to see and with the two-hour difference in time zones (eastern to mountain), travel was just easier to arrange with mostly morning flights. Also, with their METRO Light Rail service, zipping through the area would be easy and would eliminate the need for renting a car, thankfully.

With a plethora of hotels to choose from, I chose the Hilton Garden Inn Phoenix Airport North and I couldn't have been happier with my choice. Relatively new (built in 2009), it was across the street from a METRO station and more than matched my standard for cleanliness and kindness. Upon landing at 4:15 p.m. MT, I contacted the hotel for the shuttle to pick me up. Another lady boarded at the same time and it turns out that she was from Charlotte in Phoenix on business all week. It's a small world.

The weather was amazing with sunny skies and temperatures in the mid-70s. There was no way I could resist taking advantage of weather like that so I grabbed my backpack and headed straight for the train station to travel to the Whole Foods Market in Tempe. I cut across the Gateway Community College campus as a short cut to the station and was there in mere minutes.

After reading the ticket dispenser instructions, I purchased a 3-day pass for $10.50 and began a conversation with two guys also waiting. They were natives of the area so we talked about how great their weather is all year long.

Also, they said the metro officers hardly ever ride the trains and check for tickets. I bristled when they said this because someone told me that same thing several years ago about the bus system in Las Vegas. Sure enough, the very time I did not purchase a ticket, an officer was on board checking and I had to get off at the next stop. I was determined that would never happen to me again no matter where I was, so I told them thanks for the heads up, but I would have a ticket with me at all times that weekend.

And wouldn't you know it, as soon as we sat down on the train, the officer came around to check for tickets. Several people were escorted off at the next stop, and when I looked over at those two guys, they just smiled and shrugged. I was glad I totally ignored their advice on that one.

I think I rode for about 7 or 8 stops before getting to the Rural Road stop at the ASU stadium. Since the race ended in the stadium, I wanted to get a look at the area before Sunday's race so I got off the metro there.

I walked around and could see why Arizona State University has one of the largest enrollments of any postsecondary institution in the country. With the great weather and expansive campus, it is a very inviting place. I didn't dawdle too much since it was getting late and I knew I'd spend much more time there on Sunday after the race, so I returned to the station to find the bus I needed to take to get to Whole Foods. I asked around and found out that I needed to take bus # 72 going south. With my 3-day pass, I boarded the bus and rode it for about six stops before being let out right in front of the Whole Foods door on Rural Road.

I really liked this area and this part of town. Tempe had a vibe to it that I found appealing mostly because I love college towns. While there was much more to this area than ASU, the pulse of this city was still very much geared toward the younger, educated crowd, which is always to my liking.

After walking around, I finally made my way to Whole Foods and was impressed with its size and variety. I picked up all my staples: yogurt, watermelon, cantaloupe, cottage cheese, and Kombucha and some hot vegetables and chicken from the hot bar for dinner. I ate outside before getting back on the bus and then light rail to the hotel. As I was walking across Gateway, it started getting dark and I was thankful for a wonderful first day in Phoenix. I couldn't wait to see what the next day would bring.

On race morning, I was up by 6:00 a.m. for the 8:30 start. It was another gorgeous day weather-wise and since the hotel shuttle was taking runners to the METRO station, I was able to take my time and stay totally relaxed.

I boarded the train at 7:48 and it was crowded. There were no empty seats so I had to stand with many others until we reached our stop. From there, it was a 1-mile walk to the runner's village where we would start. I was prepared for this since the pre-race literature made it clear but it was still a longer walk than I would have liked to make before a race. Also, I had to use the restroom, which is why I prefer races where my hotel is within walking distance to the start; no public restroom needed.

It took a while to find where the gear check trucks (it was a nice day but I still needed to check my jacket) were located and the lines for the porta-potties along the way were a mile long. I saw one woman duck behind some bushes and although I would never do that, I certainly understood her need to do so. You see men doing this all the time in races, but of course, it is much easier for them to get away with it.

With over 25,000 participants in the half and full, it was necessary to institute a wave start. My corral number was 2 but the gear check trucks were located near corral 30, so I had to weave my way through 28 corrals to get there. While in route, I noticed some port-a-potties off to the side with barely anyone in line. I was in-and-out within 30 seconds and able to check my jacket with about 5 minutes to get back up to my corral and start the race. I definitely cut it close, but I made it.

My corral started at exactly 8:32 a.m. Because the course was mostly flat, I really wanted to finish in less than 2 hours. I completed the first mile in 8:15 minutes but slowed to 8:50 minutes for mile 2. The tiered start prevented the usual bottlenecking for the first few miles so I was able to establish my pace right away. I was concerned that it had been over 1-1/2 months since my last half marathon distance, nonetheless I was right where I wanted to be.

By mile 7, I was just 10 seconds past the 1-hour mark so I was happy. Around mile 5, I ate an electrolyte candy I picked up at the expo and was fine until mile 8.5 when I drank some Cytomax. By this time, we were crossing into Scottsdale from Phoenix and for some strange reason, my legs starting getting heavy. I thought I might have some trouble with my foot, but not my legs. Nonetheless, the heaviness grew so I drank more Cytomax at mile 9.5.

I was fine until the uphill portion of mile 11. Out of nowhere, I felt a sharp pain in my right knee just above the kneecap. It was hurting like crazy, and all I could think was "What's going on here?" Not since the early days on this journey had I experienced all these pains and it was really confusing me.

The thought of stopping the race occurred to me for about ½ of a second before I dug in deep and committed to finishing this race. I started the race too strongly to finish poorly.

As I pushed toward the final miles, the spectator support really picked up as we entered Tempe. My energy level kept increasing as I made that final turn between ASU's Sun Devil and Sun Angel stadiums. I finished in a time of 1:57:27 and I couldn't have been more thankful.

After collecting my beautiful finisher's medal, I saw a woman wrapping people in ice so I asked if she would wrap my knee. I can't express the relief it provided. I felt good as new even though I had a big ice pack attached to my knee. I left it on for the next hour while in the runner's village until I started walking to the light rail.

One of the race photographers was taking pictures of runners throughout the village so I stopped to have my picture taken before checking out the post-race food tables. I picked up a bag of chips, box of raisins, and a bottle of water and Cytomax before getting my jacket from the gear check truck. It felt so good to warm up even though it was in the 60s by that point.

After the race, fully rested and ready to take advantage of that beautiful sunshine, I decided to take the light rail to the Mill Avenue District in downtown Tempe. I was told I'd find some of the most quaint retail shops, best food, and entertainment in the area. It was an easy ride on the light rail and I enjoyed Mill Avenue very much. Having very much of the "college" feel to it, I found the many shops to be interesting and fun, With so many runners in town, it was even more crowded than it usually is with all the college students.

The main sponsor of this running event was P.F. Chang's and as a participant, I received a 10% discount card that I decided to use while in town. I was terribly hungry by this time and since it was right in front of me, I thought there was no better time than the present to have something to eat there. Practically full, I took a seat at the bar and watched some of the playoff game between the Patriots and the Jets while enjoying some wonton soup and edamame. Several other runners were at the bar as well, and we all agreed the race had been great in just about every way. It felt good to have it completed and to enjoy the fellowship of others who were equally excited about their weekend in Phoenix.

Every aspect of the weekend in Phoenix was great. I wouldn't have changed a thing about this part of my journey. I knew that if this first race of the year was any indication, I was going to have an amazing seven remaining races. I was looking forward to every single one of them.

Race 45

Hyannis 10k

Hyannis, Massachusetts - February 27, 2011

Who Needs A Boston Marathon When You Have Snow and The Kennedy Compound?

The most common question I've been asked since I started road racing is "When do you plan to run the Boston Marathon?" Usually, this question is asked by those unfamiliar with the running world. Those more informed understand that in order to run in the Boston Marathon, one must either qualify by running in a certified marathon within a certain time limit or by raising a certain amount of money through a pre-designated charity program.

Nonetheless, because of its popularity, the Boston Marathon is the only association the average person has to running, so for that reason alone, I purposely avoided any races in Boston as part of my 50-state quest. For my Massachusetts race, I wanted to explore a part of the state that was steeped in history (just about the whole state qualifies in that regard) and was off the radar as a typical place to race.

Given this criteria, many places drew my interest, but just one fulfilled what I truly wanted from this experience: Hyannis. The largest of the seven villages in the town of Barnstable on Cape Cod, it is the home of the John F. Kennedy Museum, the renowned Kennedy Compound, and one of the most popular road races in all of New England.

After the personal endorsement from the runner I met at the Baltimore Half Marathon, I knew this was an opportunity I didn't want to pass up, so I registered for the race in October. Although I was cognizant of what the weather could be in Massachusetts in February, it never occurred to me that it might be severe enough to prevent me from getting to the race. In retrospect, the threat of bad weather added to the excitement and thrill of the 44th state of my journey.

I had nearly 4 months to plan for this event, and with each passing month, the excitement continued to mount. I don't know why that always seems to happen when it comes to races in New England; I think it has to do with my love for that part of the nation.

Not only did I have plenty of time to coordinate my transportation and lodging, but I was able to really research the area, identifying the places I wanted to go to and the things I wanted to see while there. In certain respects, I don't know that I've ever been more prepared for a race than this one.

My travel day started early—4:00 a.m. to be exact. It took two flights to finally land in Boston at 10:00 a.m. I arranged to take the 10:45 Plymouth & Brockton bus to Hyannis. We made five stops before reaching the Hyannis exit at 12:45. I can't tell you how much I love sitting back and observing the southwestern route to the Cape from the bus window. When you drive as often as I do, the opportunity to relax and watch the world go by as a passenger is so refreshing. I was surprised how quickly the time passed.

Once at The Depot, I took a cab to the hotel for $7.50 and checked into my room at "The Resort & Conference Center at Hyannis." Serving as the location for the start, finish, packet pickup, and pasta dinner, the convenience was unbeatable.

Although a terrible winter storm dropped several inches of snow and ice on the ground two days prior, the day before the race was fine. There were still pockets of snow here and there, but the sun was shining brightly and although still cold, it was a beautiful day in Hyannis.

I knew deep down it was going to be an amazing weekend.

Early in the morning on race day, a combination of snow and rain began to fall. The race was not designated to start until 10:00 a.m. While I would normally frown at such a late start, in this case I was thankful for it because the longer we waited, the better chance the sun would have of melting away any residual slick spots along the course.

I went downstairs to the buffet and got a nice hot cup of coffee and a cup of yogurt. It hit the spot. I looked outside and saw that it was lightly raining but not snowing, although there was snow on top of all the cars. Thankfully, the roads looked to be all clear.

I took my time getting ready and didn't leave the hotel until 9:50 since the start was literally right outside the door of the hotel lobby. Prepared for the inclement weather, I wore my long spandex pants with a pair of shorts on top of them, my long winter Nike tech shirt with an N.C. State sweatshirt and my zippered sport rain coat that I got in St. George, Utah. I wore my black toboggan with the hood of my rain coat tied tightly to my head. I really needed that because by the time the race started, the rain had turned to snow and it was really coming down.

In the first quarter of a mile, I was thankful that the road felt fine with no icy or slick areas. The inconvenience were the water puddles that left my feet soaking wet before the first mile. I didn't do a warm-up run but I didn't worry about it; had I been running a half marathon, I would have warmed up more. For the 10k, I felt confident that I would be fine.

The snowflakes continued coming down and my face basically stayed wet throughout the entire race. I had on double gloves and they were totally soaked before we made our final turn. Around mile 3, the snow became sleet and then eventually just rain, but there was some form of precipitation throughout all 6.22 miles of this race.

It was also at mile 3 that I landed in another puddle and my right foot shoe was filled with cold water. Oh well, I thought, there is nothing to do but run through it, which I did. In fact, after a while, the weather didn't bother me. I guess I got used to it because I don't remember ever being really cold in this race.

In spite of the snow/sleet/rain, the course was still picturesque and historical, taking us along Craigville Beach, Kalus Beach, the historic Hyannis Harbor, Lewis Bay, the John F. Kennedy Memorial, the Kennedy Family Compound, Officer Michel Aselton Memorial Park and the memorizing Cape Cod villages of Hyannis port and Centerville. Particularly moving to me was running in front of the Kennedy Compound. Although the weather made it hard to see much, being so near that enclave of homes I'd only seen in documentaries and Kennedy home movies was truly a racing highlight for me.

I was disappointed that I did not familiarize myself with the course better because if I had, I would have known where the 10k runners were to veer off from the half marathon course. Instead, I thought the turn came sooner than it did and I kept slowing down to make sure I didn't miss it. When it finally came up at mile 5, it was well marked and I lost precious seconds for nothing. I don't think it would have made that much difference in my time, but I always want to do my very best when I'm on the race course. My reason for slowing down here was a result of not being as well-prepared as I should have been.

Nonetheless, I was able to pick up some speed and really pour it on at the end to finish well. The medal was amazing and as soon as I collected it, I went inside where the post-race area was set up due to the bad weather.

They had a great selection of food, including some delicious soup, protein drinks, bottled water and hot chocolate. Since I was scheduled to board the 12:30 bus back to Boston, I needed to shower and dress quickly. The hotel arranged for a cab to pick me up at 12:15 so I had just enough time to check my official finish time before checking out. I was pleasantly surprised to discover that I had finished the race in 51:53 with an 8:29 minute/mile average pace. Considering the weather, water puddles, and my ignorance of where to make the final turn, I was more than satisfied with my finish time.

When I first arrived in Hyannis, I grabbed my backpack and set out on foot to the John F. Kennedy Hyannis Museum. It was just over a mile and thankfully, there was plenty of sunshine if not much warmth. I wrapped up well and got one of the maps at the front desk of the downtown area. It was a straight walk to the museum and along the way, I could tell that I was falling in love with Hyannis. I couldn't help but be drawn to the historic quality of its downtown Main Street, full of charm and sophistication.

I absolutely loved everything about the museum. As I mentioned before, I love to learn, and this museum was an education all by itself. I enjoyed taking the walk down memory lane that uncovered John F. Kennedy's youth and summers in Hyannis. Particularly interesting to me was a videotape of Rose Kennedy taking us through the history of her family, starting with her father who was a two-term mayor of Boston.

Just like the Civil Rights Institute in Birmingham and the Clinton Presidential Library in Little Rock, the JFK Museum in Hyannis added to the richness of my 50-state quest. It provided me with a wealth of knowledge and understanding that I couldn't bear to think of my life without at this point. It was hard to imagine how the day could get any better, but it did.

After the tour, I purchased some mementos in the gift shop and had a lovely conversation with the ladies who worked there. Their Boston accents coupled with my obvious southern drawl made for interesting discussion and chuckles all around. We talked about a variety of topics, most notably about the weather for tomorrow's race.

In a way, I love to "get lost" in a new town because you really observe your surroundings much more closely, but sometimes, it can be dangerous if you are not careful. The day was so beautiful and there was still plenty of sunshine to help me navigate through the residential communities.

On most of the roads, there was no sidewalk and very few cars out, but that didn't deter me one bit. I loved seeing the style of homes in this part of the peninsula. Unlike so many communities throughout the country, I saw no "cookie-cutter" homes here. Each one had its own distinct style and character, much the way I would classify Hyannis as a whole. I enjoyed being there, and in many ways, it felt like I was the only person around for miles.

As I weaved my way through the numerous neighborhood streets, I became totally lost in the peace of it all, and didn't even notice that it was getting quite dark. "Uh oh" I thought—"Am I still going in the right direction?" I finally came upon a gas station and asked the attendant if I was going the right way. He replied, "Yes, but you've got a ways to go." That "ways to go" was almost 5 miles! I must have really gotten caught up in the moment because I was way off course. So I started double-timing it for another 45 minutes or so before taking a left turn on the main road and finally seeing my hotel. It was exactly 6:15 and the pre-race pasta dinner started at 6:30, so I had just enough time to quickly freshen up before the meal was served.

I sat with a very nice lady named Anita and her young son, Travis. They were from Long Island and two of the nicest people I think I've ever met. Eventually, a young couple from Boston joined us and they too were super nice. I loved our conversations and the food was delicious, especially the meatballs. In fact, I had two helpings!

Jack Fultz, Boston Marathon winner in 1976, was the guest speaker. His stories on winning the Boston Marathon and several other races were interesting and motivating. But because my stomach was so full of pasta, and because I had traversed quite a few miles that day, I got sleepy toward the end of his speech.

Everything about this event is top notch. From an outstanding website to an awesome finisher's medal, there was no guess work needed on the part of the participant.

As I reflected on the weekend, all I could do was smile. I could not have enjoyed my time in Hyannis more. There is a regal and intelligent quality to this great town that appeals to me very much. I love places like Hyannis and I'm in total peace when I become a part of their community, if only for 24 hours.

There's no such thing as a perfect weekend but mine in Hyannis certainly comes close. What a blessing!

Race 46

Shamrock Run 15k
Portland, Oregon - March 13, 2011

The Only 15k Out of All 50

D ue to the many years of success of the track and field and cross-country teams at the University of Oregon, there are many who regard the state of Oregon as the running capital of the United States. It is home to the Nike headquarters. Many elite runners choose to train in Oregon, so, needless to say, there is no shortage of races to choose from.

Having never been to Oregon before, I wanted to find a race that was different from any other event on my journey up to that point. So when I discovered an event called the "Shamrock Run," I knew it was the one for two reasons: 1) It took place in Portland, the largest city in the state, and 2) the distance was 15k (9.32 miles), the only 9+ mile race in my 50-state quest. Meeting most everything else on my wish list, I didn't hesitate to register nearly 2 months before the race.

For races where I have to travel across country, I will always spend a minimum of two nights, and usually more. The 3-hour time change from west coast to east coast kind of make it a necessity, and besides, I had never been to Portland and didn't want to rush through this city. So I arranged to arrive in the early afternoon on Saturday and fly back on Monday.

As usual, my travel day started early for the first of two flights to Portland. I had enough points for a free ticket with Southwest Airlines so I was able to save on airfare. Moreover, I had enough points through the Hilton Honors Program to get both nights at the Embassy Suites Downtown for free. So actually, this was one of the most economical cross-country trips of the journey so far.

The host hotel was Hotel Fifty, 4 blocks from the start and finish lines. Since I had the points for a free stay with a Hilton property, I searched until I found one (Embassy Suites) that seemed to be in the same vicinity. I wrote the race director about it and he was wonderful with his responsiveness, indicating that while the Embassy Suites was three blocks west of the start line, it was 11 blocks (about a ½ mile) from the finish line. I weighed the odds of distance vs. cost and decided to stay at the Embassy Suites with was an easy walk to the start line. I figured I'd work out the details of getting back to the hotel after the race when that time came.

We landed 5 minutes early in Portland at 12:35 p.m. and I headed straight to the MAX, Portland's light rail system. You know by now that I love to use public transportation when I travel and Portland has one of the most extensive, including light rail, commuter rail, buses, and streetcars. For $2.25 I purchased a 2-hour pass for the light rail that was more than sufficient to get me downtown. I was on the train for nearly 15 minutes before we finally pulled off. By then, it was 1:15 and the expo was to end at 3:00.

While every race provides time in the early morning hours on race day for people to pick up their running bibs and timing chips, I always prefer to attend the expo the day before the race if possible. It is just a good way to ensure that all of your information is correct without having the wait to the last minute if something is wrong. Moreover, I enjoy meeting the race officials and perusing the vendor tables at the expo. To me, it is a pleasant part of the whole racing experience.

However, with it being 1:15 already, I wasn't sure how much time I would have to check into my hotel and then make my way to the Portland Convention Center where the expo was being held. My guess was that I'd run into serious time constraints considering that the expo ended in less than 2 hours. Just then, I received revelation and looked at the train schedule I picked up before boarding. In doing so, I noticed the convention center stop was before the stop to my hotel, so I stopped at the convention center first to make sure I didn't miss anything pertaining to the expo.

I had my suitcase and backpack with me but I knew the expo wasn't going to be that big so it really wasn't a hassle. I picked up my packet, scanned my timing chip, picked up my tech shirt, and observed the tables of the few vendors in attendance before reboarding the train for the stop to my hotel.

In 4-5 more stops, I was near the hotel and even though it was a block away, I still had to ask for directions. When I finally got there, I was pleased with the suite and the location of the hotel which was important considering that I was going to be there 2 days.

I received a wake-up call at 6:45 but I was up way before that since I was still operating on Eastern Standard Time. Moreover, we turned our clocks up one hour due to Daylight Savings Time so I was just all over the place that morning.

At 7:00, I decided to have a light breakfast at the hot bar in the hotel. Normally, I just stick to my yogurt but I had a feeling it was going to be a slower than usual run for one primary reason —RAIN. To quote the cliché, it was raining cats and dogs. So my race attire was very similar to what I wore last month in Hyannis; tights with shorts on top, my Nike tech shirt, my thin Louisville pullover, and my short rain jacket. I didn't add a sweatshirt and I'm glad because it was nearly 50 degrees and rising, so it wasn't cold—it was just rainy.

I did my stretches in the room before praying to the good Lord for a safe race. I jogged to the starting line for my warm-up run and as I got near the front, it was only 8:25, so I stood under a canopy along with several other runners.

As they were stretching, I asked them if they were running the 15k (there was an 8k and a 5k taking place also) and they said they were. Then one of them asked me if I had ever run the 15k before, to which I replied no and further stated that I was from the east coast and had never run in Oregon before.

When I said that, it seemed like all of them in unison said "Then be aware that this is a VERY hilly course." I knew from the pre-race literature that it wasn't an easy course but they made it seem like it was equivalent to climbing Mt. Everest.

I left the canopy and was in line by the start at 8:35. Surprisingly, I ran mile 1 & 2 in 13 minutes. I knew that I was going way too fast and if I tried to keep that up, I was going to have a miserable finish time.

I have no idea why I started like that; my guess is that I was anticipating those big hills I was told about, so I wanted to make up for the time I knew I'd lose trying to do all that climbing. Nonetheless, I took it down and not a moment too soon because after mile 3 near Portland State University, we started at steady uphill climb of about 500 feet that lasted about 3 miles.

I was not shy about taking little walk breaks in between the strides, especially inside Marquam Nature Park. We ran there for about a mile before eventually turning onto Barbour Street. This was significant because the people I stretched with under the canopy said that once you reach Barbour Street, it is all downhill from there. So around the 6.5 mile mark, we entered Barbour Street and I tried to pour it on for those last two miles since I knew I had run the middle part of the race very slowly.

I was so thankful to cross the finish line for this one because the combination of rain and hills made it more difficult than most races. As soon as my foot hit the finish pad, I shouted louder than usual "Praise the Lord" and drew some interesting looks from a couple of people. I hope my exclamation moved them to know who He is if they didn't already. One of the volunteers put the finisher's medal around my neck and I was so impressed with the unique design in the shape of a bottle opener.

I knew by my watch that I had finished somewhere in the 1:24 area but I couldn't find the results booth in order to get my official time. Besides, the rain was really pouring down by this time so I made my way over to the food area hoping to get some of the clam chowder I was told about but when I got there, it was too crowded and just too wet. I couldn't even find some bottled water so I decided to start jogging back to my hotel since it was a good 11 blocks away.

One of my friends who had run a race in Portland the previous year told me about the Portland Saturday Market which is a huge outdoor arts and crafts market located in downtown Portland. So, the day before the race I went to take a look. I had not originally planned to attend, but since there was about an hour before it ended, and the rain looked to be staying away for the moment, I decided to stop by.

Although it was slowly closing down, it appeared to be nearly 250 artists and exhibitors there showcasing goods and services in just about every category. Though interesting, it was very similar to hundreds of street fairs I've attended all over the country.

After that, I decided to walk to the start line to make sure I knew where to go in the morning. There were lots of people milling around downtown Portland that day and I remember thinking that this is one vibrant city. I liked it right away and felt very comfortable there. At the Westside Riverwalk, I strolled along the Willamette River and found it easy to see why the residents of Portland thought a lot of their city. I did too.

With still no threat of rain, I kept walking the downtown streets hoping to see as much as Portland as I could. From Washington to Adler to 9th to 5th to Burnside; you name the street, I walked it.

Along the way were great restaurants and more retail than I expected. I came upon a great bookstore called Powell's Books. It caught my eye because so many people were going in and out of it.

I needed some postcards so I decided to join them. I purchased five for $1.00. Since there is no sales tax in Oregon, it came to exactly $1.00 and I was reminded how much I admire states that cut out excess taxes.

I enjoyed Portland, Oregon and look forward to returning one day. It would have been nice to spend some time after the race exploring it a bit more, but I experienced enough to know I was glad it was one of my destinations on the 50-state quest.

Race 47

Albuquerque Half Marathon
Albuquerque, New Mexico - April 16, 2011

Some of the Best Races Are Wrapped In Smaller Packages

In April 1998, I drove solo from North Carolina to California in 4-1/2 days and unwittingly, gave birth to the 50-state quest, or at least the desire to see this nation.

I was far from being a "walker" at that time, much less a runner. My plan was to stop in Flagstaff, Arizona on my 3rd day of the trip and drive north from there to visit the Grand Canyon. However, an unexpected snow storm 80 miles east of Albuquerque drastically changed my plans. Without much warning concerning its severity, I-40 West quickly turned into an ice rink, causing an accident that left me and hundreds of other drivers stranded on the interstate for nearly 2 hours.

Once we started slowly moving again, the trauma of the past two hours caused my enthusiasm for the Grand Canyon to be supplanted with the desire to get off the road for the day and just relax. Once I reached the interchanges for Albuquerque, I decided to wing it and see what this city was all about. As a result, I had an amazing time in a part of the country I knew nothing about, enjoying a wonderful dinner and a movie near the hotel I chose for that evening.

I don't know if it was the spontaneity of it all or just the charm of Albuquerque, but I was determined to return to this city and see more of it. Thankfully, I would get the chance to do just that when I elected to run a half marathon there, nearly 13 years to the date of my first visit.

The Albuquerque Half Marathon is a perfect example of how a smaller race can be just as, and often more, exciting and rewarding than races with tens of thousands of participants. I had never heard of this race before I discovered it via the Internet. Once I started inquiring about it within the running community, I heard nothing but good things. When the reviews of a race are overwhelmingly positive, it mostly has to do with a great race director, an informative website, a nice finisher's medal, and kind volunteers. I'm thankful to say this race had all of those qualities—and more.

Although the course was an out-and-back (my favorite), there were hardly any lodging options within walking distance of the start and finish, mostly due to it's location. Instead of being located in the downtown area near hotels and restaurants, this half marathon took place north of downtown in the Village of Los Ranchos de Albuquerque.

As you know by now, logistically I prefer to be within walking distance of everything pertaining to the race, even if that distance is up to 6 miles. However, with this race, I made an exception because I was excited about running in actual neighborhoods and seeing how this city really looked. I had already seen the downtown area when I stopped in Albuquerque in 1998—now, I was interested in getting beyond the city limits and exploring the more scenic, less populated areas.

With a course that included the Albuquerque Open Space, the Casa Rodena Winery, and the scenic Rio Grande Blvd. (adjacent to the Rio Grande River), I knew I couldn't go wrong with this race. Moreover, it was one of the flattest courses in my tenure of running. Even though I would need to rent a car, this race was still my number one choice for my New Mexico event.

My wake-up call was scheduled for 5:45 but I was up well before that time. I had a really good night's sleep and a long one, so I was as refreshed as I can ever remember being for a race. I even prayed in bed before rising which is always a sign for me that I am relaxed and unrushed. I went downstairs at 6:00 and got some coffee to slowly sip while eating some of my yogurt.

I stuck to my plan and was out the door by 6:50. Thankfully, I had no problem finding a parking space in the recommended Presbyterian Church parking lot. How unique that God was in this race, right down to the parking.

I talked to a man in a car beside mine about when to start walking to the start area. I needed to pick up our timing chips and to check my jacket in at the gear check area. He and I had the same idea - to stay in our cars with the heat on until the last possible minute. Although it was expected to get into the mid-70's, at that time of morning it was barely in the 40s.

Around 7:30, I started my walk to the start, which was farther than I thought, and not such an easy stroll. The path to the start was a long ½ mile trail on a part-dirt, part-sand road. Needless to say it was not a fun walk to make so early in the morning.

Once at the starting area, I stood in line to get my timing chip and then to baggage claim to check my jacket and gloves. It all went smoothly but then we had to walk back down the sandy trail about a quarter of a mile to get to the actual start line. On the walk back down, I stretched a little and jogged the rest of the way and that was the extent of my warm up. It wasn't much but I felt good and confident that it was going to be a good run.

The first mile was really tough because the road was narrow, so everyone was jumbled up together even though this was a smaller race (506 total runners). Also, the dirt and sand were tough to maneuver through. I didn't read the notes on the course's terrain and started to wonder if the entire course was trail and not road. At that point all I could do was try and pick up the pace because I ran the first mile in 9:30 minutes, well off my usual pace.

Thankfully after 1.5 miles, the course turned to road surfaces and I was in my element. I started picking up the pace and was pleasantly surprised that I was only 1.5 minutes over the one hour mark once I reached mile 7. Given the extremely slow start, I didn't mind being a little behind my normal half marathon pace.

The middle part of this race was typical with miles 8 through 10 being rather quiet and uneventful. I took my first drink of Gatorade at mile 8 and was pleasantly surprised by how cold it was. By the time we got to mile 11, the course turned to all downhill until we crossed the finish line.

I knew from my watch that I had finished in the 1:56 range and I was thrilled! I lifted my hands to the Lord in thanksgiving (as I do after every race) and praised Him audibly because I knew He had everything to do with my victory that day. I had no pains or discomforts of any kind in this race; it was a healthy run and I felt incredible afterwards.

With my lovely finisher's medal around my neck, I made my way over to the baggage area to put on my jacket. I saw the race director's wife whom I had talked to the day before at the packet pickup. I asked her if I could find out my official finish time because I had to catch a plane and could not stay. She told that the official times wouldn't be ready for another hour, but if I did place in my age group, I would receive the prize in the mail. She even wrote down my address and bib number just in case.

She and her husband turned out to be two upstanding people. Sure enough, with an official finish time of 1:56:41, I placed 3rd in my age group and not long after that weekend, I received a lovely medal prize in the mail. There was also a note from the race director congratulating me on my run. To me, that personal touch is what turns a good running event into a great one.

When I picked up my rental car, I programmed into my GPS system all the places I wanted to visit while in town, and proceeded straight to my hotel. Because location wasn't that important since I had a car and didn't need to rely on public transportation, I sought a hotel that wasn't too old and not terribly expensive. Thus, I chose a great Hilton Garden Inn about 10 miles from the start of the race. My room wasn't ready when I arrived so they upgraded me at no charge to room with a Jacuzzi. I was very pleased with the cleanliness of the room. Hilton Garden Inns seldom disappoint.

First, I decided to get some lunch at one of the two Whole Foods Markets in Albuquerque. Although the hot bar was no great shakes, I was able to get my staples and enough to satisfy my appetite until I could get to the other location.

From there I went to Fleet Feet, a popular running shoe store where the packet pickup was held. As advertised, this was just a packet pickup; no large expo with lots of vendors. This was simply a table with your registration packet, cotton t-shirt, runners bib with safety pins, and flyers about other local events.

Although it was disappointing that we couldn't receive the timing chip until the morning of the race, I appreciated the good organization surrounding this event.

From the packet pickup, I decided to drive to the start area to make sure I knew how to get there in the morning. The parking area was a decent walk to the start line so I walked it off to time it and recognized that I would have need to leave the hotel no later than 6:45 to secure a good parking space and prepare for the race without being rushed.

The area was beautiful and I was impressed with the North Valley neighborhoods. There is something very appealing about the southwestern adobe-style homes you find on nearly every street and it occurred to me as I walked past schools, churches, and homes that I could find myself being quite comfortable living in one of those communities. The kindness of the people combined with the natural beauty of the terrain makes it an easy place to appreciate.

I made my way back to the car and drove to Sports Authority to buy a new watch with a built-in heart-rate monitor (my old one died about 35,000 feet in the air) before heading to the other Whole Foods Market for some soup and vegetables.

By the time I drove back to the hotel it was 8:15 and I couldn't imagine where the time had gone. Since I was still on Eastern Standard Time, it was really two hours later for me. I was exhausted and knew that I needed some rest in order to be ready for the race the next day.

I loved my return visit to Albuquerque and am so thankful that the Albuquerque Half Marathon was the event I chose for the state of New Mexico.

My memories of this wonderful city and state bring me a lot of joy and blessing and that's why it is a place I plan to visit often in the future.

I couldn't have had a better experience in my 46th state of my journey.

Race 48

Cox Providence Half Marathon
Providence, Rhode Island - May 1, 2011

One of the Best Birthdays I've Ever Had

I f you recall, this whole "running thing" started on April 30, 2005, my 40th birthday. At that time I had no idea this avocation would take me all over America. At this point in 2011, almost exactly 6 years later, I was four states from accomplishing my goal of running a long distance event in all 50 states.

When I discovered that one of the remaining states, Rhode Island, held one of its most popular events the day after my birthday, it was a no-brainer that I would participate in this race. Since I fell in love with Rhode Island during my first visit there at the age of 12, I couldn't think of a better place to spend my birthday, and oh was I right!

On my birthday in 2011, I was up at 4:30 in preparation for my trip to Providence and I couldn't have been more energized. Literally everything about this trip excited me. I can't express how much I was looking forward to being there.

Logistically, you couldn't ask for a better race, with everything taking place in the lovely downtown area. I took the time to learn about this city and identify the places I wanted to make sure I visited. I didn't want to miss a thing.

Since Providence is one of the oldest cities in the United States and the capital of Rhode Island, there is a great deal of history to glean and I wanted to observe as much as I could. One of the first things on my "to do" list was tour the Brown University campus. After having such an amazing experience at Yale the previous autumn, I couldn't pass up the opportunity to visit another Ivy League university (I would tour Harvard as well but after my completion of the 50-state quest), so my plate was full for the next two days.

Upon landing around 10:30 a.m., I caught a shuttle to my hotel, the Hampton Inn & Suites Providence Downtown. This hotel was just minutes from almost everything including the start/finish line, the expo, Brown University, Providence College, shopping, food and all the other things that add fun to a race. It was a perfect location and I loved how it was situated on a cobblestone road.

So far, the Lord had been very generous to me on my birthday. He had allowed me safe passage to Providence and gorgeous weather for the entire weekend. I couldn't wait to see what else He had for me that day. As soon as I put my things in my room, I started my day of exploration at the expo at the Rhode Island Convention Center.

Now for a race of nearly 2400 half marathon participants and another nearly 1200 full marathoners, I expected a decent sized expo, but surprisingly, it was nothing more than a packet pickup.

Nevertheless, everything was in order for the race the next day so from there, I ventured to the closest Whole Foods Market about a mile away on N. Main Street and had a great lunch.

I don't know how, but I just knew that the race the next day was going to be one of my best.

Up at 6:00, I immediately went downstairs to the breakfast bar and got some oatmeal to go along with my yogurt. I checked the temperature outside. Although it was a cool breeze blowing, it was not freezing and I knew I'd be okay in the long-sleeve tech shirt I got in the Kansas race and the Providence t-shirt they gave me at the expo. I also wore a pair of black shorts that I like a lot and my "Jesus" cap.

Now I knew that the starting line was barely .35 miles from my hotel so I didn't have to rush; however, I almost pushed it too far. I took my time stretching and staying warm and departed the room at 7:51 right after praying. I slowly jogged to the starting line and just as I got into the thick of the crowd, I heard the announcer say "2 minutes." Oh uh, I thought. The runner's area was barricaded off from the spectators (which is normal) and for the life of me, I couldn't find an opening. I searched and searched and didn't see one, so just as I was about to jump the barricade, I spotted a very small opening that I thought I could squeeze through. Just as I brought my leg up, the announcer said "30 seconds." Wow, now that is really cutting it close.

My energy level was good right from the start. I felt refreshed, and since it had been only two weeks since my last half marathon in New Mexico, my body was well-trained and prepared to take on the 13.1 miles ahead. For the first 2 miles, the full marathoners and half marathoners ran together, which made for a total of almost 3,600 runners in tandem; however, overcrowding was never an issue. There were a few inclines; one at 2.5 miles that continued up to mile 5, and another around mile 7.5. While challenging, this was a relatively flat course and I was right on pace for the most part. Surprisingly, I did break my normal routine and get something to drink at mile 5 instead of waiting to mile 7. Even though I just took one gulp, it was enough to make a difference and got me back on track.

By this time in the race, we were running in some upscale neighborhoods and for some reason I was reminded of the races I did in Baltimore and Knoxville. I'm not sure why but these three races had the same "look" about them and I found that interesting. As we ran through certain neighborhoods, I could tell that I was running faster than I had in my last two races. Sure enough, when I reached mile 7, my watch indicated that I was 59:30 minutes into the race. It felt good to know that I was running ahead of schedule by 30 seconds. I stopped for water and Gatorade at the liquid station just before mile 8 and took about 30 seconds to take a gulp of both.

Miles 8-11 are usually difficult in any half marathon because that is where the fan support is the least, but in Providence, there were some spectators along the way at just about every major area of the race. Moreover, the sun was bright and the light breeze made it an excellent day to run. Just as we were coming around Blackstone Park, I drank one last time before focusing on a strong finish. I knew I was running well so I poured it on at the end as much as I could to a great finish time of 1:53:45. Not bad, I thought, for a person who turned 46 the day before! What a great additional birthday gift this race was!

An interesting thing happened at mile 11. There was a girl walking, or rather hopping, along the side of the course in obvious pain. She had a long, lean build and it was easy to tell that she was in great shape. However, as I watched her hobbling, I knew instantly that she was suffering from an IT band injury—the same injury that plagued me in my early races in San Diego, West Virginia, Arkansas, and Memphis. I could so relate to her discomfort so as I went past, I lifted a prayer for her and thanked God that my legs had remained healthy and strong for quite some time.

One of the volunteers handed me my finisher's medal, which was top-notch—and I immediately headed over to the finisher's village and got not one, but two cups of hot chocolate. It was so good and I continued to sip on it as I headed back to the hotel.

Once I showered and dressed, I walked back to Main Street and got a light lunch at Whole Foods before returning to the finisher's village and talked to some other runners about the day. We all agreed that it had been an amazing race and for me, it had been an amazing weekend and birthday. I truly wasn't ready to leave Providence but I had a plane to catch.

After lunch at Whole Foods, I was anxious to tour the Brown University campus. Although it had turned a little cloudy while I was on Main Street, the sun was starting to come out again and it was warming back up to where I like it to be (a great birthday gift from God). By the time I crossed the street to enter Brown's main campus, the sun was brilliantly shining and I was able to take a ton of video recordings of the campus and much of the residential areas near the school.

Just observing the students relaxing on the picturesque grounds made me think about my life and the poor choices I made regarding my education. Don't get me wrong—I'm thankful to be well-educated and to hold both an undergraduate and graduate degree from prestigious universities. However, if I'm being truthful, the Bridget in her 40's would have never chosen the schools or majors I did when I was in my late teens. Sadly, my decision-making skills were shallow in those days and based on nothing substantive. If I could start all over again, I would have definitely attended college somewhere in New England. I love the area so much. I would have majored in what brought me the most pleasure and where I had the most talent, which was the fine arts.

Unfortunately, I lacked the maturity and the proper guidance at 17. Yet, even though I didn't go that route, I am still blessed to be able to spend time in these places and appreciate them just as much as an alumna would.

I saw several African American girls walking along the courtyard having an intelligent conversation; so poised and so mature, I believed that they were my daughters. If I'd ever had a daughter, I know that she would have been just like these young ladies: beautiful, gifted and intelligent. If their own mothers weren't proud of them, I certainly was.

Needless to say, I loved walking through this historic campus and decided to keep walking along Waterman Street toward the Seekonk River. The residential dwellings along this walk were full of charm and warmth that I found quite appealing. It was an easy and satisfying walk, passing a lot of college-style town homes and row houses.

It was starting to get dark and I was a bit tired. As I began my walk back to the hotel, I kept thanking God for such an amazing birthday. I really understood that day how privileged I was and I strive to never forget that truth.

As I closed my eyes that night, I realized that the half marathon I would run the next day would be my first at the age of 46! All I could think of was "what a blessing!"

As I began the walk back to my hotel the evening before the race, I inadvertently stumbled upon a part of the race course where they were setting up tables for one of the water stations. You would be surprised to see all the hard work that goes into putting a race together. The job of the race director is often a thankless one and they all have my utmost respect and admiration. The race director for the Cox Providence Rhode Island races is one of the best in the business.

This was an amazing weekend. I turned one year older and ended up receiving some of the best birthday gifts imaginable. I was blessed to see places I'd only read about on this trip.

On top of that, it was one of the fastest half marathon runs in my entire 50-state journey. I left Providence that day knowing that I was a blessed woman and all I could do was thank the Lord for this wonderful quest.

And thank you Providence, Rhode Island. You are and will always be very special to me.

Race 49

23rd Annual KeyBank Vermont City Marathon
Burlington, Vermont - May 29, 2011

Saving the Best Full Marathon for Last

Having completed two full marathons on my 50-state quest, I wanted to get in at least one more before reaching the end of my journey, and with just three states left, there were few options. However, Vermont made it an easy choice because the event I wanted to participate in only offered the full marathon. That event was the KeyBank Vermont City Marathon.

The KeyBank Marathon is an event I followed for almost two years before submitting my registration. Held in Burlington, Vermont's largest city, I don't know if I was more excited about running another full marathon or about returning to New England, a region of the country I simply adored. I'm sure it was a combination of the two, as well as the fact that I had never been to Vermont and couldn't wait to step foot on its soil. I registered before Christmas the previous year.

I invited my mother along since I knew she had never been to that part of the country. She accepted before I could finish extending the invitation. I knew it was a place that would bring blessing to both of us so I began making our arrangements well in advance of the Memorial Day weekend marathon.

Logistically, this was one of the best courses in my running tenure. Beginning in Battery Park overlooking the beautiful Lake Champlain and the Adirondack Mountains, you get to enjoy one of the most scenic routes of any marathon through residential communities and parks before finishing in Waterfront Park, adjacent to Lake Champlain. So I chose to lodge at the Hilton Burlington and we could not have been in a better location. Situated on the waterfront, we had the most amazing view of the lake and mountains, and I was just steps away from the start and finish line. It was my ideal layout for a race and the unequaled views was pure icing on the cake.

Up before my 6:00 wake-up call, I knew how important this particular Sunday was to me. I would be running in my first full marathon since June 2008 in Kona, Hawaii, and while I had a great run in Kona, I really wanted to improve my time with this marathon. Some may have suspected that my goal was unrealistic since I had not run more than 13.1 miles in a race or in training since the marathon in Kona. Admittedly, this is not a training method I'd recommend to anyone; however, I knew that I was more physically fit and running better than ever, so I didn't panic about not being ready. Instead, I was determined to do my very best and to enjoy the experience of running the 26.2 mile distance again, no matter how I might struggle.

One thing is for sure: I didn't choose an easy race to reintroduce the full marathon to my system. The KeyBank Vermont City Marathon, though not the hilliest marathon out there, is definitely not the flattest either. It is challenging to say the least, so a tad more preparation probably would have been wise. Oh well, I thought. Only time would tell at this point.

Upon waking I went downstairs to test the weather and all I could see was rain, rain, and more rain. I always pack a throw-away poncho whether the forecast calls for rain or not. This was one morning I needed it.

Several runners had already gathered in the lobby, one being an elderly gentleman who I could tell was in great shape. I asked him which direction was the start line which prompted a 10-minute conversation about the entire course from start to finish. I paid attention because it was obvious that he knew the details, including where to expect hills and sharp turns. He seemed surprised that this was my first KeyBank Marathon and I chuckled wondering what he would say if he found out that this only my 3rd marathon ever.

As I headed out the building, there were so many spectators that I wasn't sure which way to go to the start. I must have looked stressed because a girl asked if I was looking for the starting line. When I told her yes, she informed me that I was going in the wrong direction. Uh oh, I thought. I thanked her and started running in the opposite direction when a guy ran up beside me and yelled "Where's the start... where's the start?"

I told him I had no idea but it had to be the way we were going so we started running together and picked up 3 other runners along the way. It must have been hilarious to see this group of runners jetting along the sidelines trying to get in line before the sound of the horn. Although I don't recommend it, this was certainly one way to get in a warm-up run.

We heard the announcer yell "30 seconds." Finally, I saw the runners lined up but I couldn't find an opening through the barricade. The guy running with me climbed through a small hole in one of the barricades, and just as I was about to follow him, someone said that there was an open gate just ahead. They were right and I was able to just walk right in and join my fellow runners. In less than 15 seconds, I was going to be running in my 3rd full marathon in state #48 of my 50-state quest. God is good.

At exactly 8:03, we were off and running. My initial strategy was to maintain a much slower pace for the first half of the race in order to have some energy for the second half. With the rain coming down steady, I was right on target, completing the first mile in 9:30 minutes.

I picked up the pace in mile 2 and found it hard to keep slowing down. I felt incredibly energized for some reason so I thought that if I could handle going faster, why not do so. Thus, I kept my normal 8:30-8:45 minute/mile pace for as long as I could.

I'm glad that I had the conversation with the man in the lobby because his description of the course turned out to be accurate. It helped me feel more at ease knowing what was coming up next.

At mile 3, we looped back to the start through the pedestrian Marketplace lined with bricks that Mom and I would get to know much better later that evening.

Just as we began a 4.5 mile out-and-back section through the Northern Connector with amazing views of the Green Mountains, the rain stopped. I was all too happy to ditch my disposable rain-coat. My arms loose from the poncho, I picked up more momentum and reached mile 7 in 62 minutes, just a bit slower than my normal half marathon pace. So far, so good.

I took my first sip of liquid at mile 8 and unlike my half mara-thon races, I drink at just about every remaining liquid station until mile 25. That was due to the increasing temperatures throughout the morning. The humidity was a beast. It got so hot —and that means a lot coming from me. I don't typically get as hot as most runners do, but this time, I was right up there with them. Thank-fully, the sun didn't come out. That may have been too much to withstand.

At mile 8.2, we returned to the city streets a second time through the Marketplace and by mile 9, we were close to where we started. As we made the loop through Burlington's South End closing in on mile 13, I knew the really hard part was about to begin.

Miles 14-16 were the toughest for two reasons. First, because my body was so used to being done by mile 13, going beyond that distance for the first time in 3 years was tougher than I thought it would be. Second, this stretch of the course was a brutal uphill siege that took everything I had to climb. Yes, my body was definitely hit-ting a wall and all I could think was with over 10 miles left to go, it was way too soon to hit any kind of wall.

Right at the end of mile 16, fatigue was starting to come into play as we ran through the nice neighborhoods near North Avenue. I started walking a bit and wolfed down water and Gatorade when-ever it was offered, sometimes two at a time. Those cool liquids helped me out quite a bit as I tried to pick up my pace again.

By mile 17, I was just plain irritable. I was tired of running and I wanted to be done with this race already. Every part of my body was starting to ache and I was puffing and blowing harder than I can remember in any other race. Moreover, I was no longer encouraged by the scenic views or the spectator support even though some residents turned on their sprinklers to give us some relief in the immense humidity. I was ready to see that finish line.

Once I hit the 3-hour mark, my goal was to run 6 more miles by noon, putting me at mile 24. Thankfully, at mile 21.5, we entered the Burlington Bikepath and got a slight reprieve as the course flattened out. When I reached mile 24, it was 12:08 p.m., so I was only 8 minutes off my goal, but I was totally exhausted. At that point in the race, it was all about walk and jog, walk and jog. I was so tired that I had to put my hands on my hips because they were too heavy to swing anymore. Several times someone would come along and bump into my elbows sticking out on my hips so I had to let my arms drop.

Finally, I saw the marker for mile 25 but I couldn't even get excited because it meant I still had 1.2 miles to go. Man, it just seemed like this course would never end! Desperate to finish, I skipped the last liquid station and tried to keep going with no more stops. I realized that if I could finish in 4:30, I would improve my last full marathon time by 15 minutes.

The finish to this race was fantastic. At mile 25.5, I was just walking. I tried to run but I just couldn't anymore. I was visibly tired and irritated. All of a sudden, a young lady with the sweetest voice said, "Come on. It's just a bit farther." There was something magical about her voice, so sweet and so gentle, that I responded to it right away and surprised myself when I started running alongside her. It wasn't much of a run given how tired I was but it was more than a walk.

Still irritated, I said "Where is mile 26? I don't see mile 26?"

Without hesitation, she said, "There it is right there" and when I looked up, I saw the sign. Praise God was all I could think.

By this time the crowd support was great and I began looking to my left for Mom. who was supposed to be near the finish line 4 hours into the race. Then the announcer called out my name which was a blessing because Mom told me later that when she heard him say my name, she started looking more intently for me. Just as if it were written in a movie script, Mom was there smiling and cheering for me. She told the people around her who I was and they were cheering for me as well.

Just as me and my new friend crossed the finish line together, I hugged and thanked her so much for her kindness and help in getting me to that finish line. I really don't think I could have finished that last ½ mile without her.

The race officials arranged for all finishers to have their final steps of the race videotaped as part of the photography package you have the option to purchase. I purchased mine primarily because it shows me and my friend crossing the finish line and embracing one another as we completed the race. That 30-second piece of footage will always be very special to me.

I have never been so happy and thankful to finish a race in my life! My official finish time was 4:33:45 and I couldn't have been more pleased with my final full marathon of the 50-state quest.

My official average pace was 10:27 minutes per mile, so with each full marathon, I improved—5:48 in San Diego in 2007; 4:45 in Kona, Hawaii in 2008; and 4:33 in Burlington, Vermont in 2011. Part of me wonders how good my time would be on a flat course, but at that moment, all I cared about was that I had reached my goal and I didn't have to think about running for a few days. Words escape me when trying to describe how great I felt in that moment.

I received my well-earned finisher's medal, as well as some water and chocolate milk that I chugged down pretty quickly. I then exited the runner's area with perfect timing because as I did, I saw Mom approaching me. She was very proud of her daughter and I was so happy to share that moment with her.

We walked together up the steep hill from Waterfront Park to the hotel. After running 26.2 miles, that hill to the hotel seemed criminal, but I took my time and basked in the joy of finishing.

The moment I checked in, I saw a view that was simply amazing. It is hard to miss the beauty of Burlington, especially when your backdrop is Lake Champlain. The only thing putting a slight damper on the situation was the overcast skies and the threat of rain; however, I wasn't about to let that ruin my first day in this wonderful city.

Since the expo was 2.7 miles from my hotel, I took my time to walk there and stopped to tour the University of Vermont campus along the way. As always, campus tours provide moments of great blessing for me and UVM was no exception. The campus and the lovely neighborhoods surrounding it were just lovely.

Mom and I enjoyed walking around Burlington both before and after the race. Once I took a shower and rested a bit from the race, I was ready for a good, relaxing meal. No health food that day. I was ready for the kind of meal I treat myself to only a couple of times a year. I deserved it after that arduous marathon!

The hotel was only two blocks from the Church Street Marketplace, an open air pedestrian mall with every kind of fine dining, shopping and entertainment option a person could want. The cobblestone walkway was packed, mostly with runners and their families and friends, as people filled the restaurants and shops, as well as the outdoor benches and eating areas. Mom and I decided to try a restaurant our shuttle driver suggested. We got a great table facing the walkway so we could see everyone milling around. I got a salad with shrimp and Mom got the prime rib. Of course, I took a couple of nice sized bites of her steak and it was delicious!

After lunch, we decided to walk through the Marketplace from one end to the other. It was so nice to stroll slowly along the cobblestone street talking to other runners (many of us had our medals around our neck for easy identification) and enjoying the fellowship of the day. I couldn't have asked for anything better. We eventually made our way over to the City Market and purchased some Kombucha for later before strolling back to the room to rest a bit.

There wasn't anything I didn't adore about Vermont, Burlington, or the KeyBank Vermont City Marathon. Literally everything - the people, the hotel, the lake, the mountains, the beauty, the kindness everywhere - was extraordinary.

The next morning I woke up early and decided to take a walk on what had to be the most beautiful morning I'd seen in a long time. Long gone was the rain and clouds, gloriously replaced with blue skies, plenty of sunshine, and total peace.

I walked up to the Marketplace and mailed some postcards I had addressed the night before. Then I walked down to the banks of Lake Champlain and found it hard to believe that just 24 hours prior, that entire area was filled with people, food, and every kind of sound known to man. Now it was quiet with only the sound produced by nature. I was there alone with the exception of two runners who passed by me. While I appreciated their dedication, I was so thankful that I wouldn't be joining them that day.

I thanked the good Lord for His rich provision and for blessing me beyond measure.

I had two states to go before completing my journey. While I looked forward to them, I knew a special piece of my heart during this quest belonged only to Burlington, Vermont, and that truth will continue to bless me for the rest of my life.

Race 50

Missoula Half Marathon
Missoula, Montana - July 10, 2011

The Most Scenic Views in the Country

efore this journey, I had never been to Montana and really never thought of ever going there. My limited knowledge of this state relegated around its largest city Billings, and its capital city, Helena. Even then, it was just the names of the cities I was familiar with and nothing more.

Then, one evening while watching a show on HGTV, I saw some of the real estate in the western part of the state and thought it was just beautiful. Essentially a river valley surrounded by mountains, I knew that wherever that place was, that's where I wanted to run.

That place was Missoula, and once I discovered that it annually plays host to a major running event, I did not hesitate to register. The Missoula Marathon and Half Marathon consistently ranks in the top percentile for best event and medal on most running polls.

Characterized by a scenic course with breathtaking views, a caring and thoughtful race director, and a gorgeous finisher's medal, it is easy to see why this event ranks so highly with runners from all over the country. As I continued to research this race, my enthusiasm to participate reached an astronomical level. I couldn't wait to see Missoula, and now that I have, I can't wait to go back.

I used points through the Hilton program to get a free night at the Doubletree Hotel. I was pleased with the room and even more pleased with the personnel, especially a lovely young lady named Kate, whose kindness helped to make my experience in Missoula even more memorable. As I headed out the door to go to the expo, she handed me a map of the city that I used faithfully my entire time there.

With the weather so outstanding, I couldn't resist sitting outside and admiring the scenery of this city. As I sat there and watched numerous residents come and go, I thought to myself that it is hard to have a bad day in a place where the backdrop is a gorgeous mountain range. No wonder the people were so friendly.

On race morning, I awoke at 4:00 because unfortunately, getting to the start was not as ideal as I prefer. As you know by now, I'm partial to races where the start line is within walking distance of my hotel. However, in Missoula, getting to the start was not nearly that simple. Although the finish was downtown, the start line was nearly 6 miles from my hotel where parking was very limited. It was highly recommended that everyone, even Missoula residents, take one of the shuttle buses from downtown to the starting area.

The buses for the start departed from a parking garage down-town starting at 4:20 a.m., with the last bus leaving at 5:30. Since I detest standing around and trying to keep warm, I decided to catch the last bus at 5:30. My thinking was that I'd leave the hotel around 5:10 and jog to the parking garage which was about a ½ mile away.

Although I didn't know exactly where the parking garage was, I knew its general vicinity and I was sure that there'd be other run-ners heading that way too so I could just follow the crowd. Boy was I wrong. When I left the hotel, the streets were dark and empty. I saw no runners anywhere. On top of that, I forgot to bring the bag they gave us for the baggage claim. I was batting zero and time was ticking. I started jogging a little faster and the thought crossed my mind that if I missed the last bus, I might not be able to participate in this race.

That thought was just too crushing to ponder so I quickly put it out of my head and prayed that I was getting close to the buses. Finally, well in the distance, I saw the backs of two women and ran to catch up with them. I asked if they were going to the shuttle buses and they said yes. I was so thankful to see someone else walking those dark streets and the three of us bonded immediately. As we walked and talked, we eventually came upon a few other runners and by 5:25, we were on the bus along with about 30 others. I was disappointed in myself that I started to panic and also that I didn't set aside more time to find the parking garage. Oh well, that is just another interesting moment to add to the ever-growing list of unex-pected blessings on this 50-state journey.

On the bus, I met several other runners, including a mother of two whose husband was active-duty in the National Guard. Her story was interesting and was another reason this adventure in run-ning is unequaled by anything else in my life. The opportunity to meet interesting people, if but for a moment, is priceless.

It was 49 degrees when the race started but I wasn't as cold as I usually am. I wore 2 tech shirts, one short and one long, because I knew it was going to warm up once we got started. As I made my way over to the baggage claim area, they had extra bags that they were giving out so I didn't need the one I left at the hotel after all (total provision from God.) I stored my Vermont jacket and gloves and slowing headed to the start line since the race was to begin at 6:00 a.m. I secured a spot very close to the front and crossed the starting mat about 30 seconds after the race officially got under-way.

Everything about this race was top notch but if I had to make one criticism, it would be the loud cannon that sounded at the start of the race. Most events use some kind of horn to start the race, which I think is much more suitable. The sound of a gun-shot is a bit disconcerting to me, but nothing is as bad as a super loud cannon. And it didn't just go off once; the sound continued for what seemed like several minutes, almost like continuous fire-works. I thought it was unnecessary and kind of unnerved me a bit because it kept going on and on.

Eventually the noise subsided and I became focused on the most beautiful course I had ever run. Much of it looked like green meadows to me and even better, a great deal of it was downhill. Moreover, this was one of the quietest races I can recall. Usually, there is a lot of talking among runners, especially in the first few miles, as well as the cheers from the spectators. This race was un-usually quiet even in the beginning. No bands, no cheers, not even much talking with fellow runners. It was silent and I like it that way.

The course was relatively flat and without even focusing upon it, I was making very good time averaging in the 8:30 minute/mile range. Sure enough, I reached mile 7 in only 59 minutes, giving me a whole minute to play with in keeping with my usual half marathon pace. I took my only sip of liquid at mile 8.2 and walked for about 30 seconds in order to finish the last half of the race strong.

There was an older gentleman who started running right beside me near mile 8. I could tell he was well into his senior years, but for the most part he was running well, although he was panting very heavily. In fact, he was breathing so hard I thought for sure he'd have to walk a little bit, but he maintained a nice running pace for much longer than I expected. Eventually, he did start walking and I didn't see him again. As I passed him, I thought to myself that I hope I'm still on some race course somewhere in the world when I'm in my 80's and 90's. After all, age is just a number. How well I know that!

When I reached mile 9, I decided to take the rest of the race in 2's: to mile 11, and then to mile 13. Part of me wanted to speed up, but the real threat of not having enough energy to finish strong kept me in check. I stuck to my normal 8+ minute/mile pace until mile 13, sprinting that last .1 mile to the end.

I was grateful for a relatively easy race, and felt pretty confident that my time was good enough to be right up there with my Las Vegas finish of 1:53:35. Once I collected the lovely finisher's medal, I got a bottle of Zero Powerade and some trail mix. Because of the nice cool breeze that persisted throughout the morning, I wasn't as thirsty as usual, but I knew that I needed to hydrate. In the next couple of days, I found out that my official finish time was 1:54:06 which tied with Baltimore as my 6th fastest half marathon on the 50-state quest.

The expo was held at the Caras Park Pavillion along the Clark Fork River. I took a trail along the river to get there and it was quite a lovely walk from my hotel. Tied to the expo was a festival in celebration of being the Montana Tourism Event of the Year, so many people were in the park that day enjoying the live bands with family and friends. While it wasn't the largest festival I've ever attended, there was something about its lack of pretension that appealed to me. I really appreciated being there.

From the festival, I decided to walk to a place called "The Good Food Store" located on the other side of town. The shuttle driver from the hotel told me about it when he picked me up at the airport. Known for its hot bar and organic offerings, it seemed like the perfect place for me to have some lunch. The food was delicious and after a long but interesting walk through some of the Missoula neighborhoods, I was ready for some sustenance.

I also purchased my staple foods for dinner and breakfast in the morning. I went a little overboard and ended up purchasing two bags of groceries that I made sure were double-bagged. Then, with backpack in tow, I began my walk back to the hotel. I must admit, it wasn't a walk I was looking forward to because the groceries were heavy and the sun was making it toasty. Nonetheless, the weather was absolutely gorgeous so I tried to make sure the bags were as balanced as possible and began the return trip to downtown.

After about one mile, my shoulders were starting to feel it, so just as I was about to take a break, I heard a voice say "Hey, you want a ride back to the hotel?"

I turned around to find it was Kate who checked me into the hotel. I was so thankful to see her and did not hesitate to accept her offer. As we rode along, I learned that she was a native of Missoula and a recent graduate of the University of Montana. She was working at the hotel until she secured a job in her chosen field of criminology. She was one of those people you know in your heart will go very far in life.

Due to Kate's kindness, I had even more time to tour the university which I was happy about because it was a large campus. A short walk across the river was all it took to be on the campus grounds. Since it was mid-July, few students were around so it was quiet that Saturday. I stopped at the Student Center where a few people were eating at one of the cafes that was open. Already gearing up for football season, there were football schedules and calendars all over the place, so I picked up a couple.

Then I strolled through some of the dorm areas and wound up at the athletic facilities. I remembered that my one of my favorite actors, the great Carroll O'Connor (known to many as "Archie Bunker"), received his undergraduate and master's degrees from the University of Montana. I was privileged to share a special moment with this great man when I was a studio page at Culver Studios in Los Angeles and I knew of his stellar education. I kept him in mind as I strolled through the vast courtyards of this school.

As I walked back to my hotel, I reflected on how much I liked the city of Missoula. Its beauty and serenity comforted me. I was thankful to be there.

I loved everything about my experience in this breathtaking city and was so grateful for all the kindness I received from everyone there.

Before checking out of the hotel, I made sure to submit a note to the management of the hotel acknowledging the special kindness and warmth of Kate, and departed Missoula feeling blessed and humble.

It was hard to believe that I only had one more race to go to complete my 50-state journey and I couldn't have been more pleased that it was going to be in one of my favorite places on earth—the state of Alaska.

Race 51

Big Wild Life Runs – Skinny Raven Sports Half Marathon

Anchorage, Alaska - August 21, 2011

Saving the Best for Last

In 2004, I was privileged to take a 7-day cruise with In Touch Ministries (the ministry of Dr. Charles Stanley) to Alaska via the Inside Passage. It included tours to Sitka, Ketchikan, and the capital city of Juneau.

Once you've witnessed the unmistakable beauty of this state from these venues and frontier towns, you feel there can't be much more to see. In some aspects that may be true, but Alaska's largest city was always a place I desperately wanted to explore. I was blessed with the best opportunity in the world in which to do so; the Big Wild Life Runs Half Marathon in Anchorage.

I decided well over a year before this race took place that I would make the great state of Alaska the final destination of my 50-state quest. Perhaps if I had been more innovative, I would have made

Alaska the 49th state of my journey and Hawaii the 50th, since that is the proper sequencing of their admittance into the United States, but so much for innovation. Having run in Hawaii nearly 3 years prior, Alaska was the definitive choice for the 50th slot and in retrospect, I wouldn't have it any other way.

I knew I wanted the race to take place in Anchorage, preferably at a time of year when the temperatures would be a little warmer. Of course in Alaska, warm weather is not guaranteed even in the summertime, but the choice to run in the Big Wild Life event was pretty cut and dried. I registered by early February and took the remaining 6 months to plan the perfect trip and racing experience.

The same day I told my mother I was going to run a long distance event in all 50 states she said, "I will be at your final race no matter where you choose it to be." When I told her that the final state would be Alaska, she was thrilled and kept her word to go with me. I was so thankful to have Mom with me on this final leg of my dream.

As soon as feasibly possible, I began making our arrangements. Not wanting to rush through this experience, I took some vacation time to stretch out our time in Anchorage and enjoy every aspect of this picture perfect ending to a 3-1/2 year quest.

Two weeks leading up to the final weekend of my journey, I was in Orlando, Florida for a conference for my job. Every morning at 5:00, I ran anywhere from 5-8 miles in and around the Lake Mary area. I wanted to ensure my last race on this quest would be a good and productive one. I wanted to be as fit as possible.

Also, approximately two weeks before the event in Alaska, two local newspapers ran the story of my 50-state journey which prompted a feature in a Raleigh-based show called "The Tarheel Traveler." The reporter for the show came and interviewed me in my home on August 17 with an expected airdate of August 22, the day we were to travel back to North Carolina. All in all, it had been a full couple of weeks and it served as the perfect momentum to make Alaska one of the most memorable and excellent destinations of my quest.

Alaska is so big that it has its own time zone: Alaska Standard Time (AST) which is four hours behind Eastern Standard Time (EST). So our first flight departed N.C. at 11:25 a.m. EST, and after changing planes in Houston, we finally landed in Anchorage at 9:00 p.m. AST, or 1:00 a.m. EST. Needless to say it was a one long day of travel but once we hit Alaska soil, my energy level shot through the roof. I was so happy and thankful to be there.

I awoke at 5:30 on race morning and was so thankful that my stomach was not upset because I had a terrible night. I'm not sure if it was something I ate or nerves or a combination of the two, but whatever it was, it kept me up most of the night. I prayed to the good Lord for relief and He certainly gave it to me because when I woke up, I felt much better. Nonetheless, I was cautious about what I consumed pre-race and stuck with what I knew my stomach could handle: coffee and ½ cup of goat milk yogurt. Since the race didn't start until 9:00, I had time to make sure everything digested properly.

As for the weather, God is so good because all the rain we had in the two days leading up to the race were supplanted by beautiful blue clear skies. I couldn't have been happier. What a blessing!

I decided to wear my black shorts and two light tech shirts

(one I received at the expo) and my "Jesus" cap. I started with gloves but by mile 3 I discarded them. I regret to this day that I did because those were excellent running gloves that I received in the Birmingham race. But the temperature got too hot for them and I had no other choice.

I left the hotel room at 8:45 and told Mom to try to be at the finish line around 10:30 so she wouldn't miss me crossing the finish line. Since the start was near the Performing Arts Center, several other runners and I decided to warm up inside the building where it was nice and warm. Before leaving to get in line, I prayed again (I always pray in my hotel room before the race), and asked God to let me complete this race and 50-state quest in good health and in a manner that was pleasing to Him. It was just starting to hit me that this was going to be the last time I line up for a race as a part of my 50-state journey. It was a bittersweet feeling, although more sweet than bitter.

I was in line by 8:55 and by 8:59:41 (by my watch), we were underway. Because of how upset my stomach had been the night before, I wasn't sure how things would go but I just tried to relax and find my pace, regardless to what it might be that day. Thankfully, as we progressed through the first two miles, I felt strong and capable. When I finished mile 2 in 7:50 minutes, I knew that I was going to be okay for the duration of the race.

We stayed downtown for mile 1 and then merged onto a bike trail for miles 2 and 3. There we split from the full marathoners (good volunteers to let you know which way to go) and remained on the nice, well-shaded Coastal Trail along a running river. As in more cases than not, I hadn't studied the course map so I had no idea it was an out-and-back course and didn't discover it was until the overall winner was on his way back right when I had just reached mile 5 (or somewhere close to that mark.)

I tried to stick to my race plan of 8:30-8:45 minutes/mile, but it was hard because we began a steady climb from mile 5 to about mile 7 that took a lot out of me. I almost stopped at mile 6 for Gatorade but persevered so I could get an accurate time for my first 7 miles.

Once I crossed the mile 7 marker, my watch was showing 9:57:30 a.m., which meant that I was 1-1/2 minutes faster than my goal. Remember that I like to be at mile 7 within the first 60 minutes of a half marathon. Since mile 7 also represented the turnaround point, I decided to stop at the next liquid station for some Gatorade to quench my thirst and ease my left leg which was starting to cramp. That was unusual and something I hadn't experienced in several months, so I prayed and continued to forge ahead.

Around mile 7.5, we started descending and the cramping began waning until finally, it was all but gone. Thus, I picked up my speed as much as I could knowing that my time was good, perhaps one of the best so far. As we made our way along the Chester Creek Trail, the elevation continued decreasing and I decided to get one last drink of both water and Gatorade to prepare for a strong finish. However, even with the extra liquid, miles 8-10 are always difficult for me in a half marathon.

Perhaps the biggest lift at that point was seeing other runners heading toward the part of the course I already completed (that is one of the positives of an out-and-back course.) It always feels good to know that you are beyond where others have yet to go.

Once at mile 10, I struggled to keep my pace, and by mile 11.5, we had a small climb that I decided to walk instead of run. At this time, two girls passed me and said "Come on, don't walk now. We only have a ½ mile to go!" So I listened to them and picked it back up again.

I remembered that Mom was planning to be at the finish line by 10:30, so I really wanted to get there as soon as possible. In the last quarter of a mile, I ran full throttle, giving it everything I could not just for this race, but for all the races in all the cities in all the states of the past 4 years.

I ran so fast that I ended up passing one of the girls who encouraged me to pick up the pace. With my elbows reaching as far back as possible, I pushed and used every ounce of my strength to cross that finish line without leaving a thing out there on the race course.

When my foot touched the finish mat, I looked up and saw Mom right at the fence and I immediately ran over and gave her the biggest hug I could. I was so happy! I was happy to see my Mom, happy to be healthy, happy to have another successful half marathon under my belt, and happy to have this wonderful quest completed!

When a volunteer put the lovely medal around my neck, there was no removing the smile on my face.

Mom told a nice couple she was standing beside at the finish line that this race represented my completion of a race in all 50 states The man asked to take his picture with me. As his wife took the photo, he said to me, "You're going to be famous."

We attended the awards ceremony later. The good news was that my official finish time was 1:53:08, my second fastest half marathon of all time. The not-so-good news was that I finished 4th in my age group, just missing the podium by less than 2 minutes. Nonetheless, I still had the victory and nothing could take that away from me. I couldn't have picked a better way to finish my journey.

Anchorage is an exciting place and Mom and I explored it before and after the race. One of the first things we did was walk across the street from our hotel to a tour agency and arrange to take a city bus tour at 2:00 p.m. for $49.

Even though it had started raining, we walked to the Anchorage Fifth Avenue Mall, which I thought was spectacular. I guess I was expecting something more rustic and smaller, so I was surprised to find that this place had a total of five levels, culminating with a food court at the top. Every store you can think of is located in this mall with J.C. Penney and Nordstrom serving as the anchor stores. We enjoyed window shopping and comparing the prices to those in the south. We left there and stopped at several other shops before reaching the hotel. At one of the shops, I purchased a zippered jacket with "Alaska" across the front (second only to my "Vermont" and "U.S. Open" jackets.) It was getting close to 2:00 p.m., so we put our purchases in the room before heading out on the tour.

There were a total of four of us on the tour: me, Mom, and a couple from Argentina. Our stops included the Alaskan railroad, the earthquake cliff, and Flat Top Mountain. Even though it was pouring rain and had turned much colder than it was earlier in the morning, we got out and walked around at both the earthquake landing and Flat Top.

I loved talking to the couple from Argentina. They were personable, as was our tour guide Julie. She used to be a junior tennis champion, so when I told her that I was going to attend the U.S. Open in a few weeks, she was elated. She had a great personality and we enjoyed our time with her very much.

We planned to go to a nice seafood restaurant about five blocks from the hotel for dinner, but because of the rain, Mom decided to stay in the hotel and eat at the restaurant there. That worked out well for me because I wanted to explore more of downtown and have some alone time, rain or no rain.

I set out, along with a few others—mostly runners from out of town—strolling along the streets comprised of restaurants, shopping, retail, and entertainment venues like the Alaska Center for the Performing Arts and the Anchorage Museum at Rasmuson Center.

Of particular interest to me was the Delaney Park Strip, an 11-block park with courts, six softball fields, and several historical memorials. Although the rain had stopped, it was rather muddy and getting dark so my exploration was somewhat altered. I had the opportunity, however, to see it during the day with no threat of rain before my time in Anchorage came to a close.

As I took my time walking back to the hotel and reflecting on the day, it was no surprise to me how much I liked Anchorage. Based on how much I loved the cities of Juneau, Sitka, and Ketchikan, I had no doubt that I would feel the same about Anchorage. It felt so good to be there 3 more days to enjoy and appreciate it. If I could use one word to describe my being that night, it would be "peace."

As I walked down the city streets, as well as some of the neighborhoods adjacent to downtown, I had the opportunity to reflect on my 50-state journey. In some ways, it didn't seem possible that I could accomplish this goal. A girl who couldn't run 10 yards without panting and gagging for air had completed a long distance running event in all 50 states and the District of Columbia.

I have always acknowledged that the dream itself, and the determination to fulfill the dream, came directly from God because I'm not creative enough, brave enough, and certainly not at the time, athletic enough, to come up with such a lofty and challenging goal. It was all God from the beginning and I give Him all the glory and the honor.

It has been a privilege to see the United States of America up close and personal, and even more from the field of a race course. From its people, to its rich land and history, I have been amazed and blessed by every square inch of terrain I walked and ran during this nearly 4 year adventure. We are a vast and diverse nation, and I'm thankful to have had the opportunity to witness it in ways I could only previously imagine.

I have no idea what the Lord has in store for me in the future, but whatever it is, I know that this 50-state quest will stand alone in my heart. I pray that in sharing my story it will yield the same blessing to you that it has for me.

Epilogue

That's my story folks—an honest, straightforward accounting of my experience running a long distance event in all 50 states and the District of Columbia.

Rarely is a journey this long and arduous solely characterized in the positive, but that is truthfully how this great task started and ended for me. Sure, there were some minor problems here and there, but nothing too intense to minimize the benefits and blessings of this quest. In fact, the few hurdles I did have to jump only made me appreciate the journey that much more. They helped me learn life lessons that I continue to implement each day. In short, I wouldn't trade my experiences of this quest, good or bad, for anything in the world.

As I tell people daily, this was never a book solely about running. Yes, I talk about the races I participated in, but there are more than enough books on the market about running, written by people much more qualified than myself. Instead, I have always stood by the conviction that my book is an accounting of me using the gift of running to see this beautiful country called the United States of America.

It is more my story of growth and exploration through the mental and physical challenges of distance running. Along the way, I made some incredible friends, saw some amazing places, learned some life-changing lessons, climbed some gigantic mountains (literally and figuratively) and was touched in the most unassuming, unmanaged ways. I am indeed a blessed woman.

We are fortunate to live in a beautiful, vast, and diverse country. It breaks my heart when I hear someone who has been to just a handful of states talk about the expensive trip they are planning to Europe or the cruise they are taking to the Bahamas. They have the impression that they know all there is to know about the U.S. and that a real vacation takes place somewhere else in the world.

Don't get me wrong, I have nothing against international travel. I've done quite a bit of it and plan to do more, but why rush to go somewhere else when you've seen so little of the country you call home? I promise you, there is much more to the United States than you think. Our mountain ranges, prairies, coastal shores, deserts, bodies of water, urban dwellings, country estates, national parks and university campuses rival anything you could find abroad. Travel here also provides the opportunity to learn about our vast history. By visiting places like the Civil Rights Institute, the Clinton Presidential Library, the Coca-Cola Museum, the John F. Kennedy Museum, the USAF Museum, the Texas State Capitol, and so much more, I gained a greater understanding and appreciation of this place I call home. Without question, this journey has helped me realize what a privilege it is to live in the United States and how proud I am to be an American.

When I was halfway through my quest, I composed the following poem that I think best illuminates what this journey has meant to me.

The Runner

Perusing the race calendar so many to choose
Craving the challenge with nothing to lose.
Lodging and travel with ease she goes
Absorbing the beauty as the blessing gently flows.

Checking in at the expo with packet in hand
In her new favorite place nicknamed "marathon land."
Mingling with others who share the same passion
Of pushing the limits in a gut-wrenching fashion.

Later that evening after touring the town
The high from this venture refusing to come down.
Trying hard to focus she lays out her attire
Knowing the morning will yield a heart on fire.

Early wake-up call addresses the morning dark
Silent prayer slowly begins ensuring she hits the mark.
Approaching the field for warm-up to begin
Exhaling amongst a sea of anxious women and men.

Gun sounds and she gradually establishes her pace
Determination, fortitude show firm on her face.
Passing slower foes she settles in strong
Enduring the journey that's over 26 miles long.

Occasionally hydrating in order to stay the course
But never really stopping or considering divorce.

Though her body commences to ache as the miles pass by
Her spirit rejoices loudly with what they call the "runner's high."

With the ultimate goal creeping ever so close
Breathing deeply and fatigued, too soon to boast.
The final distance becomes so much shorter by this time
Crossing over to victory makes it worth the grit and grime.

A shiny new medal now adorns her tired neck
Still high from the finish, too exhilarated to stretch.
Yet she slides through the maze to her hotel she goes
Clean up, check out, smelling and feeling like a rose.

The journey back home is long and sure
As depression seeks to supplant the virtue called "endure."
The sweet smell of home gently ushers her inside
As she hangs her new medal with privilege, not pride.

Reflection and peace reside in the air
Muscles bathed and massaged only the quiet to share.
What a gift she is given
To race with no strife.
Such is an illustration of this blessed runner's life.

- Bridget Simpson
November 7, 2008

I pray my story has been an inspiration to you and I hope it has opened a new door or renewed an old dream for you. If so, then it has all been worth it.

May your journey bring you much blessing and joy!

- Bridget

Made in the USA
Columbia, SC
28 May 2018